To Chuck,
May God continue ... and yours with his ... blessings.

WILLIAM R. KIAH

Please keep on singing for Jesus in the way that you do. You are doing a fantastic job.

THE PRESIDENT And The QUEEN

William R. Kiah
June 13, 2004

A factual firsthand account of how and why former United States President Bill Clinton received and hid highly illegal quid pro quo campaign finance contributions to cover-up U. S. Treasury theft—and the problems that America faces because of it.

The President And The Queen

ISBN: 0-9710038-0-7
Library of Congress Control Number: 2001092455

Printed in the United States by:
Morris Publishing
3212 East Highway 30
Kearney, NE 68847
1-800-650-7888

Acknowledgments

This book is dedicated to four very special girls in my life: Sandy, my best friend and wife; and my three precious daughters, Sarah, Laura and Stephanie.

Contents

Introduction ix

Chapter 1 The Queen 1

Chapter 2 Much Work To Do 7

Chapter 3 The Evil Hand Moves 29

Chapter 4 The Disturbing View Through The Queen's Window 45

Chapter 5 The Emperor Has No Clothes 77

Chapter 6 The Chopping Off Of Kunta Kiah's Foot 135

Chapter 7 Bananagate 163

Chapter 8 Politicians Playing Politics 203

Chapter 9 The View From The Pinnacle 213

Chapter 10 The Quasi-slave System 233

Chapter 11 Patriot Parallels 257

Chapter 12 Stopping The Hemorrhaging 269

One of the most famous landmarks in Cincinnati, Ohio (a.k.a. "The Queen City") is a statue, the Water Genius, located on Fountain Square, a large pedestrian plaza in the absolute heart of the Queen's downtown.

Introduction

"[R]ight temporarily defeated is stronger than evil triumphant."
—Martin Luther King, Jr., Nobel Peace Prize Acceptance Speech, Dec. 10, 1964

For more than ten years, my wife, Sandy, and I owned two large and valuable investment properties in the central business section of downtown Cincinnati, Ohio's prized West Ninth Street Historic District. After signing a binding federal contract between ourselves, the City of Cincinnati, Ohio and HUD (the presidential Cabinet Department of Housing and Urban Development) to renovate one of these two properties (124 West Ninth Street), we soon discovered that we had opened a Pandora's box of White House criminal activity.

On November 5, 1992, two days after United States President William Jefferson Clinton was elected to his first term of office, I received the first in a contracted series of U. S. Treasury HUD payments via the City of Cincinnati for 124 West Ninth Street's renovation. Within weeks of that date, inexplicably, the rug was illegally pulled from underneath my HUD building renovation project, thereby, terminating it abruptly. As a result of my being suspiciously abandoned by the Clinton Justice Department, I was forced into bankruptcy and lost practically everything that I owned.

The emotional drubbing that I took in the face of the glaring procedural inconsistencies of my HUD project discombobulated me, causing me to desperately seek answers to the nightmarish financial condition that engulfed my family. Astonishingly, I discovered that a wall of silence, a well-coordinated labyrinth of implausible cover-up activities, had been erected against me. I soon found out why: I had been lured into a completely bogus HUD building renovation project that used stolen federal tax dollars from the U. S. Treasury.

However, that is only the beginning of the story. When putting all of the hidden pieces of the puzzle together, I uncovered a plethora of federally incriminating evidence and facts that irrefutably linked the cover-up of 124 West Ninth Street's stolen HUD financing directly to President Bill Clinton. It was at this point that the subterranean use of power from the White House came down on my wife, three young daughters and me like a shoe on a bug.

Well in advance of the Monica Lewinsky presidential sex scandal, I had personally presented incriminating evidence to the U. S. Justice Department showing why President Bill Clinton should have been impeached for his active participation in the HUD U. S. Treasury theft cover-up at 124 West Ninth Street. Instead of getting help from the U. S. government to expose and remedy the Treasury theft crimes that I had witnessed, a full-fledged Bill Clinton-led White House cover-up conspiracy of intimidation unfolded right in front of my eyes. In the wake of exposing this concealed federal criminal activity, my story was kept away from the national press and, in retaliation, I was publicly humiliated and physically threatened.

When I uncovered irrefutable evidence that the White House used the FBI, the U. S. Congress, the U. S. Secret Service, U. S. Attorney General Janet Reno's office, the IRS and others against me in a twisted abuse of presidential power, I knew that 124 West Ninth Street's significance went well beyond what I could have initially seen. Greater still, after Independent Counsel Kenneth W. Starr was aware that Bill Clinton had received highly illegal White House Lincoln Bedroom quid pro quo campaign finance contributions for 124 West Ninth Street Treasury theft protection and failed to prosecute the President during the Monica Lewinsky impeachment hearings, a larger threat to America began to unfold.

In the larger scheme of things, I realized that I had uncovered a Holy Grail that verified the hushed existence of a government-sanctioned form of outlawed racial discrimination that negatively affects the indigenous African-American population. Of even more importance, I saw how 124 West Ninth Street's cover-up sprang from a disturbing political trend that was negatively affecting all Americans: out of control campaign finance contributions.

In a day when the American public's expectations for the delivery of effective public service is rising while confidence in the ability of its leaders to effectively govern is falling, the rancor against public fraud, waste and malfeasance is becoming more unacceptable. Because of the way in which many politicians cloak their wrongdoings in a system of their making, it is very difficult for the American public to catch corrupt politicians with their hands illegally in America's till. *The President and the Queen* lays out a detailed trail of facts, proof, laws and evidence that reveals a clandestine modus operandi of federal corruption that has far greater implications to the American society as a whole.

As specific dates of 124 West Ninth Street's federal criminal activity are highlighted in this writing, *The President and the Queen* goes even further by providing the names of politically well-connected and financially powerful individuals who have participated in this well-documented scheme to defraud the U. S. government. At the same time, *The President and the Queen* shows the motives of those who have used their political and financial resources for illegal purposes, as they continue to attempt to hide their federal crimes through sleight of hand, stealth, and the suppression of evidence.

The President and the Queen shows how illegal political activity stretches all they way from Cincinnati, Ohio's City Hall past the Cabinet of the President of the United States of America. As it is about a threatening way of national government for the American people, *The President and the Queen* only mirrors what happened in Cincinnati, Ohio, as it is a window into how money is stolen and successfully covered-up from Uncle Sam's ability to prosecute.

Yet, it is the way in which President Bill Clinton's federally indictable stratagem backfired on his cloak and dagger activities that makes *The President and the Queen* a writing of note. Told from the perspective of a person who had a crystal-clear view of stolen HUD financing from the national Treasury, *The President and the Queen* reveals how U. S. President Bill Clinton illegally received campaign contributions and used the power of the national government to make sure that my incriminating message did not surface.

Far beyond the sexual peccadilloes of the Monica Lewinsky White House scandal, *The President and the Queen* uncovers the magnum opus of President Bill Clinton's Machiavellian ruse on America. Therein, this book highlights the duplicitous resources from within a HUD Treasury theft cover-up ring that emanated from my building renovation project at 124 West Ninth Street.

Like canaries that were used in underground mines to warn of deadly air, I wrote this book to warn my fellow countrymen of a deadly internal threat to the viability of America. Due to my detection of constitutionally outlawed public and private conduct, *The President and the Queen* elicits a warning with respect to America's looming and poisonous Treasury theft dangers.

The President and the Queen is a case study that provides its readers with a clearer understanding of the mechanics of how easily federal tax dollars can be stolen from the U. S. Treasury via HUD's Rental Rehabilitation Program (RRP). Just as importantly, *The President and the Queen* chronicles, gives insight into and shows how these illegal activities were carried out by snake-in-the-grass politicians, bureaucrats and opportunists who are positioned to systemically fleece the United States Treasury with impunity.

The incontrovertible evidence of which I speak is of public record and can be found in the following U. S. Sixth Circuit Court case files: Lower case numbers C-1-94-150 & C-1-95-219; and Appeals Court case number 95-4314. These suppressed case files bring light to a dark and sinister side of pervasive government corruption that readily provides a veritable cornucopia of incriminating facts, proof, and evidence showing how the American people have had their Treasury robbed by the Queen (the City of Cincinnati, Ohio) and many others.

*The President and the Quee*n takes its readers through the anemic building of a convoluted web of political chicanery and deep-seated influence peddling which culminated in illicit behavior that occurred in the Lincoln Bedroom of President Bill Clinton's White House. As this writing unequivocally shows that U. S. Treasury safeguards do not work and allow secret Treasury robbery, I also offer credible proof and evidence as to how many public and private individuals and organizations use cunning and duplicity to trick an unsuspecting American taxpaying populace.

In explicit detail, *The President and the Queen* uncovers a telling trail of deeply rooted federal incrimination that implicates former U. S. President Bill Clinton. In addition to many other illegally concealed felonies, this writing also reveals:

- how the Clinton administration's fanatical fundraising activities, designed to compete with the Republican Party at all costs, crossed the line into a U. S. Treasury theft cover-up ring that was initiated by the City of Cincinnati, Ohio;
- how a jaded, increasingly beleaguered and politically crippled member of President Clinton's Cabinet, Secretary of HUD, Henry G. Cisneros, was conveniently forced to resign from office while an odorous cloud of federal incrimination bil-

lowed from a failed cover-up of stolen HUD financing at Cincinnati, Ohio's 124 West Ninth Street;

- how one of President Clinton's top fund-raisers, travel companions and confidants, Attorney Stanley M. Chesley of Cincinnati's Waite, Schneider, Bayless and Chesley Co., L.P.A., was not only used to obstruct justice from within U. S. Attorney General Janet Reno's Justice Department, but how this same person was intentionally left off of the President's Lincoln Bedroom sleepover list in a failed attempt to disassociate the White House's shameless role in covering-up the stolen U. S. Treasury HUD financing used at 124 West Ninth Street.
- how Cincinnati, Ohio billionaire Carl H. Lindner, Jr. (who, as of this writing, is the CEO of Chiquita Bananas, majority owner of the Cincinnati Reds and owner of a bank, Provident, that participated in 124 West Ninth Street's HUD Treasury theft) is inextricably involved with President Bill Clinton's quid pro quo cover-up of these federally indictable crimes; and
- how a President Richard M. Nixon-appointed federal judge, U. S. District Judge Carl B. Rubin, made an shady deathbed decision to rescue Attorney Stanley M. Chesley from the jaws of certain federal prosecution—only 50 short hours before he died of cancer—in an attempt to erase a telling trail of federal incrimination that led to the doorstep of President Bill Clinton.

Moreover, *The President and the Queen* addresses a broader topic of endemic state and national government corruption while it offers a factual account of a major news event that has, heretofore, not been accurately covered by the news media. The overriding premise of this book is this: something is wrong when money is stolen from Uncle Sam and nobody does anything about it.

In Chapter One, "The Queen," a chronological tapestry is woven of Cincinnati, Ohio which shows how and why the city became a historic bastion of public fraud and ultra-conservative racial intolerance. In Chapter Two, "Much Work To Do," and Chapter Three, "The Evil Hand Moves," the reader is taken through my metamorphosis from a suburban single-family home real estate investor to a rapidly climbing real estate developer in Cincinnati, Ohio's central business district.

Chapter Three also sets the scene for White House complicity, as it describes the end result of a large 1988 racial confrontation involving many financially qualified African-Americans in Cincinnati, Ohio's population that had been repeatedly turned down for loans by the area's notoriously discriminatory lending institutions. Chapter Four, "The Disturbing View Through The Queen's Window," gives the reader a glimpse into how a marriage was made between the vindictively illegal goings-on of the City of Cincinnati, Ohio (the Queen) and the make-money-at-all-costs Bill Clinton presidency.

In Chapter Five, "The Emperor Has No Clothes," HUD's sloppy and reckless handling of federal tax dollars is presented in a way that easily reveals *The President and the Queen's* criminal deception on American taxpayers. As an embedded system of public and private political patronage was spun to produce a cloak of secrecy, this chapter meticulously unravels a convoluted web of 124 West Ninth Street's U. S. Treasury theft government involvement to show how they got caught lying. Since I let nothing stop my search for the truth, in this chapter, I give a full account of my infiltration of HUD's guarded national headquarters in Washington, D. C. Also, while this chapter establishes a nexus between a phenomenon of illegal discriminatory treatment that is continuously being leveled at the African-American population in the United States and U. S. Treasury theft, the coining of the term *Queen syndrome* is introduced.

In the aftermath of my uncovering clear-cut evidence of hidden U. S. government Treasury theft, Chapter Six, "The Chopping Off Of Kunta Kiah's Foot," tells of how punishing forces of political and financial patronage were unleashed against Sandy and I to keep 124 West Ninth Street's federal crimes hidden. This chapter also shows how my family bore the brunt of repressive activity by powerful conspiratorial forces that superseded America's laws in order to punish the messengers who dared to stand up against them. More significantly, Chapter Six describes how these repressive political activities are eroding the bedrock of this nation's highest political post: the office of the Presidency.

In Chapter Seven, "Bananagate," an accurate chronological re-creation of facts and events is presented to reveal how an embattled U. S.

President Bill Clinton illegally used the Lincoln Bedroom of the White House to cover-up crimes of his Cabinet, large campaign contributors and others. This chapter also shows that what happened at Cincinnati's 124 West Ninth Street was a portal into a much larger picture of federal cover-up corruption that was instrumental to President Bill Clinton's plan to avoid certain impeachment.

Chapter Eight, "Politicians Playing Politics," and Chapter Nine, "The View From The Pinnacle," brings unwanted attention to the modus operandi of unscrupulous politicians, bureaucrats and power brokers involved in 124 West Ninth Street's U. S. Treasury heist. These chapters also lay down a factual trail of federally indictable incrimination showing that 124 West Ninth Street's Treasury theft conspirators had the motive, the means, and the opportunity to participate in cabbaging America's Treasury while concealing their evils.

In Chapter Ten, "The Quasi-slave System," comparisons are made between America's pre-Civil War form of chattel slavery and the continued existence of an institutionally functioning remnant of that same form of slavery. In this regard, Chapter Ten lays out in detail some of the striking similarities between these old and new forms of thralldom, showing how many different aspects of America's culture remains stuck in embedded African-American discrimination.

As the heart of Chapter Ten draws inescapable analogies between America's slave system days of yore and many of today's racial practices, much verbiage is directed towards the many negative aspects of conservative racial ideology. Further, this chapter also makes comparisons as to how African-American treatment resembles U. S. foreign policy to Third World nations, and how the cause of this treatment is symptomatic of classic mental disorders. Greater still, as the hamstringing of my immediate family is but a mere microcosm of the greater African-American experience, I also show in this chapter how and why the institutional marginalization of the vast majority of America's Negroes is beyond the pale of constitutional law.

Just as American Revolutionary War patriots and others were forced to fight a threat to their homeland, Chapter Eleven, "Patriot Parallels," compares my little known of U. S. Treasury theft reaction to the reputations of selected American patriotic heroes. I use poetic license in this chapter to tell the story of how I saw the nationally injurious theft, misuse and cover-up of federal tax dollars and, when no one did anything about it, how and why I was forced into fighting the immense power of an evil ruler alone.

Chapter Twelve, "Stopping The Hemorrhaging," poses some serious questions, and offers some viable solutions, to concerned American citizens regarding the thesis of this writing. While it makes some necessary recommendations for America's self-survival, the underlying theme of this chapter is that America will eventually bleed to death if a true constitutional tourniquet is not applied to stop our decline.

As a full analysis of American government corruption and racial discrimination is far beyond the scope and intent of this writing, it is my fervent wish that *The President and the Queen* will be read objectively and weighed on the indisputable facts, federal laws and evidence that are presented herein. It is also my impassioned hope that this book plays a part in contributing towards an ongoing American dialogue that will ultimately be responsible for bridging the existing gulf of institutional racial intolerance which destructively separates the American people, and makes a mockery of the U. S. Constitution.

Even as federally orchestrated exertions continue to attempt to browbeat me into silence, I am still moved into action knowing that untold millions of African-American lives are being wasted, while many billions of the nation's scarce and precious dollars are being squandered in illegal racial folly. It is for this reason that, at the end of the day, *The President and the Queen* reverberates with the apropos dictum of an unknown philosopher, who once said, "It is not the act that costs…it's the cover-up." Hence, whereas the means exist that allow all American taxpayers to be quietly robbed and mismanaged to our overall disadvantage, it is toward the uplift of America that this book was written.

With a strong belief in God and country, it is the hope of this writer that the indisputably hidden federal criminal activity that *The President and the Queen* exposes will serve a useful purpose in the necessary defense of the United States of America. In this regard, and above all, it is my most sincere prayer that this book will only be interpreted as the heartfelt expression of national concerns that it was intended to be.

If this writing helps to stem the danger of the rampant corruption that threatens to consume America from within, and if my timely observations can contribute towards this nation's betterment as a result, my supplications will be answered beyond measure. Just as surely as the particular brand of racial and U. S. Treasury theft politics that *The President and the Queen* brings attention to must not remain unchecked, I emphatically maintain that it is we Americans who must stop our own self-destruction.

William R. Kiah

Chapter 1

The Queen

"A good name, like good will, is got by many actions and lost by one."
—Lord Jeffrey

From the time that it was first carved out of ceded British lands in 1788 in the rush of settlement of the Northwest Territory following the American Revolutionary War, divergent factors caused the city of Cincinnati, Ohio to acquire several nicknames. As a longtime east-west Ohio River transportation center, and as a major north-south overland travel artery, Cincinnati was called "The Crossroads of the Nation" as well as "The Gateway to the South." As it moved from the nation's chief meat packing center in 1835 to the world's largest pork packing center in 1845, Cincinnati was also known by the name of "Porkopolis." Many vestiges of this name remain today.

However, the suitably well-drained and fertile Ohio river valley hillside vineyards of one of America's best vintners of the middle eighteen hundreds, Nicholas Longworth, would prove to have a direct bearing on giving the city a nickname with supreme staying power. After receiving a much appreciated gift of high quality wine made from Longworth's Cincinnati grapes, the renowned American poet, Henry Wadsworth Longfellow (1807-1882), referred to Cincinnati as "the Queen of the West" in his 1854 poem "Catawba Wine".

Due to Longfellow's fame, Cincinnati, Ohio's predominant nickname, "The Queen City," has stuck ever since. Today, everywhere one turns in Cincinnati, Ohio, the name of "Queen City *this*" or "Queen City *that*" can be seen. Currently, in Cincinnati's telephone directory, there are well over one hundred listings of businesses that begin with the words "Queen City." So widespread is the nickname today that it is quite commonplace to hear eighteen-wheel interstate truck drivers referring to Cincinnati, Ohio on their CB (Citizen's Band) radios as "the Queen."

Over the years, however, due to sticky negative reputations that were generated by racial ultra-conservatism and rampant public corruption, the majestic connotation of the Queen's sterling and regal nickname has fallen into disrepute. In retrospect, it can readily be seen that several convergent historical determinants have been directly attributable to the Queen's propensity towards its adverse municipal behavior.

As its overall character is a direct by-product of its distinct history, it is not hard to understand why Cincinnati, Ohio's attitude to racial relations is the way that it is. Deeply rooted in its American past, the ultra-conservative racial attitude that Cincinnati is recognized for had its genesis at a time that began long before the Civil War and Longfellow's writings, deep into the days of chattel slavery in the United States.

Up until the Emancipation Proclamation in 1863, Cincinnati, Ohio was, geopolitically, a Northern, industrial and free American state that was separated by several hundred yards of the powerful Ohio River from Kentucky, a Southern, agrarian and slave holding state. As escaping Negro slaves unceasingly entered into the freedom land of the North by crossing the Ohio River into Cincinnati, the Queen became a portal that was abuzz with activity from the Underground Railroad.

During that day, typically, local Cincinnati businessmen, because of their strong economic, cultural and social ties to the South, opposed most causes that might have offended their neighbors on the other side of the Ohio River. After the Civil War ended, the Queen's proximal relationship to the South continued to be fertile ground for its development as a bastion for racial ultra-conservatism. Today, Southern sentimentalities and racial traditions, like the Ohio River, continue to run deep in Cincinnati, Ohio.

A second major contributing factor to the Queen City's racial attitudes resides within the cultural makeup of its population. As Cincinnati was peopled by large influxes of European immigrants during the nineteenth century, great waves of people from Germany and Ireland settled there. They not only brought with them rich social cultures which significantly contributed towards giving the Queen it's distinct municipal identity of today, but they also brought with them the fiercely conservative and clannish attitudes of their native lands.

It is from these wellheads of cultural identity that the Queen City also sprang a reputation for racial insensitivity. Within the context of the formation of its municipal character, the concomitant historic relationship that exists between the Queen's geographical positioning and its peopling is largely attributable to the development of its far-reaching reputation for being racially intolerant.

But ultra racial-conservatism was not all that the Queen City would become known for. By the early 1900's, a pattern of present-day municipal corruption and malfeasance had already begun to manifest itself. After many years of turn-of-the-century city bosses and their administrations who questionably operated the Queen City, by 1927, Cincinnati city politicians had literally thrown away six million dollars into 2.2 miles of never used underground subway tunnels that were dug into the city's central core.

Although scores of indictments were served on city and county leaders for skimming county funds, these idle, rotting and decaying tunnels still ominously lay in mute testimony to the long-standing and persistent nature of public corruption in the Queen.

Yet, singularly, it is not the Queen's communal signature of racial intolerance that is buttressed by its historic corruptive activity that brings this story to the fore. Instead, it is the unique set of circumstances that destined my life's path to cross that of the Queen.

Having been raised in the segregated southern United States during the racially tumultuous 1950's and 60's, when domestic civil rights tumult was the norm rather than the exception, my direction in life was determined at an early age. Not having to look so terribly far back in time to be sadly reminded of the staunch racial barriers that persistently remained in America, my personality was formed from the sum total of my life's experiences.

Caring parents constantly reminded me that, unlike white Americans, my life was being negatively impacted due to the color of my skin. With so much that was wrong, unequal and unjust within America's black community, I took it upon myself to become part of the solution, instead of part of the problem. As I felt internal and external forces directing my life's course, I knew that in some way, some how, I was on a mission.

As far back as I could remember, my parents taught me that this nation's institutional racial bigotry, like a recurring virus that is resistant to cure, was still a burdensome cultural pestilence infecting the American landscape. They also taught me that it was best to approach these types of racial barriers by understanding the bigger picture, and by turning those types of negatives into positives. The issue that was instilled into me by my parents was not that racism existed; instead, the question posed by them to me was what was I going to do about it?

During the Vietnam War era, when I experienced rampant racism while serving in the U. S. Army between 1969 and 1971, little did I realize that my destiny was headed towards a collision course with the powerful Queen that would give new definition the word *discrimination*. By the time I had graduated from Norfolk State University in the spring of 1976 with a BS in Business Administration and Marketing, it bothered me greatly that, regardless of the civil rights advances that had been made during my lifetime, intractable economic, social and political conditions naggingly continued to plague African-Americans. In viewing this as a significantly more important American problem rather than just an African-American problem, I felt compelled to do something about a vexing national predicament whose solution was much larger than myself.

In my well-intentioned determination to contribute towards the resolution of America's race problem, I started with an analogy of the causal factors that were at hand. With human nature being what it is, it was quite clear to me that no one was going to take care of African-Americans like African-Americans themselves.

I also knew that racial impediments continued to exist which thwarted African-Americans from equally entering into the mainstream of the American economy. It pained me to see that equal opportunities and employment were not sufficiently being created to get African-Americans out of the economic hole that the legacy of America's racial past was continuing to maintain. I made a commitment to myself to do something about it.

With my life's mission in mind, I moved to the Queen in the summer of 1976 after accepting a position to sell computer systems as a Marketing Representative with IBM. Arriving in Cincinnati with the fresh and unclouded perspective of an outsider who had the American dream in his heart and youthful exuberance in his veins, I was undaunted by the Queen's ultra-conservative reputation for race relations that had preceded my entrance into the city.

After my arrival, I began to measurably and persistently follow my dream of personal and professional business development in preparation for my goal of being a job-creating entrepreneur who could help to create much needed jobs within the black community of America. Having entered the corporate world for the first time as an eager and optimistic twenty-six year old bachelor on a self-appointed mission, the exposure that I achieved allowed for my rapid professional growth in the business world. As I learned and explored innumerable possibilities, I began to methodically put together the pieces of the puzzle that would help me to meet my goals.

By 1979, I had purchased my first piece of real estate located at 12066 Hitchcock Drive, in one of Cincinnati's suburbs. In the same year, Cincinnati's city manager appointed a Working Review Committee to devise a redevelopment program that consisted of a series of downtown goals for the remaining years of the 20th century. The creation of downtown housing in the blighted historic Garfield Place section of Cincinnati's central business district was key to this redevelopment program. By the end of 1979, there was no way that I could have seen the collision course that I was heading towards with the Queen, as the quiet go-ahead for Garfield Place development had already begun.

Chapter 2

Much Work To Do

> "We are not here to play, to dream, to drift;
> We have hard work to do and loads to lift;
> Shun not the struggle—face it, 'tis God's gift."
> —Shaftesbury

Owning a home meant more to me than having a place to live: it meant that I owned a piece of the rock. As real estate nationwide had undergone healthy appreciation levels for decades, the purchase of my home in 1979 started me well on my way towards using it as a financial leveraging base from which I could purchase other real estate. Time just seemed to roll on as I explored other possibilities.

After I married my beloved wife, Sandy, in 1980, I gained other invaluable professional sales experience while being in the employ of such corporate giants as Digital Equipment Corporation and Xerox Corporation. All along, Sandy and I remained focused on our highly desired entrepreneurial objectives while she taught school.

We both knew that my working for corporate America was rewarding within its own right, but it did not compare to our dream of eventually wanting to veer off into our own real estate development business. True to plan, we started a small specialty-contracting business while I got my license to sell real estate in the State of Ohio. By 1981, in addition to the house that we already had a mortgage on, Sandy and I bought our first rental property and started a real estate investment and development business that was designed to buy distressed single-family rental property in need of renovation.

As we were successful in turning this first piece of rental property into a positive cash flow producer, we quickly realized that we wanted to take advantage of the economies of scale that multifamily housing could bring. Despite its racially intolerant reputation, Sandy and I began to entertain the concept of looking immediately in and around the Queen's downtown for other real estate opportunities.

Like myself, Sandy was raised and nurtured in a family that taught understanding the responsibilities that one had to oneself, one's race and to one's nation. Although we both experienced the daily ugliness of racial segregation in Tidewater (Southeastern) Virginia, we were reared to believe that we had to earn our respect in life by the sweat off of our brows.

From our perspective, and regardless of the lingering racial polarization that persisted, we did not give up the ship of believing that America, with all of its flaws, was still the best country on earth. If anything, we felt that it was our duty as American citizens to do something about the racial problems that were having an adverse effect on the daily lives of most African-Americans. We had much work to do.

Sandy and I only had to look back in time from within our own families for archetypes. As our forebears had confronted the type of rigid racial barriers that we could only read about in history books, we were told how they had experienced a much more difficult time with overall racial intolerance and indifference than we ever did.

Both of our fathers, for example, served in the segregated U. S. Army during World War II. My father received a head injury while fighting the Nazis in France during World War II and Sandy's father was at Iwo Jima in the Pacific theater during the same war. At early ages, our mothers and fathers imparted upon us that giving up our rights as citizens (particularly in the face of adversity) was not an option. Imbued with a perspective that was a result of our upbringing, Sandy and I envisioned ourselves as answering a call to our country by helping to correct a national racial misdirection that was patently anti-constitutional.

Owning real estate in downtown Cincinnati became much more desirable for us when the Queen made moves to inject large sums of money into an area of its central business district that we had eyed. In 1982, as the City of Cincinnati realized the ongoing need for Garfield Place housing development, a formal document was generated named the *Cincinnati 2000 Plan*, incorporating at its heart the municipal housing goals from its 1979 redevelopment program.

"There is not a significant number of people now living downtown," the Cincinnati 2000 Plan's report declared. It went on further to say, "Some 2,800 residential units are dispersed in isolated pockets that provide little sense of neighborhood identity." The need, the plan suggested, might be for as many as 6,000 new residential units downtown.

Guided by a growing real estate business savvy and prowess, we looked forward to having the opportunity to expand our young investment business by incurring increased levels of calculated mortgage risk. The most important caveats to Sandy and I were threefold: the financing numbers had to be right; the real estate projections had to be sound; and, most of all, we had to have a warm and fuzzy visceral feeling about any additional financial commitments that we would make. We proceeded to do all of the types of things that readied our financial house, e.g., formulating a business plan, attempting to establish lender contacts, etc.

As we had pulled together a fairly sizable war chest that allowed us to make a sizable down payment on the purchase of additional real estate, like Christmas shoppers with cash in their pockets, Sandy and I began to look all around the Queen for the right real estate investment opportunities in 1983. We eventually decided to concentrate our buying efforts in the heart of the Queen, the central business district of Cincinnati's downtown. On September 6, 1983, I began talking to the City of Cincinnati regarding purchasing real estate in its downtown. My reception was noticeably cold.

Like most other major American cities of that day, the Queen's downtown skyline was strewn with construction booms in a building frenzy, as there was a profusion of available construction financing to many large concerns. Although Sandy and I could only marvel at having the financial wherewithal to command access to sizable amounts of construction financing, still, we, nevertheless, pressed forward to develop our own entrepreneurial dream.

From our hungry neophyte real estate investor's perspective, we fully understood that we were looking onto a double-leveled tier of bank borrowing difficulty. On one tier were the ordinary financing rigors that most people face. On another tier were the incrementally discriminatory financing rigors that most African-Americans face.

Determined not to be defeated because of our race, we prepared for the financing numbers game that we were in, as the test of whether we would win or not was based upon our success at getting suitable financing. We reasoned that the more creative opposition that we could muster against this type of illegal discrimination, the greater our chances would be to break through the barriers that borrowing through typical banking channels would present. In weighing our options, like in football, we calculated that we did not necessarily have to run through or over the barriers that were in front of us. As a result, we readied ourselves for the possibility of going around them in an end run.

Sandy and I were fully cognizant that the local Cincinnati grapevine was full of credible stories of tried and failed attempts by more-than-qualified African-Americans who were routinely kept out of owning property in the central business district—professional ball players and other well-to-do blacks included. As an avid baseball fan, I had already known that the Cincinnati Reds were one of the last Major League baseball teams to integrate. But, it was upon the expression of my desire to buy real estate in the heart of the Queen's downtown that I was reminded by Cincinnati friends and acquaintances about the extremely conservative racial attitudes that hung around the city like a dense river fog.

By the late fall of 1983, our interest had greatly spawned in the Queen's northwest downtown central business district quadrant. After inspecting the entire central business district multifamily housing inventory of Cincinnati, Sandy and I ended up with a handful of affordable and prospective investment properties that were a five-block radius northwest of the absolute center of the downtown business hub. All of the prospective buildings were large, in need of major repair and were rundown historic row houses or former historic mansions located on West Ninth Street in Cincinnati's Garfield Place area, the area that had been quietly targeted for development by the Queen.

Whereas these targeted investment properties were immediately adjacent to many mainstream downtown businesses and concerns, e.g., the City's NBC TV station affiliate (WLWT), one of the nation's top libraries (The Public Library of Cincinnati and Hamilton County), Cincinnati City Hall, etc., political pressures were continuing to build to force a higher and better use of properties in this rare residential pocket.

I also knew that the Queen's central business district core was landlocked to the south by the Ohio River, to the east and west by two large interstate highway systems, and to the north by a wide east-to-west city thoroughfare, Central Parkway, which separates it from the Queen's notorious high crime area called "Over the Rhine" (so named by German immigrants because the area was once separated from Cincinnati's downtown by a canal that reminded them of Germany's Rhine River). Accordingly, in our investment strategy, we took into consideration the fact that Cincinnati's rapid downtown development had to radiate northward in a domino effect, directly towards West Ninth Street.

Although most of the West Ninth Street buildings were structurally sound, architecturally significant and of historical importance, during 1983, they fell into a category of rundown multifamily rental housing that were populated by low income and transient tenants. Make no mistake about it; these West Ninth Street buildings were rat and roach infested. Winos regularly urinated (and sometimes defecated) on the street—even at high noon. Hookers and drug dealers solicited their business there as well.

Until this time in 1983, I had never seen rats sniffing and crawling all over a passed-out wino's body in an alley behind these buildings—or anyplace else for that matter. Not knowing if the poor fellow was dead or not, I actually chased the rats away from him while inspecting properties in the neighborhood. Fortunately, he was alive—stewed to the gills, but alive.

West Ninth Street was the good landlord's street from hell; the abode of societally damned tenants; a dark, slippery hellhole for unwary investors; a place of real estate management torment; and a decent apartment renter's netherworld. As the neighborhood had spun out of control after many decades of uninterrupted decline, the Queen's neglected West Ninth Street of 1983 was in the bottom of a downward spiral of habitability that left it unattractive to many investors and developers who were looking for opportunities that were not as challenging.

In the final analysis, investing there was a gut call. I believed that the possible benefits of owning property there greatly exceeded the negatives. Surely, West Ninth Street did not have the ideal conditions that I wanted, but it had the location that I desired, and the selling price ranges that I needed. I knew that, if I had any chance of being a successful building owner in that neighborhood, I had to figure out a way to effectively develop any property that I bought there from a losing money position to that of turning a profit.

I saw the conditions in this out of control neighborhood as only being short-term impediments to a gentrification movement that was welling unforeseen. As a fright factor to many other developers created a window of buying opportunity for me, the neighborhood's outward appearances scared away and held at bay most other investors who wielded much greater financial and political strength than I had. As all outward signs pointed to the fact that the urban blight on West Ninth Street was temporarily distracting other investors away long enough to buy us the extra time that we needed to pursue mortgage financing, Sandy and I continued to press forward to wedge an opening for ourselves.

We had a warm and fuzzy feeling that we could not go wrong. Practically any way that we looked at it on paper, investment on West Ninth Street came out in the favorable light of our being able to meet our investment objectives. Running through the financial numbers of the buildings that we had narrowed our choices down to, Sandy and I increasingly realized that the prospective buildings fit our decision criterion for having an extremely high potential for rapid property appreciation. This was of extreme interest to us because it appeared that we would be able to maximize the return on our investment dollars in the shortest amount of time. From a marketing standpoint, it was quite obvious to me that the West Ninth Street building renovations that I could effectuate could solve an unmet demand for quality living space for many downtown office workers.

My curiosity peaked when I found out about the 1970 Garfield Place plans through my real estate marketing research. At this point, I began to salivate when I discovered that Cincinnati City Council had approved this very little ballyhooed municipal plan which called for a massive infusion of federal housing and infrastructure tax dollars into the immediate area that I was interested in.

However, what I discovered next stoked the fire even more under my already existing sense of urgency. In 1982, the Queen City had placed top priority on Garfield Place development. Specifically, millions of dollars of federal Community Development Block Grant (CDBG) funding from the federal government's Department of Housing and Urban Development (HUD) would soon begin to be infused into real estate that laid within six feet of the building that I liked most on West Ninth Street, 123 West Ninth Street.

CDBG financing from HUD provides billions of dollars in monetary grants to carry out a wide range of nationwide community development activities across America. As far as Sandy and I were concerned, this was our investment go-ahead, our green light, and the clincher. Convincingly, we then knew that West Ninth Street was the spot for us to invest in—if we could get in.

Moreover, Sandy and I realized that the neighborhood was a sleeper that most opportunity-seeking real estate investors and developers that prospected West Ninth Street were not aware of. Based upon our real estate investment calculations, buying strategically located real estate on West Ninth Street also made sense to us because the purchase prices of the neighborhood's properties had fallen to their lowest points, a favorable sign that investors relish. Having identified most of the rundown properties on West Ninth Street as golden investment opportunities, we strongly felt that this area was an intentionally hushed property boom that was just waiting to explode.

The more we examined the numbers of our financial projections, the more Sandy and I were convinced that this was the area where we wanted to buy. At this point, the frantic pace of our searching for financing kicked in. We knew that if we were seriously going to approach purchasing real estate in the West Ninth Street market, we had to figure out a way to beat other attentive investors to the punch while overcoming rampant banking discrimination at the same time. Nothing drove home this point more than the cold shoulder that was increasingly extended to me as I continued talking to the City of Cincinnati regarding purchasing real estate in its downtown.

While the locals slept, maybe it was the fresh perspective that I brought to the Queen as an outsider which allowed me to see the tremendous upside potential that these properties held. Certainly, the same positive signs that I saw for favorable investment conditions on West Ninth Street were there for all to see. Although I did not fully understand why others had not exploited the property that I was eyeing, I regarded the insight that I had as an answer to many prayers, a blessing from above, a gift from God.

Even though I only let a small and select circle of friends and acquaintances know of my downtown property purchasing plans, I still heard the same old refrains like, "You can't buy property in the central business district," and "No blacks are allowed to buy property downtown." Little did they know that they only added fuel to my fire. My rationale for proceeding forward was not only bolstered by a sense of urgency to not be beaten at the draw in buying property on West Ninth Street at the most opportune time, but it was also my chance to test the U. S. Constitution which outlawed discrimination.

Fortuitously, 123 West Ninth Street held more promise for our being able to buy and develop it than any of the other downtown buildings. It was a charming four-story structure that possessed much personality and it was situated in the middle of a row of historic buildings that dated back to the middle 1800's. As it was built in a neighborhood where some of the Queen's most prominent citizens once lived, the building had many covered-up architectural features that revealed high-class amenities of a long gone era.

As its ground floor contained a 2,300 square foot commercial space that had a twelve-foot high and ornately pressed tin ceiling, passing pedestrians could plainly see its period beauty through a large glass-paned street level display window. Although, by my inspection of the building, I soon discovered that passersby could not see that 123 West Ninth Street was also designed in such a way that a twenty-five foot long by four-foot wide external light well was incorporated into the buildings internal structure.

Like the indentation that one would get by sticking the small end of a two-by-four into the far-left middle of one shoe box-sized block of soft clay laying on its side next to others, 123 West Ninth Street's light well is hidden from street view. As the building's original nineteenth-century architect created a unique structural effect by taking full advantage of the already existing four-story brick party wall of the adjoining 121 West Ninth Street, a four-sided encasement of 123 West Ninth Street's light well was created.

I was able to determine that the creation of this light well accomplished more than just bathing the top three floors of 123 West Ninth Street with a natural light source through eighteen windows with stone sills and lintels at the hidden center of the building. While this outside air canyon dropped down twenty-eight feet from the top of the building to a sunken roof at the floor level of the second floor, I could see that a large skylight used to be there that illuminated that section of the ground floor of the commercial space. As mammoth solid steel pillars with decorative capitals stood underneath and supported the heavy brick weight of three stories of upper-floor light well walls, I knew that 123 West Ninth Street was once a very special place.

Although each floor had been divided into sleeping rooms over the years, I could also see that the upper three floors were originally designed as townhouses for the well-to-do. The white Italian marble stairs that led up from the street level were only a precursor to the building's other designed luxuries. Building amenities such as oversized oak pocket doors; three-foot tall oval bullet windows that pivoted; tiled fireplace hearths; mahogany-trimmed oak stairwell banisters; large walk-in bay windows on each floor's frontage; and a skylight that lit the front stairwell made me keenly aware that the building's occupants during the 1800's were from a high economic strata. With my recognizing that it was the architectural prize that it was, I salivated even more at the prospect of being able to own it.

As fate would have it, in November of 1983, Sandy and I were able to purchase this property because of a combination of many variables, i.e., prayer, luck, timing, exhaustive research, etc. For example, had it not been for my walking down the street past 123 West Ninth Street at precisely the right moment when the owner of the building came storming out onto the sidewalk in anger, I would not have been able to purchase it.

Had our paths not crossed at that particular point in time when 123 West Ninth's owner was so terribly upset at a longtime prospective buyer who repeatedly reduced the selling price of the building (after the owner had repeatedly accepted it), he would not have offered to sell the building to me on the spot. It was because of this chance encounter on the sidewalk in front of his building that the infuriated owner of 123 West Ninth Street offered to let me assume his mortgage. Essentially, what that did was that it allowed Sandy and I to circumnavigate the normal real estate financing gauntlet that is ofttimes thrown up in front of qualified black buyers. This was the end run that we were looking for.

As the building required a hands-on type of owner—not just a passive investor, I was willing to do what was necessary to make the operation of the building a success. To make this building work, Sandy and I knew that we had to divert every available dime of our discretionary personal income into this building project. As we were deeply immersed in the process of building a coveted real estate development and investment business, this was a sacrifice that we did not mind in the least. After the building was purchased, the work really began.

As I had become a West Ninth Street property owner, the immediate challenge was then to bring into line a building that was completely out of control. First, rents had to be accurately set and collected. This, within itself, was no easy feat, as it was my job to tame a building full of mutinous and hostile tenants. As an upstart multifamily building owner, this entire endeavor reminded me of something that was as out of control as a *National Lampoon Landlord Vacation* movie would have been.

Oh, it was a mess. As the new kid on the block, I was a no-nonsense landlord who was firm, but fair, and was perceived as a threat to the pecking order of constantly loitering and habitually delinquent-paying tenants. I guess that was why I was physically and verbally assaulted on numerous occasions. In any case, while substantial building and property management improvements went on apace, the good tenants were allowed to stay and the bad ones were evicted.

Immediately, Murphy's Law took over. All kinds of problems seemed to pop up with the building's electrical and heating systems. Once, a small roach tried to crawl up my nose after I had nodded off at 3 a.m. one morning while waiting to see if a water line plumbing patch that I had installed in the basement was going to hold.

Like clockwork, within one month after I purchased 123 West Ninth Street, a rapid succession of significant public announcements began to signal the beginning of the West Ninth Street area's soaring rise in property values. On December 17, 1983, an article appeared in the Metro section of *The Cincinnati Enquirer* entitled "Housing Subsidies Topic of Hearing." The article mentioned how neighborhood activists were planning to pack a public hearing before Cincinnati City Council to support their side in a developing confrontation about the subsidization of downtown housing. The Queen's neighborhood organizations that were vying for the same scarce federal tax dollars vigorously objected to the City Manager's allocation of housing subsidies to Garfield Place.

This newspaper article went on to say that "The confrontation centers on whether 1984 federal CDBG money from HUD should be spent on several downtown sites—particularly a $1.4 million commitment to Garfield Place. The federal government provides the city with a lump sum each year—about $16 million in 1983—and with some restrictions lets the city decide how to spend it. Most of the money supports neighborhood housing and economic development."

A political storm began to brew when City Manager, Sylvester Murray wanted to spend $1.4 million of the federal money to subsidize private development of upper-middle- and upper-income housing in downtown Cincinnati's Garfield Place section that rested six feet away from 123 West Ninth Street's property line. But the Community Development Advisory Council, whose members were appointed by Murray, and who were neighborhood activists, rebelled against the proposed expenditure, and recommended no money at all for Garfield housing.

The article concluded by saying, "There are really two issues involved in this vote of rebellion by the advisory council. First is a philosophical one—whether these federal dollars should be used to benefit the well to do at all. A second one is whether the Development Department should be allowed to have money for relatively undeveloped projects. There is no private developer on line yet to build more Garfield Place housing, and the city hasn't yet chosen a specific site in the area on which it wants the new housing built."

In this same vein, on December 19, 1983, an article appeared in the Editorial section of *The Cincinnati Post* entitled "The need for housing." This article brought to the public's attention that there was a drastic need for decent and affordable downtown housing, due to the fact that most of Cincinnati's downtown residential units were unfit or dilapidated. The article went on to say that, because most of the downtown residential population too often were the poor who could not pay enough taxes to support schools, city services and human needs, a new approach had to be taken.

The Mayor at that time, Arn Bortz, a real estate developer of Towne Properties, was featured in the editorial. In the opinion of *The Cincinnati Post*, this editorial further stated, "Cincinnati has a space problem. Mayor Bortz suggested in his housing paper that a complete inventory of city-owned land be made to find out what is available for middle-income residential development. The mayor is a real estate developer himself. He knows housing. We believe he has started in the right direction and we urge him to stay the course."

The crescendo drumbeat of Garfield Place real estate development activity that began to catapult Sandy and I into an orbit within the

Cincinnati real estate development milieu went on into the beginning months of 1984. In a defensive move that was designed to keep the $1.5 million (instead of the anticipated $1.4 million) of recently allocated CDBG funding in the Queen's Garfield Place section, the Garfield Neighborhood Association (GNA) was incorporated on January 17, 1984. By this time, I had established my office in apartment number one of 123 West Ninth Street.

At the GNA's initial meeting I was appointed as Chairman of the Membership Committee. Soon after this initial meeting, our new organization applied for legitimate neighborhood status recognition with the Queen. The GNA was formed to politically establish a legitimate vehicle for the receipt of federal financing to a formally structured neighborhood organization. The Association was formed to protect the interests of its members and to affect positive change in the place that its members worked, lived and owned property in the Garfield Place area.

The object of this organization was to preserve and develop the Garfield community as a delightful in-town residential and business area for all citizens. The GNA recognized that Cincinnati's Garfield Park had a traditional charm; that the future of a valuable community like the Garfield Neighborhood area should not be left to chance; and that its growth and development should be guided by actively interested residents and business people.

The organization concerned itself with development, zoning regulations, housing code enforcement, traffic patterns, shopping and recreational facilities, attractive appearance, maintenance and other measures designed to preserve and upgrade the area known as the Garfield Neighborhood.

Within the Queen's downtown of 1984, the Garfield area was a distinct neighborhood with its own characteristics. Among these characteristics were the presence of two public facilities that were used by people of all incomes in the city: one of the top six libraries in the United States, The Public Library of Cincinnati and Hamilton County, and Piatt Park, the Queen's oldest Park.

Building preservation, growth and development of the Garfield neighborhood was not only important to those who resided and worked in the area, but to the City as a whole by providing market-rate housing for working people and retirees who have disposable incomes. The GNA understood that it was the voice of the only location in the Queen that possessed the tremendous potential for the development of a concentrated neighborhood of new housing for these desired residents.

The GNA concentrated its initial efforts on the Queen's City Council. We applied pressure upon them in order to get the City to stimulate additional capital investment into the neighborhood by applying money from HUD (which was at its disposal) to take advantage of Garfield development opportunities that had been on the shelf thirteen years theretofore.

As the politically connected unit that we were, the GNA was astutely aware that the City had to take the initial step, which was to assemble the Garfield area's properties into a formal neighborhood for new housing development. Prior to our incorporation, this step had been deferred, often in the interest of simply abating the dueling interests of the outlying neighborhoods versus the downtown central business district argument that was fueled by competition for the allocation of scarce federal tax dollars.

As a small and struggling entrepreneur who was part of an organization that consisted of prominent, wealthy and influential individuals and businesses in Cincinnati's body politic, I was an anomaly who was caught up in a true-to-life real estate monopoly game. I was fully cognizant of plans to infuse many millions of public and private investment dollars into properties that were all around 123 West Ninth Street.

As a member in good standing in the GNA, I had an inside track to understanding that my West Ninth Street building was in the center of a federally subsidized area that was designated to be the focal point for residential development targeted to become the city's first and only residential community in the heart of downtown. The boundaries of the GNA's area encompassed from 7th to 9th Street, and from Walnut to Plum Street. At the GNA's inception, City Council was composed of: Mayor Arn Bortz; Bobbie Sterne; David Mann; Marian Spencer; Ken Blackwell; Charlie Luken; Sally Fellerhoff; Guy Gukenberger; and Peter Strauss.

Although our non-scientific (but accurate) assessment was based purely on the local grapevine, Sandy and I were fairly confident that we were the only blacks who owned property outright in the Queen's central business district. By the same token, we knew that the strongest opposition to CDBG funding into the Garfield Place area came from neighborhoods that were predominantly black. Knowing this, Sandy and I watched at how I had been eagerly recruited to join the ranks of the GNA's conservative group of property owners and businessmen for my showcase value.

On January 18, 1984, while glancing at the streetscape through the large ceiling to floor bay windows of the second floor front apartment that I had converted into my office, I saw the owner of the building that was directly across the street, 124 West Ninth Street, being verbally assaulted by one of her tenants. Having a crow's nest view, I witnessed a large barrel-chested and athletic shirt-wearing male tenant of 124 West Ninth Street verbally accosting the emotionally distraught divorcee building owner, who was quickly retreating from the premises to her car that was parked on the street in front of the building. To my seasoned eyes, I immediately recognized that this was obviously another West Ninth Street building that was out of control.

Upon going down to the street to both console and talk to her, I quickly learned that she had a change of heart for West Ninth Street building ownership and desperately wanted to get out of the landlord business. With all of the creative financing options that I had recently become familiar with in getting my Ohio real estate license, I began a running dialog with her to see if arrangements could be made for her to sell her building to me.

In the January 30, 1984 GNA meeting, it was resolved that the City Manager should be notified that we were officially in business and should be added to the list of Cincinnati's Neighborhood Groups, and as such, should be entitled to all of the rights, privileges and obligations of Cincinnati's other neighborhood organizations. After each Trustee of the GNA corporation (myself being one of them) took an oath of office at the conclusion of the organizational meeting, we marched two blocks en masse, passing 123 West Ninth Street, to a City Council meeting that was convening.

There, the GNA bird-dogged and pressed the Queen's City Council hard to publicly acknowledge and confirm the allocation of $1.5 million in the 1984 CDBG funds from HUD for the acquisition of a housing site in Garfield Place, as their decision had wafted under pressure from other neighborhood groups. Succeeding in that regard, we also got City Council to confirm its funding in the Garfield Place and Cincinnati 2000 Plan by committing to an ongoing program for development of our neighborhood. Ironically, as have-nots who owned property on West Ninth Street for a little more than two months, Sandy and I found ourselves on the side of the haves, who wanted to use the $1.5 million of federal money as a springboard to subsidize private development of upper- to middle-income housing in Garfield Place.

As a GNA member, I had access to closely held neighborhood development information that gave me a full appreciation of the investment potential that I had in my building at 123 West Ninth Street. GNA members routinely discussed strategies as to how to get our share of additional federal HUD CDBG financing and were exposed to a whole host of local real estate development facts and considerations. Therefore, I knew that Garfield Place had become a federally subsidized area that had been designated to be a focal point for massive amounts of new and rehabbed residential development in the Queen's downtown well in advance of the public being informed.

On February 2, 1984, *The Cincinnati Post* printed an article in its Metro section entitled "Park's future bright." It reported how Cincinnati's Department of Economic Development had recommended that the Queen's City Council hire Chicago developer Charles H. Shaw to prepare a master plan for the future of more than 1,000 units of housing on five sites in the Piatt Park area—the two blocks along Garfield Place between Vine and Elm streets.

The article mentioned that, at this point, the City had already applied for $1.5 million in CDBG funds. Using a large graphic that displayed the sites for 1,000 proposed housing units from the Cincinnati 2000 Plan, the article also featured a photograph that presented a view of the two-block stretch of Garfield Place looking west between Vine and Elm streets, designated to become a downtown residential center with apartments, shops and night spots.

On March 21, 1984, Cincinnati's City Council passed legislation for the allocation of $1.5 million in CDBG funds for a housing site in the Garfield Place area. It was satisfying to me to know that I had played an important role in the politics of getting Cincinnati City Council to approve this hard fought for allocation. It was at this point that Sandy and I knew that we had become real players in the Queen's downtown real estate game. From the inside of a organization that had strong political connections, for the first time in my life I was seeing how the powerful flexed their muscles to have their way.

On Sunday, March 25, 1984, I saw how the GNA's cause was helped by an Editorial page leadoff article *The Cincinnati Enquirer* entitled, "DOWNTOWN, Garfield Place housing deserves the highest priority from the city." This article stated that "...a major goal of the (Cincinnati) 2000 Plan has been the development of additional downtown housing. The development of a residential neighborhood in the central business district is important for several reasons. For one, downtown housing makes it unnecessary for men and women employed downtown to commute from outlying neighborhoods. For another, an expanding, permanent population downtown means increased viability for all of downtown and generates still more business development. Garfield Place offers an extraordinarily attractive and available arena for residential development."

On the next day, March 26, 1984, the well-mobilized GNA met at 11:45 A.M. at the Cincinnati Club. We knew that City Council was under heavy pressure from other neighborhoods to eliminate or cut the proposed $1.5 million request for Garfield area housing. By 3:00 P.M. of the same day, we were in the Finance Committee meeting in City Council chambers doing battle. As several councilmen were wavering and considering a $400,000 cut from the city administration's recommendations, we held our ground.

By April 25, 1984, only five months after purchasing 123 West Ninth Street, the factors of prayer, luck and timing came into play again for Sandy and I. We executed another financial discrimination-thwarting end run by purchasing the building which is directly across the street from 123 West Ninth Street, 124 West Ninth Street. Even though it was structurally sound, the march of time had taken its toll upon 124 West Ninth Street by the time that I had purchased it. As its once rich glow had been significantly downgraded to the squalor of a 21-room drug, roach and rat infested tenement slum, it had become a place where common prostitutes often did their dirt.

Built in 1850, ten years before the start of the American Civil War, 124 West Ninth Street (formerly the Thomas Morrow mansion) was an unaltered embodiment of a three-story Greek Revival townhouse. Although it was neglected for years, I also salivated at this building because of its marvelous architectural characteristics. Some of the important features of this building were: its vermiculated Dayton limestone facing; its severe Grecian influences; its rusticated foundation; its stone shelf lintels and dentils; and its skylight-lit classic stairway entrance.

Although there were countless layers of paint over everything, and many anachronistic sleeping room wall divisions that had been erected to form squalidly cramped living spaces in spacious areas that were originally designed for opulent living, my eyes detected hidden period amenities that were still of architectural significance. As it still showed signs of its originally being gas-lit throughout, viewing the ornate marble and cast iron fireplace mantles, along with its intricate woodwork and moldings, could easily take a historian back in time. As a well planned residence that emphasized creature comforts, 124 West Ninth Street also had a stand-alone two-story servant's quarters at the rear of the building's ninety foot long brick-paved side courtyard.

Other features let one know that the building was special in its heyday. The rear of the second floor housed a prayer room that contained a large leaded glass transom that featured, among other things, beveled gothic arches. But I thought that the grandeur of the premises was reflected most in its twelve-foot ceilings. Not only did these ceilings give the building a sense of delightful spaciousness, but that same feeling of airiness was amplified when walking into any one of the four twelve-foot bay windows that overlook the building's side courtyard from three different floors. There was also a picturesque brick wall that enclosed the property's courtyard that was ninety feet long, six and one-half feet tall and one foot thick.

While we cut corners to save, Sandy and I poured every available dime that we had into both buildings to keep them afloat. In order to meet the constant business expenses of paying utility bills, legal expenses and insurance premiums, and while buying carpeting, refrigerators, stoves, kitchen cabinets, toilets, lumber, office and maintenance supplies, roofing materials, paint, drywall sheets, plaster, screws, nails, etc., Sandy and I determinedly reinvested the ever-increasing rent receipts that we generated back into the buildings that we were improving.

For us to have achieved some modicum of success, we continued to deny ourselves many of the creature comforts of life. Although we had long outgrown our house with our growing family, we stayed put in order to conserve our available cash for downtown renovations, until suitable building financing could be arranged. We began to feel a bit Neanderthal in a nuclear age from denying ourselves so much for so long. But, we were contented because we were on track with the entrepreneurial goals of our American dream.

In the process of cleaning up the buildings to increase their rent appeal, I cosmetically changed the indoor appearance of the buildings by buying paints that were on clearance and carpets that had been used. We even bought secondhand draperies with white backings in order to give the windows in the front apartments of both buildings a more attractive street appeal.

Taking full advantage of the horticultural interests that were instilled in me by my mother, I transformed the lackluster urban streetscape of my block into a veritable oasis of floral beauty. Like the sudden appearance of a garden of roses in a barren desert, I gave these two center-of-the-block buildings new personalities by emblazoning their fronts with long window boxes and planters filled with the lush greenery and color of cascading floral arrangements consisting of hanging vinca vines, petunias, asparagus ferns and geraniums. By the summer of 1984, I was awarded the first of almost yearly building beautification awards from a prominent downtown organization by the name of Clean Cincinnati.

Thereupon, due to the improvements that Sandy and I made to these downtown properties, the apartments became increasingly demanded by tenants with higher incomes, as the West Ninth Street neighborhood went through a steady and inexorable metamorphosis.

From a real estate speculation standpoint, Sandy and I could not have been more correct in our predictions in purchasing these two buildings. In 1985—just two years after we first bought downtown, these properties became part of the Ninth Street Historic District and, as part of this designation, were placed on the National Register of Historic Places. Subsequently, due to the increased recognition that I received as a successful real estate developer, the President and Trustees of The National Trust for Historic Preservation announced my election to a full vested membership in its National Trust.

As both buildings were directly in the path of central business district development that was radiating northward, West Ninth Street properties became some of the fastest—if not the fastest—appreciating real estate in the City of Cincinnati, Ohio. The HUD CDBG money that had begun to be infused into the Garfield Place area ushered in an era of public and private investment that set off a chain reaction of real estate development activity which moved ahead at a frenetic pace. In the several buildings that are right next door to 123 West Ninth Street alone, a torrent of millions of private investment dollars began to flow into those historic properties, as very healthy levels of gentrification ensued.

Within two years of the time that Sandy and I purchased our first downtown building in the Queen, the cheap sleeping rooms and squalid tenement slum apartments that were in the same block as our properties began to be transformed into upscale apartments with spiral staircases, balconies and wood burning fireplaces. Soon, other businesses such as an advertising agency, lawyer's offices, an interior designer's office, headquarters offices for a commercial printer, a computer consulting firm, and headquarters for a philanthropic organization that supports the fine arts in Cincinnati moved into the block.

On September 22, 1985, *The Cincinnati Enquirer* printed an article entitled "Cincinnati Club Renovation Mixes Old, New Touches". For the GNA members and Garfield place area property owners, this article made an earth shattering development announcement about the old Cincinnati Club and Phoenix buildings that were located approximately 200 feet east of 123 West Ninth Street.

Mention was made of how the renovation was a project of the Ameritas Company, an Atlanta-based firm that specialized in restoring old buildings. The article went on to say, "Ameritas purchased the two buildings from the Cincinnati Club in May, 1984, for $4.6 million, and will transform them into 175,000 square feet of office space...The $18 million renovation project, now called the Piatt Park Office Center, is an extensive one."

Development on West Ninth Street moved ahead at breakneck speed. By February 24, 1986, GNA members received inside information that the City had disbursed $265-285,000 for updated drawings on energized Garfield Place activity.

As I was an exception to the rule of white real estate ownership in the Queen's downtown, I became somewhat of a news item and was thrown into the limelight of local attention. On March 9, 1986, a large 5"x 8" picture of me was published in a newspaper article on the top front page of the Sunday Real Estate section of *The Cincinnati Enquirer*. As the large heading of the front page reflected the pace of development activity around my downtown buildings, it was captioned,

"West Ninth Street enjoys a revival: Garfield Place plans, rehabbers push up property prices."

By early 1986, a $50 million, two-block wide office development, Centennial Plaza, began construction beside Cincinnati's City Hall. This new construction site was approximately 800 feet away from 123 West Ninth Street.

As the Garfield Place real estate phenomenon became an ever-growing news event, local newspapers regularly heralded the latest developments of the area's targeted development prize. On May 13, 1986, the front page headline of *The Cincinnati Post* read, "$3 million plan to give facelift to Piatt Park." Although the actual cost was $3.75 million, Piatt Park on Garfield Place is located only 90 feet away from 123 West Ninth Street. The renovation was presented as part of the city's large housing redevelopment plan for the two-block area at Garfield Place.

In addition to the extensive landscaping, new sidewalks, city streetlights, soft park lights, new benches, planters, new trees, new paving and stonework that was planned, the newspaper article announced that Piatt Park was targeted by the city to undergo a major renovation that included moving the mammoth equestrian statue of President William Henry Harrison to a European-style plaza and the construction of two new granite encased fountains.

Besides the moving of the Harrison statue from the intersection of Garfield Place and Vine Street to the plaza at the west end of Garfield Place at Elm Street, the newspaper article mentioned that the City's plan called for the large bronze statue of President James Garfield, then in the middle of Garfield Place at Race Street, to be placed where the Harrison statue was. "The Harrison statue is larger and more impressive when seen from the full distance of the east part entrance at Vine Street," city planners were quoted as saying.

The article went on further to say that the city had long been planning construction of middle- and upper-income condominiums and apartments at Garfield Place as part of its commitment to increasing housing downtown. Not long afterwards, on June 10, 1986, Cincinnati's *Downtowner* newspaper printed an interview of me entitled "Bill Kiah sees his vision of downtown paying off."

With one mandate to produce units of low-income housing, the City of Cincinnati brought Wayne Chapman into office on November 1,

1986 as the Director of Neighborhood Housing and Conservation (NHC). As the City was under pressure from the neighborhood groups, Chapman was told to build them anywhere, and build as many as possible.

On January 7, 1987, *The Cincinnati Post* printed a front page headline that read, "Downtown land values soar." On March 4, 1987, *The Cincinnati Post* printed an article entitled "Piatt: future oasis in 'urban canyon.'" This article announced that Piatt Park would soon receive a $3.5 million facelift as part of the city's plans to line Garfield Place with upscale inner-city housing.

The article went on further to say that "Garfield Place, which is divided by Piatt Park, was scheduled to have a portion of onc of thc two narrow traffic lanes on each side to be used to widen the park, leaving one wider traffic lane and one parking lane." As an indication of the upcoming real estate boom that was about to take place within six feet of 123 West Ninth Street's property line, the article continued by writing, "City plans eventually call for a $202 million project that would create 1200 housing units on five sites along and near Garfield Place...The city began to acquire land for the first phase of the housing project at Elm Street and Garfield Place."

With the rapid appreciation of our downtown properties, by March 27, 1987, Sandy and I had a net worth of $216,535, with total assets of $541,901 and total liabilities of $325,366. Try as we did, the sad irony of our financial standing was that we were forced into being real estate rich and cash poor because of illegal discrimination by the banks of the Queen. Finding it next to impossible to borrow money based on our positive net worth, or our stellar positions in the community and our good credit standing, the question remained: What were we going to do about it?

Throughout this long and arduous process, when building repairs were needed, or when bills needed to get paid and there was no money, prayerfully, Sandy and I began to draw upon a dual reservoir of determination and creativity in order to forge ahead. All along, we were fervently convinced that the hand of Providence continually guided us through the numerous financial straits and obstacles that we had no solutions for. We painfully remained saddled with the unlawful burden of discriminatory lending practices by the Queen's banking industry that stymied our upward progression.

Tending to concentrate on the brighter side of things, Sandy and I knew that we were urban pioneers who had paid their dues by being on West Ninth Street before the first wave of construction and building rehabilitation activity rolled through the neighborhood like a Pacific tsunami. With the valuation dynamics of our downtown properties being what they were, we were comforted to know that we were riding the crest of a rapidly swelling real estate appreciation wave that was unavoidable and had to be responded to.

Knowing that we had bought right, there was no denying of the excitement that we felt as the values of 123 and 124 West Ninth Street skyrocketed. Despite the lending roadblocks that had been placed in our way by the Queen, there was no denying of the sense of pure satisfaction that Sandy and I felt, as we knew that we were creating significant amounts of equity by the sweat of our brows. Knowing that a level playing field was being denied to us, we worked even harder to not be denied.

As construction finally began on the renovation of Piatt Park in May of 1987, a fissure of race-based opposition to our ownership of West Ninth Street properties widened significantly and silently beneath the surface. While sinister forces skulked in the wings of the Queen's lending institutions, deeper, more powerful hidden forces directed a well-coordinated effort of broad-based and intolerant municipal policy against Sandy and I.

In the face of it all, West Ninth Street took on a larger significance for me. Having placed a heavy mantle of civic responsibility upon my shoulders, I believed that I had much work to do in the limited amount of time that I had in this life on earth. This challenge was my fate. This fight was my calling.

Chapter 3

The Evil Hand Moves

"We sometimes learn more from the sight of evil than from an example of good; and it is well to accustom ourselves to profit by the evil which is so common, while that which is good is so rare."
—Pascal

It was a time in the Queen when my real estate investment and development business had been perpetually locked into a patently illegal bank lending environment that was almost a half-decade long. Like an apparition materializing from a fog, it was also a time when the winds of change blew across the Queen to reveal the larger hidden presence of pervasive racial discrimination that stealthily hung over an increasingly vocal African-American community.

Even with the outstanding equity position that we had by owning a real estate investor's dream, Sandy and I had no doubt that we were being systematically cut off at the knees by Cincinnati lending institutions that would not let us borrow the much warranted financing for reinvestment into our prized investment properties. Contrary to the federal lending compliance measures that they touted, Sandy and I knew that the Queen's banks were being allowed to operate out of bounds. My investigation furthered in order to see why this was so, and how the Queen was illegally doing it.

The ongoing common talk that there were no other central business district property owning blacks in the Queen confirmed the suspicions of Sandy and I that African-Americans, regardless of their economic standing, were, in effect, still being kept out of real estate ownership there. From our perspective, the exclusivity of our downtown real estate status was not a source of pride but, if anything, a sad reflection of the state of racial affairs in the Queen.

There were bank-wide refusals to recognize the stark surplusage of collateral that existed in either one of our West Ninth Street properties.

The nonsensical rationalizations that were repeatedly used to deny us warranted access to development financing became even more odious when viewed for what they were: abstract redlining.

Based upon the characteristics of the neighborhood, redlining was an unlawful credit discrimination that got its name by lending institutions literally drawing red lines around an area designated for non-lending. As my two desirably located buildings sat in the center of the block on both sides of West Ninth Street, it was easy for us to visualize how imaginary red lines were opportunistically drawn around the property line of each of our buildings due to our racial characteristics. Sandy and I were experiencing the brunt of a planned financial cut off where there was, otherwise, a free flow of money.

With the equity in the downtown property that we had, any qualified lending institution in the Queen would have been in a win-win situation to lend Sandy and I the financing for the nominal building improvements that we requested. Even in the worst case, had we fallen flat on our faces in failure, the trifling amount of needed building financing that we would have borrowed would have been more than enough to adequately cover the loan.

Greater still, the out-and-out windfall that would have been gained by foreclosing on some of the most desirable real estate in the greater Cincinnati, Ohio area should have been an additional incentive for the Queen's lending institutions to do business with us. Just as surely as Sandy and I were repeatedly expected to jump through craftily designed lending hoops that were designed to be exercises in futility, lending stealth in the Queen began to lose its cover.

When many in Cincinnati's African-American community began to compare notes, a disturbing pattern of citywide banking lending discrimination began to publicly emerge: we were all being stung by the same bee. As scores of us verified that we were not being fairly lent money by a recalcitrant banking lending establishment, a strategy was designed to combat this illegal banking activity. Collectively, we focused on the City of Cincinnati itself, due to the fact that it deposited, on a regular basis, millions upon millions of its public tax receipts into the local banks that were racially discriminating against us.

All of this was happening at a time that the Garfield Place area was very visibly awash in public and private development financing activity, and was receiving a substantial amount of news coverage. It is for this reason that Sandy and I gained a tremendous amount of recognition from within Cincinnati's black community, as our buildings sat noticeably untouched, while those around us went through major renovations.

Events of the day made it such that the unfair banking behavior that was being force-fed to Sandy and I coincided with that which many black Cincinnatians knew of and could relate to. The dilemma that I faced at 123 and 124 West Ninth Street came to epitomize the plight of the Queen's African-American community.

As part of this collective strategy of confrontation that was designed to force the Queen and its local banks to abide by the law, I was chosen from the ranks of many in Cincinnati's African-American community to be a salient example of the jutting injustices of local unfair bank lending practices. The obviousness of the illegal racial restrictions that had been imposed upon Sandy and I made it blatantly clear that we had become a cause célèbre.

It was obvious to concerned Cincinnati African-Americans that my downtown properties were gold mines. With all of the press coverage that had been given to me, they could plainly see that I had what it took to consummate a suitable development financing deal by being able to come to the lending table with something of substance that could be offered as collateral.

As my destiny unfolded in front of me, I was seeing that my personal commitment to do something with my life to improve the lot of African-Americans was coinciding with my lot as a victim of lender discrimination in the Queen. The banking inequities that made my downtown buildings stick out like a sore thumb were the root cause of my being chosen by my peers. Not only did I see this as a very serious opportunity for me to do my part as a concerned American citizen to bring to the public forum the national social evil of embedded racial discrimination, but I was honored to be able to do so as well.

For many weeks on end, as a result of an upsurge of mounting and visible resentment toward local banks and the City of Cincinnati by scores of disgruntled black folks, many African-Americans regularly showed up in meetings in the Queen's City Council chambers. We had one agenda in mind: bringing attention to the lending discrimination that was negatively impacting our lives.

As a well-orchestrated group that was headed by the current Secretary of State for the State Ohio, J. Kenneth Blackwell, Cincinnati

African-Americans applied a considerable amount of pressure by issuing an ultimatum to the Queen: either lend us money based on equal merit or stop depositing our tax dollars into those local banks. Extensive radio and television news coverage of the growing numbers of irate black Cincinnatians added to those pressures on the Queen and its banking industry.

As a result of our visible protests, the Cincinnati black community won a small victory from its political exertions when the Cincinnati Banking Disclosure Act (Ordinance 363) was begrudgingly adopted on September 21, 1988 by the Queen's City Council. Seen as a major inconvenience by powerful banks in the Queen which had not been required to disclose the amounts of their City of Cincinnati tax dollar receipts, one provision of this Act was that there be a public accounting of City tax dollar bank deposits.

Ordinance 363 was reluctantly accepted by many infuriated banks that had been in the practice of receiving large amounts little-disclosed tax dollar deposits from the Queen. Although it put a crimp in their operations, effectively, Ordinance 363 was a watered-down regulation so full of holes that it did not hold water.

Ordinance 363 required the banks of the Queen to appoint a panel, The Committee on Reinvestment, which was to have been empowered to oversee that banks lent to local blacks fairly. As it turned out, it was a rubber stamp organization consisting of handpicked figurehead puppets that did not set banking policy. With little or no dissent or discussion, it did nothing more than to endorse the programs and policies of the Queen's banks to make it appear that the Cincinnati banking community was allowing oversight of its banking operations. Even with the public eye upon them, the Queen's banks continued to go through disingenuous motions of lending compliance.

Even though it was a toothless piece of City legislation that continued to allow banks to feign adherence to banking laws that outlawed discriminatory activities, the net result of the 1988 Cincinnati Banking Disclosure Act was this: the Queen was forced to move when it did not want to. Angered, Cincinnati's banks quietly retaliated by underhandedly becoming more creative in shrouding their illegal banking lending discrimination practices.

A dirtier, quieter and more evil hand began to move as the Queen's ire was raised. From the hidden recesses of a powerful and ultra-conservative city banking industry that was collectively embarrassed, humiliated and set in its ways, a greater, more far-reaching process was set into motion that tied the arrogance of the Queen to the influence of its money.

It is from these corruptive beginnings that the trail of much greater federal criminal activity to the White House of the United States of America would be made clear. With its history of corruption, this is where the Queen became my secret nemesis. This is where the Queen began to lay in wait for me, as it prepared for the right opportunity to execute its particular brand of furtive retribution.

It was because of my drive to make America a better place for all Americans that I was singled out as a costly cause of embarrassment to a vindictive Queen that was hopelessly trapped in its own obstinacy. Like breaching the moat of an evil castle, I had entered a forbidden zone, a place that exposed the Queen in a way that it wished to be kept secret. Like a wicked and cunning storybook witch that was evilly peering into a cauldron of desires from the inner sanctum of a well-insulated ivory tower, it was as if the evil Queen began resorting to incantations to call up forces beyond its power in its refusal not to abide by the federal lending discrimination laws that applied to 123 and 124 West Ninth Street.

But the internal fuming of the Queen against me did not stop the hurried pace of real estate development and investment in the Garfield Place area. Horse drawn carriages had already begun their regular taxiing of many of Cincinnati's tourists down West Ninth Street, which had become a municipal showcase of the Queen. On October 21, 1988, at 3:40 P.M., as part of the National Trust for Historic Preservation's annual meeting, a very large pedestrian crowd from the downtown Cincinnati Architecture Tour passed between 123 and 124 West Ninth Street stopping, gazing, taking photographs and pointing, like out of town tourists in New York City.

During the month that Vice President George Bush was elected President of the United States, a newspaper article, "OK, park 'em: Restored presidential statues swap spots as they return to rejuvenated Piatt Park", appeared in The *Cincinnati Enquirer*. On November 8, 1988, this article showed a full color photograph of the large, newly polished and restored bronze equestrian statue of President William Henry Harrison, ninth President of the United States, being lowed into place in Garfield Place's Piatt Park. The statue sat approximately 150 feet from 123 West Ninth Street's property line.

Illustrating Cincinnati's pride in the renaissance of the Garfield Place area, the article mentioned that "The bronze horseback statue of [President] Harrison, formerly at the east end of Piatt Park, was returned to the park Monday at the west entrance on Elm Street. It will be the centerpiece of a new European-style plaza. A statue of [President] Garfield was reinstalled in the park at the Vine Street end, switching places with the Harrison statue…New fountains designed by Cincinnati sculptor Stuart Fink will go on each side of Race Street in the middle of the two-block park on Garfield Place."

Concurrent to all of these escalating West Ninth Street real estate boom developments was the continuation of my not being able to tap into the large amount of equity that I had amassed. The two Cincinnati, Ohio lenders who held mortgages on both of my buildings refused to lend Sandy and I additional warranted financing on either of our two West Ninth Street buildings. While other banks and savings and loans refused to extend lending to us as well, the only bite that I got was from a hesitant, strained lender, Suburban Federal Savings Bank (SFSB), that had provided development financing for a building two doors down from 123 West Ninth Street.

Of the two buildings that I owned, I concentrated my efforts on 123 West Ninth Street, due to the larger return on investment potential that it had. Even though I was able to effortlessly justify costs to rehab the entire building, which included nine efficiency apartments and the 2,300 square foot unoccupied commercial space on its ground floor, I was still unable to obtain a bare minimum of financing.

In a fall back position, I reasoned that, if I could not tap into all of the equity that was available in my downtown properties, I would, instead, attempt to get a lesser amount and obtain a larger development loan at another time. Therein, I decided that 123 West Ninth Street's commercial space would be rehabbed, due to the relatively larger income potential that it possessed. I also decided that the front of the building would receive cosmetic changes, i.e., exterior painting, front door reworking and refinishing, and front landing tile work, to greatly enhance the building's street appeal.

Sandy and I found out through our struggles to get suitable financing that there were many ways in which bank lending discrimination took form. One very convenient method that the banks used to deny justifiable financing to us was to negatively alter our true collateral position through the underappraising of our properties.

Strapped for available cash to pay for the types of extraneous appraisals that we were required to have performed, we had no other choice but to rely upon the appraisals of disinterested banks. Confined to a position where we had to accept a ridiculously low valuation of 123 West Ninth Street to get development financing, we were forced—out of the economic necessity of survival—to make the most of a situation that would allow us to have access to the large amount of equity in the first downtown building that we had bought.

On January 24, 1989, 123 West Ninth Street was appraised by SFSB at $280,000. Based upon a conservative market value, 123 West Ninth Street should have been appraised at $422,500. 124 West Ninth Street was worth at least $329,150.

After we lodged our disagreement with SFSB and saw that it was going nowhere, we were caught into an economic stranglehold that forced us to begin to make the most of a very negative do-or-die situation: either take the $45,000 driblet of limited financing that they offered us or sell the building. Forced into a predicament where we had no other option, lest we would have surrendered to the withering effects of lender discrimination without a fight, Sandy and I made a calculated move to accept the only financing that was available to us. As unfair as it was, we saw it as being our only hope to turn this negative situation into one that would give us a fighting chance to keep our valuable real estate.

Taking full advantage of the scarce dollars that were available to me—when there was a requisite need for much, much more, I was able to make each dollar look like three dollars due to my construction and dollar-stretching know-how. With a signed long-term commercial lease in hand, I was able to complete 123 West Ninth Street's commercial space renovation on time and under budget. Consequently, 123 West Ninth Street was successfully transformed into an investment property that generated significantly increased income. Even though I had demonstrated my ability to successfully develop my highly prized real estate, I still found it next to impossible to acquire the warranted financing that was necessary for additional improvements.

Unceasingly, the steady drumbeat of rapid development in the West Ninth Street area moved apace. By early 1989, the $50 million, two-block wide office development that was 800 feet away from 123 West Ninth Street (on the other side of Cincinnati City Hall), Centennial Plaza, was completed. Further, the completion of the landmark construction of Piatt Park in May of 1989 signaled the neighborhood's arrival as a very hot development area.

I had to constantly keep thinking ahead in order to avoid many immediate pitfalls. In mulling over my next move, I knew that I needed to shift gears to clear my mind and to get a fresh perspective of the lay of the Queen's land. In completing the final leg of doing research for a book on my African genealogy that I had started to write, in July of 1989, I ventured to the epitome of a faraway place, to the land where Timbuktu is: Mali, West Africa.

After a refreshing and introspective twenty-one day trip that took me to four West African countries (Mali, Ivory Coast, Liberia and Sierra Leone) and three European countries (France, Holland and England), I came back to the Queen refreshed and with many positive results for my writing research. As well, I also came back with an invigorated mindset that was necessary for me to challenge the Queen's culture of corruption and racial discrimination that had negatively impacted my American dream.

By September of 1989, The Year 2000 Review Committee, a blue-ribbon panel of political, corporate and civic leaders began its fifteen-month effort to review and rewrite Cincinnati's Year 2000 Plan. Led by the City's Director of NHC, Wayne Chapman, Cincinnati's housing program designers made their first attempt at fashioning a long-term housing plan to guide the Queen into the next century. With respect to HUD's CDBG Entitlement Program, Wayne Chapman was also the powerful City of Cincinnati official who had been designated under federal law to have the primary responsibility as the Chief Executive Officer for the conduct of the city's governmental affairs.

A 97-page document was created as the Housing Sub-Committee Report of the 2000 Plan Review Board recommended that the restoration of historic row houses—like 123 and 124 West Ninth Street—be established as a primary goal. This Board's housing blueprint embodied the Queen's commitment to rebuilding deteriorated neighborhoods and increasing home ownership.

Notwithstanding the soft real estate marketplace throughout Cincinnati and the nation during a significant part of the late 1980's and the early 1990's, 123 and 124 West Ninth Street maintained very healthy appreciation levels due to the extraordinarily strong government and private real estate development in the immediate vicinity. Pride in the neighborhood by those who owned property on West Ninth Street made us all feel that we were walking around wearing blue ribbons on our chests. Realizing what we had, on January 10, 1990, a group of us got together and inaugurated the Ninth Street Historic District Foundation.

Many others were noticing what was happening to the soaring values of my downtown properties. It was during this time that the Queen's Director of the Department of Economic Development, Nell Surber, wrote a letter to me that said "The north frame of the City is, in my opinion, going to take off like a comet over the next several years. It was very astute of you to invest when you did."

Elsewhere, while the Queen's financial blackballing of me went onward, I continued to prudently invest every penny that I could muster into 123 and 124 West Ninth Street, where my investment dollars took quantum leaps in value. As an illustration, after the City would not plant decent trees on my West Ninth Street block, I bought my own trees because of the aesthetic and financial effect that they would have on my properties. On May 14, 1990, I drove over the Ohio River to a Northern Kentucky tree farm and purchased four five-inch (at the base) locust trees, two for each side of the street.

With the breakneck acceleration of property values in the Garfield Place area, spending money towards capital expenditures on my downtown properties had gotten to a point where it was not like spending money at all. I was immediately doubling, tripling, or quadrupling my money, if not a lot more. In the case of the trees, which was the case for many of the capital expenditures that I made to my buildings in a neighborhood that was shooting up from the ashes like a phoenix, my money increased at least fifty times.

Realizing that Sandy and I had been effectively stonewalled by the activities of the Queen, and in an attempt to turn over yet another stone in search of banking fairness, I decided to personally approach the richest man in Cincinnati, billionaire owner of Provident Bank, financier Carl H. Lindner, Jr. I armed myself with a portfolio of newspaper articles and other correspondence about my much publicized involvement in the West Ninth Street real estate boom and went to his office on

June 7, 1990 to make a personal appeal to him for help in breaking the lending logjam that blocked me.

At his office, although I could not see him, I met Ms. Sandy Heimann, Carl Lindner's assistant and Vice President of American Financial Group, and explained to her who I was, what I had done as a downtown property owner and the difficulties that I was facing. I later found out that my efforts were to no avail, as I called his office after not hearing back from them by September and November of 1990. In the end, the only real comfort that I derived from my contact with Carl H. Lindner, Jr.'s office was knowing that I was giving my lending problems the old college try.

In December of 1990, Cincinnati's long awaited and revised Year 2000 Plan was unveiled by The Year 2000 Review Committee as the blueprint to rejuvenate the Queen's downtown central business district. While it revealed that downtown housing proposals were only being funded at less than ten percent of the minimum level required, and with less than ten years to go, The Year 2000 Plan acknowledged that there was a pent-up housing demand in the Garfield Place area that was being unmet. The report also stated that Cincinnati needed to build or rehab about 15,000 dwellings by the Year 2000 in order for the City to maintain targeted population levels.

The ironic became the ridiculous when I continued to not be able to get the City's financial assistance to help me to develop the type of sought after housing that it said that it was in great need of. Although I had a seven-year track record of being a successful landlord and building developer in the City's central core, the Queen's reserved coldness turned into arrogance as I was repeatedly misled by City officials, ostracized and treated like my property was insubstantial in the scheme of things.

As Sandy and I knew that something had long been terribly afoot, it became even more obvious that there was a much larger dynamic at work that did not auger well for the Queen's use of public financing. Even more, as white developers and property owners all around my buildings openly benefited by having access to the many millions of dollars of capital that flowed into the neighborhood due to its rapid nascency, my financial strangulation continued without interruption.

While I continued to be a downtown presence by doggedly holding on to my real estate, I remained as an unwanted fly in the ointment and a burr under the saddle to the pigheaded Queen. More and more, a covered trail of egregious financial lending missteps became visible to the public's eye as a wayward Queen and its lending institutions angrily stamped down a familiar culture path of overt racial discrimination, the law be damned. Even in the wake of Ordinance 363, like a stumbling stone in a loathing Queen's self-righteous path, my underdeveloped buildings at 123 and 124 West Ninth Street stood out, revealed illegal lending activity and amplified the pressure for citywide financial lending compliance.

Forced into a corner, the irately incompliant Queen cursed and shook its fists to the legal heavens by seeing to it that my vividly red-letter Garfield Place area real estate remained underappraised. Like the rumblings underneath an enlarging volcanic dome before an ominous explosion, revealing fissures began to appear in the disingenuous bedrock of the Queen's bigoted real estate lending machinations. Though, try as it did, the tide of current events proved to be too great for the Queen's successful contrivance.

When the local news regularly covered the rapid rise in Garfield Place area real estate values, the public's access to information became a two-edged sword to the Cincinnati political machine. In a positive way, due to the abundant infusion of millions of federal and private development dollars into the area, the rebirth of the City's central business district was widely lauded, while civic pride significantly increased. In a negative way, due to its inability to shake the pressures of its illegal handling of 123 and 124 West Ninth Street, the dark side of the Queen's iron-fisted clinging to its outlawed past behavior steadily became an unwanted focus of attention, thereby, placing it in legal jeopardy.

On January 7, 1991, increasing light was brought to the open lending discrimination that was being used against Sandy and I when a newspaper article in the Business section of *The Cincinnati Post* headlined, "City pushes hotel conversion." Like the pulling of a necessary support card from the base of a house of cards, this newspaper article punctuated the collapse of the Queen's perennial rationalizations for undervaluing my buildings.

It was a time when the City was concerned about the politically sensitive issue of the elimination of low-income housing in the rapidly developing Garfield Place area. This breaking news story reported how

Cincinnati city officials recommended that acquisition of the 115-room Milner Hotel continue as planned so as not to disrupt a plan for new apartments on Garfield Place.

The Milner Hotel, a 115-room longtime haven for low-income central business district tenants, was the only building that stood on the southern half of the same rectangular block where 123 West Ninth Street stood. Facing Piatt Park, it sat only twenty-five feet away from 123 West Ninth Street's property line.

Flanked on both sides by undeveloped surface parking lots, the Milner Hotel site was part of an elongated and highly valued landmass for Garfield Place development. As the Milner Hotel site was located immediately north of Piatt Park between Elm and Race streets, 123 West Ninth Street's property line was only seventy-two inches from this large area of land where city officials were hoping to see Phase II of a new inner-city residential complex.

The City planned to acquire the Milner Hotel and lease it back to its owner, E. R. Milner, until construction began on the site or until the city could implement actions to help the building's occupants move to other low-income buildings. In this article, *The Cincinnati Post* scooped that the acting City Economic Development Director, J. Martin Griesel said, "In order to meet the terms of our agreement with Towne Properties [the City-chosen preferred developer that was awarded the right to develop all new Garfield Place construction] and not slow down their momentum in developing the Garfield housing project, the city's acquisition process [of the Milner Hotel] should proceed."

This pivotal *Cincinnati Post* article continued by writing, "The city has agreed to provide Towne with more than $3 million in Community Development Block Grant funds to make the project feasible…The city, which has been planning housing around Piatt Park for 10 years, is obligated to Towne to buy the hotel and two adjacent properties by June 1992."

Even though it had long been widely rumored that the Milner Hotel would be torn down as part of an integral revitalization plan by the City for upscale downtown housing on Garfield Place, as an active GNA member, I knew that the Milner Hotel's demolition had already been a forgone conclusion. However, it was through the printing of this article that the general public was made aware that the financial floodgates of millions of federal and private development dollars were about to be opened up within inches—instead of feet—of 123 West Ninth Street's property line.

The significance of this *Cincinnati Post* newspaper article is that it confirmed that the Queen knew all along what the true values of my West Ninth Street properties were. As a result of the Queen's plan to spend many millions of federal HUD CDBG tax dollars (not to mention the many more scores of millions of private development dollars) so close to 123 West Ninth Street's property line, the article publicly underscored the fact that the ongoing under-appraisals of my Garfield area properties were illegal stints to deny the justified financing.

On top of how much this newspaper article added fuel to the fire that drastically increased the already skyrocketing value of the real estate that Sandy and I owned on West Ninth Street, it was the printing of another newspaper article less than three months later that sent positive development shock waves reverberating throughout the entire Garfield Place area.

On April 3, 1991, the Queen's *Downtowner* newspaper printed a verbatim copy of the Queen's Economic Development Department's summary report to the City Manager and City Council on the current status of downtown projects that the City was involved in. This issue of the *Downtowner* publicly announced the long-awaited commencement of the $16 million Phase I apartment complex, The Gramercy on the Park (located 170 feet away from 123 West Ninth Street's property line), which would contain upscale housing, underground parking and retail stores.

Quotes from this April 3, 1991 *Downtowner* newspaper article describe what was reported best: "The first building of the Garfield Place Apartments will be located on the northeast corner of Elm and Seventh streets. It will consist of a 429-car public garage, 148 apartment units located atop and adjacent to the garage, a clubhouse, exercise facilities and a pool."

The article continued by reporting, "Four agreements, associated with the construction of the public garage and the developer's apartment units, have been reviewed and approved by the developer [Towne Properties] and the [Queen's] Economic Development Department. They have been forwarded to the City Manager for submission to City Council for approval so that construction of the public garage can begin by April 15, 1991. The apartments should be ready for occupancy by the summer of 1992."

With the printing of this article, counter to the false postulations of the Queen, the close to one million dollar combined value of 123 and 124 West Ninth Street—that I had long known of—became more known about to the public at large. This was a time when unprecedented real estate appreciation in the Garfield Place area took off to usher in an incremental wave of land and building development. This was also a time when the Queen's contrivance to maintain the illusion that Sandy and I did not have the real estate collateral and equity position to justify a development loan to rehab our downtown properties was rendered impotent.

In the doldrums of going through a period where I was still doggedly holding on to my property, and when there was nothing but real estate financing rejection due to my race, a reprieve came to my emotional slump in a surprising way. As construction activities began in earnest at The Gramercy on the Park apartment complex site on April 15, 1991, the earth literally began to quake from the steady and staccato drumbeat of a pneumatic construction pile driver that was pounding building supports into the ground, some 200 feet away from 123 West Ninth Street's property line. Realizing the significance of feeling vibrations through the earth in the privacy of my 123 West Ninth Street office, I watched with a West Ninth Street pioneer's gleeful amazement, as concentric circles pulsed to-and-fro in a glass of water on my office desk.

In the stillness of my office, my joy was that much more intense from the unexpected way in which it occurred. I never would have dreamed that the rippling of tiny and undulating rings of water would be an important confirmation that I had truly bought my West Ninth Street properties at the right time. I knew that large-scale Garfield Place development had finally arrived.

In the meantime, my development accomplishments produced more positive results. On June 5, 1991, I received a letter from the Downtown [Cincinnati] Residents' Council. The letter was as follows: "The Board and its members extend to you a sincere "THANKS" for the attention you have given to your apartment buildings in the way of flowers. This is the type of commitment that all downtown residents so selflessly strive for in promoting urban living. We can only hope that your example will catch on throughout downtown. Your clear passion to make the city a "FRIENDLIER" place to live, to visit, and to shop does not go unnoticed by the Residents' Council."

Twenty days later, after having received numerous annual awards and letters for street beautification and building improvement since 1984, 124 West Ninth Street was given the highest award that can be given to any downtown business or property owner, the Sterling Award. Sandy, my three daughters and I were presented this coveted award at a large weekday noontime gathering on the Queen's main pedestrian plaza, Fountain Square. Regardless, I still could not get financing for my downtown properties.

The November 5, 1991 Cincinnati City Council elections yielded the following results: Dwight Tillery was elected as Mayor and Peter Strauss was elected as Vice Mayor. The remaining City Councilpeople were as follows: Roxanne Qualls, Nick Vehr, David Mann, John Mirlisena, Bobbie Sterne, Nell Surber and Tyrone Yates.

Chapter 4

The Disturbing View Through The Queen's Window

"Politicians think that by stopping up the chimney they can stop its smoking. They try the experiment, they drive the smoke back, and there is more smoke than ever; but they do not see that their want of common sense has increased the evil they would have prevented."

—Borne

In the years following the passage of the Cincinnati Banking Disclosure Act, the prevailing banking discrimination in the Queen that was exacting a financial toll upon Sandy and I remained in place. With increasing public awareness of the West Ninth Street lending irregularities staring it in the face, the Queen faced mounting pressures to act lawfully by ceasing the slow and methodical restriction of the economic lifeblood to our showcased downtown buildings. Seeing absolutely nothing to make us believe otherwise, Sandy and I knew from the feeling in our bones that, somewhere behind the scenes, a city's racially indifferent attitude stole behind a municipal façade of legitimacy.

By January of 1992, due primarily to the colossal gain in value of our downtown properties at 123 and 124 West Ninth Street, Sandy and I had a net worth of $629,612, with total assets of $987,990 and total liabilities of $358,378. Even though we possessed an undeniable bonanza of cherished real estate as useable collateral, we were even turned down time and time again for small amounts of extremely low-risk financing in the $10-15,000 range by the Queen's banks and savings and loans.

As the Queen's lending institutions inexplicably refused to budge from their intractable position, they made desperate attempts to construct a phantasm that was intended to put 123 and 124 West Ninth Street, unlike the other pieces of real estate in the neighborhood, into an unfavorable light. Calculating that it would only be a matter of time before we would wither away at the vine as an ongoing concern, the Queen remained hell-bent to get rid of us by going deeper and deeper into illegality.

Unmoved and confident of its cultural ability to use its extensive political power to corrupt, the Queen pressed forward to play the waiting game of financially imperiling us through a type of economic starvation that it considered to be innocuous. As Sandy and I held on for dear economic life, the Queen's chosen coup de grace was the reliance on its old mainstay of denying us suitable development financing by distorting the method of accurately appraising 123 and 124 West Ninth Street. In the face of the burgeoning 1992 market conditions in the Garfield Place area that drove real estate values to heights far beyond the norm, a stance of deception and trickery was fallaciously maintained. Even in the magnified glare of the public spotlight, the insolent Queen only tightened its chokehold on us to hasten economic death's calling.

Whenever the rapid escalation of West Ninth Street real estate values came into appraisal discussions with the Queen's lending institutions, universally, they always acted as if those considerations did not exist. Whenever mention was made of the millions of dollars of private and federal CDBG funds that had been—and would be—spent only inches away from 123 West Ninth Street, deaf ears were extended to this relevant factor as well.

However, diametric to its racially self-serving and wicked intentions, the Queen's hard-line ploy backfired, as it slid further down a slippery slope of unwelcome public scrutiny that was brought on by flagrantly visible ethical and legal inconsistencies. On January 28, 1992, I sent SFSB (123 West Ninth Street's mortgage holder) a fourteen-page financing proposal that showed the following: current and projected income and expenses; how the money was to be reinvested in their property at 123 West Ninth Street; an architect's drawing of the building; and the uses of and the income that would have been generated from the requested financing. From this point on, SFSB only continued to underappraise 123 West Ninth Street.

Growing racial overtones from the visible lending discrimination that was leveled against me became an ever-growing source of irritation for the Queen. On the heels of a special report that was presented in a February 3, 1992 newspaper article in the Focus on Downtown section of The Cincinnati Business Courier entitled, "City leaders declared urban housing a high priority", inconsistencies abounded as the Queen's banks continued to not lend me development financing.

In view of the fact that this newspaper article highlighted a picture with 123 West Ninth Street in it, and wrote that "City planners, business leaders and Downtown residents were excited about the spurt in downtown residential development", a lack of consistency was made plain as the Queen's racial culture stopped me from exercising my Constitutional rights of equal treatment under the law.

As Garfield Place development moved ahead speedily, on February 13, 1992, a topping-out ceremony was conducted at The Gramercy on Garfield when the highest structural member on the building was secured and a pine tree was attached. In construction tradition, the rea son why it was done that way was to bring good luck. I was just hoping that some of that good luck would have drifted some 200 feet over to my property.

Even though I had previously distributed many business plans to Cincinnati financial concerns, at the advice of a friend, I began to compile an even more ironclad business plan that was updated and of an impeccable nature. Utilizing my corporate marketing experience for making oral presentations and preparing written proposals, by March 2, 1992, I had prepared and distributed comprehensive business plans all over the Queen. Leaving nothing to chance, I included practically all of the types of personal, business and financial information that a lending concern could possibly require.

This business plan was my masterpiece of thoroughness, simplicity, and professionalism, all in an easy to understand format and language. It had full-color bar charts and diagrams, color photographs of 123 & 124 West Ninth Street; an executive summary; an introduction; a description of the principals (Sandy and I); our mission statement; our philosophy; goals; market analysis; competition; the principal's uniqueness; a marketing plan; income projections; detailed use of financing; financial projections; attachments; exhibits; and references. Also included in this business plan was a signed letter of intent from a very interested firm that would have increased the lease income for the 2,300 square foot commercial space at 123 West Ninth Street from $1,500 to $4,500 per month.

Looking at practically every aspect of my rehabbing cash requirements and the service on the debt that would have been incurred, I proposed logically sound and businesslike requests for development financing needs. Placing my primary emphasis on totally rehabbing 123 West Ninth Street, I planned on doing more extensive renovations to 124 West Ninth Street later on. On even ground, the procurement of development financing that I proposed should not have been a problem. Still, ominously, there were no takers, as the financial stranglehold against Sandy and I by the Queen hurtfully persisted.

Unwilling to give up my rights as an American citizen, and determined not to blink in the waiting game of legally pursuing warranted development financing, I continued to press the Queen to abide by the law. After initiating an exhaustive search that was followed up with telephone calls, appearing in City Council Chambers, letter writing, going to banks and participating in local radio talk shows, the mounting pressures that had been exerted by me on the Queen's lending bias became so great that the Queen blinked.

By April of 1992 the Queen's NHC contacted me and made me aware of a federal government housing program, the Rental Rehabilitation Program (RRP), that it was administering for HUD out of Washington, D. C. NHC also informed me that HUD's RRP had been established by the federal government to increase the available housing stock in American cities by providing incentives for the creation of decent housing to qualified property owners, such as myself.

I listened attentively as NHC told me that the provisions of this grant stated that this federal financing would come in the form of a non-repayable government grant, providing that I maintained acceptable living conditions in the building for the tenants. While interested in what I was hearing, at the same time I was somewhat disappointed when the City told me that the parameters of HUD's RRP would only encompass the renovation of 124 West Ninth Street, a property with seven apartment units, and not, as I had hoped, 123 West Ninth Street, with its nine apartment units and commercial space on its ground floor.

At first, this was viewed as a setback to my long thought out plans to simultaneously rehab both of my downtown buildings. But, in considering the dearth of other development financing opportunities that were being offered to me, I pursued the federal availability of financing for 124 West Ninth Street as a recourse designed to give me access to investment capital.

The more I talked to NHC, the better it sounded. As my interest increased, NHC also told me that HUD would give me specific per rental unit financing amounts (not specified at that time) provided that matching funds from a participating private lending institution would be part of the financing package. Encouraged, from what I had heard, I left the conversation with NHC to do my homework.

I reconfigured my building designs, reworked my required development finances and had my building plans redrawn. Without hesitation, On April 8, 1992, I formerly applied to the Queen's NHC for a HUD RRP grant of $169,250 to rehab 124 West Ninth Street. One week later, on April 15, 1992, I received a letter of commitment from the City of Cincinnati which stated that NHC would award me a federal grant of $45,000 from the government of the United States of America (HUD's RRP) to rehab 124 West Ninth Street.

Besides, with the receipt of forty-five grand of free money from the United States government, it would have been suicidal for any lending concerns in the Queen to reject my development financing requests further. Also, from our understanding of the range of possible financing calculations that we had already laid out on paper, Sandy and I realized that the additional $45,000 of matching funds from a local lender would give us $90,000, an amount that we could significantly stretch by making it look like at least twice that figure. It was a far shot from the financial package that I had anticipated, but it was much better than not having any financing at all.

With the possibility of receiving money from a federal program, for the first time, the view of the bank-lending panorama that we had faced in the Queen abruptly changed. In one fell swoop, no longer was the exclusively tight financial realm of the Queen's banks the only consideration that was before us. From all outward appearances, the NHC letter, with all of its federal safeguards, was an indication that yet another end run had opened up, allowing us to get around the suppression of the Queen. I was suddenly talking about considering the expansiveness of the big leagues...HUD...the American government...a Cabinet Department of the President of the United States.

Surely, I thought, I could not go wrong in a deal that was bolstered, backed and guaranteed by the faith and credibility of the federal government. Surely, I believed, the Constitution would protect me, as its laws, regulations and guidelines spelled out how HUD financing from the U. S. Treasury could be disbursed, used and reported. Surely, I believed and trusted that the rule of law—the bedrock supporting the foundation of America as a nation of laws—would protect me.

Admittedly, as I was moderately leery about entering into a financial transaction at a place where so much ill will had been shown to me in the past, I did not let my skepticism of the Queen hinder me from exploring an offer from the feds. Truly believing that federal laws would protect me from any local malfeasance, I moved forward in negotiations with the Queen's NHC.

Unbeknownst to me, however, the Queen's trap had been set. While unseen gears of corruption were silently turning against me, I had already commenced my nibbling at the bait in the Queen's hidden snare. In retrospect, with all of the financial benefits and federal guarantees that were extended to private lenders who participate in United States government operations like HUD's RRP, I did find it to be rather queer that only one bank in the Queen availed itself to participate with me in this federal program.

Out of the dregs of humanity stepped forth the Queen's Provident Bank with a HUD matching funds offer of $46,000. Owned by the local billionaire financier Carl H. Lindner, Jr., I had visited his office in a personal appeal for financial assistance some twenty-two months prior. As the combined financing amount of $91,000 for the 124 West Ninth Street rehab project did not give me the contingency cushion that I wanted, I needed further assurances from HUD's agent, the City of Cincinnati, to ensure my success.

Upon meeting with the City and expressing my intense objection to their paltry offer of inadequate federal financing, I was reassured that, if need be, I would be allowed to tap into the substantial equity that I had in my properties at 123 and 124 West Ninth Street. In referring to the federal regulations that guided HUD's RRP to allay my fears of possible project cost overruns, NHC went on to tell me that they would come forward, without hesitation, to make up any difference between estimated and actual project costs. Sandy and I had the collateral; we knew it, and so did they.

This was a consideration that I did not take lightly. In seeking an outside opinion, one of my uncles told me to "beware." In reminding me of the treachery that was known to exist in federal bureaucracies, he told me that "there is good, there is bad, and then there is the law." In considering the safeguards that would be provided by the federal government, I thought long and hard as to whether or not to accept the offer of government financing assistance that was coming through the Queen.

After all, it had not been that long ago since I had listened to national news coverage of HUD corruption in high places. I was fully aware that my pre-financing activities with the Queen began during a time when George Bush was President and former Congressman Jack Kemp had been appointed as HUD Secretary, replacing Samuel Pierce. I also remembered that Samuel Pierce had been President Reagan's infamous HUD Secretary, who was found to be an agent for politically favored special interests. As if it were yesterday, I recollected that many from Samuel Pierce's well-publicized HUD scandal were ultimately sent to jail for felonies concerning the misappropriation of U. S. Treasury tax dollars in HUD's care.

As Samuel Pierce's "HUDgate" became all the rage and Congress held hearings to root out corruption, I recalled that HUD Secretary Kemp vowed to "restore honor and integrity at the Department." He even promised to personally watch "every dime" to make sure that none of them were misspent. Yet, I reminisced how, when six audits took place during his tenure as head of HUD from 1989-92, persistent and systemic waste, fraud and abuse were found.

A *Washington Journalism Review* story later marveled that Secretary Kemp managed to avoid accountability for financial mismanagement that rivaled any in HUD's history. The story also mentioned that Republicans did not want to criticize one of their own, and Democrats were too bedazzled by the stupefying number of new programs that Secretary Kemp initiated to complain. Out of my view from the Queen, billions of taxpayer dollars were being ground up in HUD's corrupt and bureaucratic federal machinery.

The Department's numbers alone were telling. As head of HUD, Secretary Kemp made the agency the fastest growing cabinet level department, increasing its budget by an astonishing 48 percent. President Johnson's HUD budget was a mere 2.5 percent of Secretary Kemp's last budget. By the end of the Kemp tenure, and at the time I began negotiations to enter into a HUD contract via the Queen, Secretary Kemp had managed to balloon the agency into a vast and sprawling $28.1 billion monstrosity.

In addition to my unawareness in stepping into a HUD quagmire that was of Secretary Kemp's making, it was also a time when development lending contract negotiations with Provident Bank were visibly conducted under dubious conditions. When I met with Provident Bank's Assistant Vice President, George Fulford, I explained to him my disapproval of the City's rejection of my $169,250 development-financing request.

As his pontifical eyes revealed that his bank was walking in lock-step with the City, it was clear to me that he knew that no other lending institution in the Queen had made an offer to me. His bank's true intentions were written all over his face when I saw that he knew that I was dependent upon $46,000 of private financing from his bank in order to make 124 West Ninth Street's development work under the Queen's HUD RRP plan.

In particular, whereas the federal government's HUD was guaranteeing that Provident Bank would not lose a cent at my 124 West Ninth Street RRP building renovation project, Provident Bank's George Fulford crystallized his lending institution's recalcitrant position even further when he refused to look at my total net worth. Instead, he only used the greatly under-appraised value of 124 West Ninth Street in determining his imprecise mortgage risk calculations. Through its criminal immurement, Provident Bank had me where it wanted.

With the type of eye and facial expressions that are so often given to African-Americans behind closed bank doors, George Fulford told me to "take it or leave it." Had it not been for the further assurances that were given to me by the City of Cincinnati with respect to its standing by me in the event of cost overruns or unforeseen rehab problems, I would not have pursued the consummation of a questionable relationship with Provident Bank that was fabricated under duress.

Regardless, knowing that intractable racial and lending problems were deeply infixed in the draconian politics of the Queen, I was from Missouri. Not believing that the Queen was powerful enough to disregard, render null and void the rigid federal rules, regulations and laws dictating the issuance and use of U. S. Treasury tax dollars from HUD, I had to be shown otherwise. This became my test of the U. S. Constitution—whether or not I would be allowed full participation in America's society as an African-American. All things being even, I knew that if I was given the $91,000 dribble of money that the Queen was agreeing to federally contract to me, I still felt that the chances of 124 West Ninth Street becoming a successful HUD building renovation project were greater than not.

On May 5, 1992, I met the City of Cincinnati's employee who was mandated by federal law to have HUD RRP supervisory responsibility at the 124 West Ninth Street building rehab site, the Queen's NHC architect, Charles Alexander. With respect to 124 West Ninth Street's compliance to the federal laws which would have allowed it to be a legally bona fide HUD RRP site, his supervisory cost and building project verification job was to make sure that all of the *i*'s were dotted and all of the *t*'s were crossed. On this date, a Preliminary Scope of Work (PSOW) for 124 West Ninth Street was completed.

The PSOW was an estimate that described the specific construction rehab areas in 124 West Ninth Street that required repair or replacement to meet the federal housing code standards that are of particular importance in adhering to HUD regulations and guidelines. The City estimated at this time that the cost of renovation was $78,987, a contradicting figure that greatly differed from the $91,000 figure that the City had agreed to help finance twenty-one days earlier.

This estimate was based on minimum rehab construction of the site. Based upon the City's unwillingness to resolve the discrepancies between what they were saying, doing and federally responsible for at this point, it was easy for me to see that things were increasingly running afoul within the Queen.

Unknown to me, all of these negotiations were going on at a moment in the Queen when the helm was being manned by a peculiar mix of politicians and bureaucrats who had the power to illegally open and close the doors of the U. S. Treasury—at will—via the HUD RRP. While the Queen's legislative political body, City Council, led the City, the Queen's NHC bureaucracy was led by its Director, Wayne Chapman. NHC's HUD RRP Supervisor and Manager for 124 West Ninth Street were, respectively, Charles Bronson and Michael Jackson. Frank A. Dawson was the Director of Finance and Gerald E. Newfarmer held the important City Manager's position.

By the last part of May, 1992, Provident Bank ordered an appraisal of 124 West Ninth Street. Like a sea captain of old who was about to set sail to embark across a perilous ocean, I came closer and closer to embarking upon a course of financial involvement with the Queen's

HUD RRP, not knowing what storms would exist over the horizon. I knew that I was armed with the financial, property management and construction know-how that was required to successfully steer my RRP building renovation project to its successful completion. I looked beyond the Queen and legally relied upon the U. S. government to guarantee 124 West Ninth Street's safe passage through duplicitous straits.

Gingerly, I took the Queen's hidden cajoling that "nothing could or would go wrong at the 124 West Ninth Street HUD RRP building renovation project" with a grain of salt. In so doing, I continued to press ahead in pursuance of a federal financing deal believing that the receipt of a HUD grant from the U. S. Treasury would not be fertile ground for the shenanigans of the Queen. On July 29, 1992, Sandy and I refinanced 124 West Ninth Street's mortgage as we closed with Cincinnati's Provident Bank for $195,000. Of this amount, $46,000 was to be applied towards the federally required private lending institution contribution at the HUD RRP renovation project at 124 West Ninth Street, and the remaining balance was used to refinance the old mortgage. Sandy and I still could not see how Provident Bank was illegally in control of the Queen.

Even though the paralytically venomous teeth of the Queen's financial artifice unknowingly sank deep into our almost ten-year downtown real estate operation, from this point, providentially, the ambush began to lose it stealth and backfired in a long succession of dumb and sloppy mistakes.

For starters, as everyday Americans who had never been involved financially with a city—not even mention the federal government, there was a lot that Sandy and I did not know about the misuse of power by corrupt individuals. To illustrate, we were not aware of the existence of a Cincinnati City regulation having the force of law which required that 124 West Ninth Street's Provident Bank closing should have happened simultaneously, on July 29, 1992, with the City of Cincinnati's HUD RRP closing.

The Queen legislated this municipal rule that dealt with details of procedure to ensure that all HUD RRP projects would get off on a good financial footing. By design, the Queen intentionally attempted to illegally scuttle the 124 West Ninth Street HUD RRP building renovation project from its outset, even though it had committed federal financing to me in writing. On top of this faux pas, the Queen bungled to a much larger extent.

Just like the City of Cincinnati, Provident Bank bit off more than it could chew when it began to illegally delve into the federal realm. Had they kept the artifice of their discriminatory building renovation financing of 124 West Ninth Street restricted to a completely state or local financing deal—instead of involving the federal government, Provident Bank stood a much greater chance of carrying out its scheme against Sandy and I. Since it actively and knowingly engaged itself as a co-financier in a completely bogus HUD RRP building renovation project that lured us into a designed trap that used U. S. Treasury financing, the Queen's Provident Bank let its racially biased obstinacy stand in the way of what was best for its stockholders.

As it conspired to release a two-fisted financial and political punch upon two unsuspecting federal program participants, the Provident Bank loan closing set into motion a series of events that was intended to make Sandy and I succumb to the daunt of facing overwhelming odds. But unlike a pummeled circle jerk that futilely stands in a bad situation by running in all directions to apprehend the most recent deliverer of a series of incessant blind-siders, I countered by merely stepping outside of the Queen's closed circle of doom. Instead, I remained adamant in insisting that I remained grounded in the much wider circle of full federal accountability and enforceability that the Queen was beholden to.

At first, I wanted to think that the Queen's mishandling of the situation was ineptitude that was susceptible to correction. However, as the waves of inconsistencies began to turn into a flood of wrongful patterns, I found out that its actions were a prelude to more sinister things to come.

On August 4, 1992, six days after I financially committed myself to a new mortgage with Provident Bank for 124 West Ninth Street's private RRP development financing and was eagerly waiting for HUD's public financial participation, the Queen's NHC delivered a bombshell to me. Cavalierly informing me that its RRP was under a "freeze notice" before I had received one red cent, I was told that all money from the Queen's RRP had been immediately cut off, and that the federal program had been suspended by HUD.

I did not have to be a rocket scientist to figure out that these were the classic workings of a swindle by the Queen. When I soon found out that the City of Cincinnati was under a RRP freeze notice when it first received my RRP application four months earlier on April 8, 1992, the view through the Queen's window became increasingly more disturbing.

Upon immediately contacting the Queen's powerful confidence man, NHC's Director, Wayne Chapman, he told me that he "was sorry for the problems that HUD was causing me," and did absolutely nothing thereafter to render assistance. Like in the past, nothing had changed. Just as all of the Queen's telltale signs were there, it was easy for me to see that Chapman was being disingenuous, and that the Queen was only going through the motions to make it appear that it was doing what was correct within the law.

The Queen watched me squirm in discomfort. As an integral operative for the Queen's play, NHC's Chapman slyly told me that I "should take it upon myself to ask Cincinnati City Council for an Emergency Ordinance", knowing that it would take too long for that to happen, thereby continuing the economic strangulation that I was trying to avoid. When Chapman then told me that he "would notify Provident Bank of the situation", it was as if my sixth sense allowed me to hear the Queen guffawing over the successful setting and the springing of their HUD RRP trap.

On the next day, August 5, 1992, in desperation, I called the Cincinnati City Manager's office, lividly complained, and was told that they would look into the matter. I never heard back from the City Manager's office either. I even called Provident Bank's 124 West Ninth Street contact person, Assistant Vice President George Fulford, and, expectedly, was given the royal runaround. Fulford told me that "Provident Bank's loan was predicated upon the City's matching funds being in place, and that none of their money could be released until the City moved." The Queen had me coming and going.

After being led astray in a succession of unreturned telephone calls and dead-ended recommendations by the City and Provident Bank, in utter frustration, on August 6, 1992, I contacted the Washington, D. C. office of the then Secretary of HUD, Jack Kemp, where I was channeled to four other HUD offices, including the State of Ohio's HUD office in Columbus. Between August 6-28, 1992, I lived on the telephone with anyone from HUD that would listen to me.

Somehow, the pressure that I had applied forced the Queen to move.

After I received a telephone call from Ron Williams in HUD's Columbus, Ohio office on August 31, 1992, the go-ahead for the 124 West Ninth Street HUD RRP financing was given to me on September 1, 1992 by the City of Cincinnati. As the 124 West Ninth Street Provident Bank financing had already been deleteriously set in place, the only thing that was left for Sandy and I to do was to have a forgivable grant loan closing with the City, which would have completed the financing deal.

But, behind the scenes, in an orchestrated plan to financially destroy me, the Queen kept on blundering by ungainly stumbling forward. On September 14, 1992, Charles Alexander, the Queen's federally required architect for 124 West Ninth Street, was forced into giving a final go-ahead for the HUD building renovation project at the RRP pre-construction meeting. In the same shadow, NHC's RRP Manager, Michael Jackson, acting at the behest of his watchful and insulated superiors, slithered into position to ramrod into existence an illegal federal startup time for my RRP project.

As an American lay person who was not familiar with the intricacies of correct HUD RRP procedure, I could not see that the Queen had begun a slipshod criminal operation in a federal HUD program by using a victimized City employee (Alexander) as a go-between. In the fluster of it all, I could not have also seen that a series of federally indictable events had begun its course in the clandestine handling of my HUD RRP building renovation project. There was no way that I could have seen that the Queen had begun to invest millions in an expansive 124 West Ninth Street cover-up scheme.

On September 22, 1992, the day before Sandy and I signed the federal contract with the City for $45,000 in HUD grant financing, I was unaware that I was swallowing the evil Queen's death potion, both hook, line and sinker. On the eve of a day that I believed would be a very special day, it was like Christmas Eve for me, full of eager anticipation and hopeful expectations. In a mental state that rested between starry-eyed excitement and cautious optimism, I made it a point to reiterate my concerns to NHC regarding the under-funding of 124 West Ninth Street.

Like a department store manager reassuring a lost child that a parent will be found, the City reiterated to me that additional financing would be made available in the event of cost overruns, due to the worth of my downtown properties. In the height of deception, the Queen kept the attraction of its lure intact by falsely allaying my final hour concerns, assuring me that HUD would not let me down.

On September 23, 1992, a binding contract between HUD, the City of Cincinnati and Sandy and I was signed for $45,000 of federal government grant financing for 124 West Ninth Street. This HUD RRP contract was the one document that Sandy and I had yearned for as a precondition for dealing with the Queen as it gave us the full federal accountability and enforceability that we needed to offset the localized wiles of the Queen. The $45,000 in federal government grant financing that Sandy and I signed for was not to have been received in one lump sum: its terms dictated that the money was to have been drawn down upon in increments, based upon the degree of job completion.

124 West Ninth Street's HUD RRP grant closing was just how the Queen wanted its allurement to be: unforeseen, beguiling and lethal. As Sandy and I were oblivious to walking into its far-reaching web—a web that was far more extensive than we would have ever dreamed of, the Queen had its way.

The Queen's behavior reminded me of the nineteenth-century poem written by Mary Howitt (1799-1888) entitled "The Spider and the Fly." Just as the opening stanza of this indicative poem begins with "Will you walk into my parlor said the spider to the fly?," the Queen acted similarly by luring Sandy and I into its "dismal den" of financial corruption. However, unlike the fly, Sandy and I had a way out of the deceptively sticky strands of the tangled web that the Queen had spun at 124 West Ninth Street: we had an enforceable federal contract that protected us.

Contrary to what it desired, the significance of the Queen's involvement at 124 West Ninth Street became just as much about the bungled trail of federal incrimination that it left behind as it was about the illegal trap that was set. The Queen did not anticipate that it would leave connecting evidence showing a well-coordinated scheme that involved the felonious falsification of HUD documents that gained it illegal access to U. S. Treasury financing.

For all intents and purposes, as HUD's duly designated RRP representative, the Queen's NHC was HUD. As HUD's agent, NHC was legally bound to all of the terms, conditions and provisions of the federal rules, regulations, guidelines and laws that governed that federal department. Sandy and I were legally protected under the binding terms and provisions of federal contract Number 25X0130 that was between HUD the Queen and us. This legally binding contract that governed the who, where, when, how and why's of taking money out of the U. S. Treasury for 124 West Ninth Street gave us a revealing means—a life rope, if you will—to pull ourselves from the evil clutches of the clandestine Queen's web.

Still and all, I was completely ignorant to the actual depth of the plot that was continuing to evolve around me. I suppose it was my trust that allowed me to think that everything was correct and in order when the City of Cincinnati's Department of Buildings and Inspections endorsed the commencement of my HUD RRP project by officially affixing its receipt stamp upon my building plans on October 1, 1992.

The day after President William Jefferson Clinton was elected to his first term of office, November 4, 1992, my trust in the City of Cincinnati, Ohio grew when its Department of Buildings and Inspections approved my building plans that it had received thirty-four days earlier. While rehabbing began in earnest at 124 West Ninth Street, Garfield Place development moved interestingly ahead.

Also in November of 1992, construction was completed on the first phase of the Garfield Place housing project, known as The Gramercy on Garfield. The electricity in the air that was generated from its completion only matched the impact that was felt upon the area's property valuations.

The Gramercy on Garfield was a brand-spanking new 16 million-dollar jeweled showpiece in the Queen's crown that highlighted efforts to rejuvenate its downtown. Notably, my two downtown properties, along with the other properties that immediately surrounded it, were part of a central business district real estate base, upon which The Gramercy on Garfield was mounted. The following seven paragraphs, excerpts from a contemporaneous newspaper article in *The Cincinnati Enquirer*, gives an indication of the excitement and the influence of The Gramercy on Garfield's opening:

> "Phase I of the City of Cincinnati's Garfield Development project, The Gramercy on Garfield apartment complex, was completed and opened to downtown renters and retailers. The Gramercy was the first phase in the redevelopment of historic

Garfield Place, a two-block street between Elm and Vine [Streets], and an important anchor in Cincinnati's urban regeneration. It became the catalyst for subsequent residential and commercial development on Garfield Place."

"Piatt Park runs down the middle of the two-block length. The strip is planted with grass, trees and flowers, lined with park benches that were built into granite encasements which serve as the base for the elevated planters, and is highlighted by larger than life presidential statutes at each end, and twin fountains in the center that lie on each side of Race Street."

"The Gramercy is an architectural marvel that wrapped a combination of residential units and commercial frontage around a secured parking structure that is buried inside the building. This parking lot is barely noticeable from the street and accessible through unobtrusive entrances on Elm Street. On the north, townhouse units face Piatt Park. On the west and south, a variety of retail establishments—including a food market, restaurants, dry cleaners and other services—front Elm and Seventh Streets."

"On the third-story (above the parking structure), four floors of spacious sunny studios, and one- and two-bedroom flats form three sides of an open court. The court, with its swimming pool and landscaped terraces, does more than augment the social interaction of residents. This unexpected oasis, with its luminous southern exposure, serves the function of a semi-private urban back yard and offers a combination of freedom and security. The apartments are conventionally laid out but create variety with modest design choices, such as the expansion of interior living spaces into bay windows or, alternatively, small outdoor terraces."

"Unlike many new urban buildings, The Gramercy presents an engaging face at the sidewalk. Townhouses along Garfield Place have wide, recessed entrances leading to warm wood-paneled front doors several steps above the sidewalk. Entryways, protected by thick roof planes on freestanding piers, are flanked by large bay windows. Stacks of bay windows on the third floor enrich its form sculpturally. At Elm and Garfield Place, a corner pavilion rises slightly higher than the six stories of the main block. Capped by a flared roof of standing seam metal painted deep teal, the tower gives The Gramercy a dramatic presence at the west end of Piatt Park. The form of the roof is ambiguous enough to stimulate curiosity and make the building memorable, especially when glimpsed from Central Parkway or the east end of Garfield Place. It also relates The Gramercy to surrounding structures where towers in a variety of shapes animate the skyline."

"The most striking quality of the exterior is the character of its materials and color. Recognizing that the principal north and west facades would be almost constantly in shadow, the architect considered this an opportunity to exploit material and ornament for richness and chromatic interest. Exterior walls are deep red brick, a material found throughout historic Cincinnati. Contrasting tones of teal, aqua and white are introduced in glazed tile, painted metal, pre-cast concrete elements and synthetic stucco paneling. This palette of materials and colors relates the building to the late Victorian Waldo Apartments (on the northwest corner of Eighth and Elm) and to other nearby buildings."

"Ornamental patterns in smooth glazed tile and textured panels articulate the three levels of the building—base, main block and attic—and tie them together optically. The colorful materials and the geometric decorative elements do not represent significant additions to the building budget; but their thoughtful inclusion distinguishes The Gramercy from less fortunate monochromatic neighbors such as the stark gray Garfield Towers next door."

As the immediate West Ninth Street desert of blight was being transformed into an oasis of new development right in front of my eyes, it was my belief that I had launched my American dream, albeit somewhat shakily, as the HUD RRP project at 124 West Ninth Street got off the mark. In preparation, I had meticulously assembled a hearty and capable team of skilled craftsmen in the construction trades who needed the work. More meaningfully though, I had assembled a sympathetic group of artisans at 124 West Ninth Street who generally understood the great challenge that confronted me. They developed an appreciation of the pressing need that I had to accomplish a lot of work on a very limited budget.

To the consternation of those who sided with the Queen's evil intentions, the successful coordination of 124 West Ninth Street's rehabilitation went like clockwork, putting my HUD project well ahead of schedule. Everyday, the streetscape in front of the building was abuzz with truck activities of all kinds. Trucks were pumping concrete, removing construction waste, unloading HVAC units, plumbing supplies, electrical stock in trade, drywall, lumber, building supplies, etc. Yet, something still did not smell right.

On paper, my financial position improved with the supposed availability of $91,000 in construction financing. In attempting to seize the moment while I believed my financial momentum was on the upswing, I contacted most of the Queen's lending institutions with the hope of tapping into the large and uncommitted equity pool that existed in 123 West Ninth Street. The silence continued to be deafening.

Logically reassessing my position, I reapplied to the two captive lending institutions that held the mortgages on my downtown pieces of real estate, Provident Bank and Suburban Federal Savings Bank. Even after new financial, marketing and neighborhood data was factored into my financial position, both of these banks acted as if nothing had changed. They both illogically turned down my reasonable requests as I sat on many hundreds of thousands of dollars of free and clear equity.

As the strategy of their illegal plot to continue my economic strangulation became more manifest, Provident Bank continued to insist that 123 West Ninth Street not be used as collateral for my additional financing for 124 West Ninth Street. With all of the nearby development that had radically transformed the neighborhood, Suburban Federal Savings Bank continued to not lend me development financing by underappraising 123 West Ninth Street, illegally insisting that it's value was still $280,000—the same woefully under-appraised value that it had determined three years earlier!

Even before I went to the Finance Department at Cincinnati City Hall at 3 P.M. on November 5, 1992 to pick up my first HUD payment draw of $3,562 (which was deducted from 124 West Ninth Street's $45,000 of RRP grant financing), the Queen had already begun to methodically execute its Trojan horse plan to hamstring me. Just as the Greeks of old left a large, hollow wooden horse filled with Greek soldiers, and introduced it within the walls of Troy by a stratagem during the Trojan War, the Queen left a surreptitiously calculated and completely bogus HUD RRP project within the walls of 124 West Ninth Street.

Too, just like the Greek soldiers who came out of the Trojan Horse at night to open the gates of the City of Troy to the Greek army, thereby conquering the city, the Queen clandestinely attempted to perform a comparably intended sneak move. Pretending to abide by federal laws that governed the administration of the RRP, the Queen released its building inspectors, which formed the basis of a shaky justification for the illegal termination of the 124 West Ninth Street HUD RRP project.

Positioned to release the full fury of its pent-up anger by inflicting its own distinctive kind of Queen City injury upon Sandy and I, the evil Queen began to slowly and methodically execute its nefarious plan to cause the profuse terminal hemorrhaging of 124 West Ninth Street's HUD operation. Knowing the tremendous difficulty that I faced in getting downtown development financing, the Queen used a whole host of its construction inspectors to escalate the renovation costs of renovating my HUD RRP project so high that it had to go belly up.

First, the Queen sent in a succession of rapacious City building inspectors; who were followed by covetous City plumbing inspectors; who were followed by ravenous City HVAC inspectors; who were followed by voracious City framing inspectors; who were followed by gluttonous City electrical inspectors.

Not long after project start-up, a trickle of illegal RRP project undermining by the City's inspectors turned into a torrent of crippling activity that led to the hopeless stagnation of 124 West Ninth Street's renovation. In no time, the Queen's inspectors had caused the RRP building costs to whiz from $91,000 to more than $329,000—a figure that was, under the circumstances, undoubtedly, out of my reach to refinance.

While the evil Queen superimposed its will over the federal laws that guide HUD's RRP, 124 West Ninth Street began to illegally wither on the vine. As additional requirements were imposed upon me that were not part of the original stamped and approved City building plans, time began to prove to me that the Queen's actions were only part of a larger culture of racial discrimination that imposed anti-constitutional requirements on most African-Americans.

Amid a national controversy on November 13, 1992 that reflected its intolerant racial reputation, the Queen was exposed broadly to negative news coverage over the racially insensitive comments that were made by one of its prominent civic leaders, then- President and CEO of the Cincinnati Reds, Marge Schott. As a representative slice of the Queen's ultra-conservative racist mentality surfaced, the world news media was filled with reports that she had called two of the outfielders on her baseball team, Eric Davis and Dave Parker, her "million-dollar niggers."

By December 9, 1992, Marge Schott's racial insensitivity resurfaced again in the national press when she apologized publicly for making "insensitive remarks", including the statement that she was alleged to have said, "I'd rather have a trained monkey working for me than a nigger." On the very next day, December 10, 1992, the Queen gained more national news attention amid the controversy over the City approving an application from the Ku Klux Klan to erect a cross on Fountain Square from December 21-30, 1992.

While all of this was going on, I was irretrievably caught in the throws of the Queen's subterranean death grip that was slowly draining the life out of 124 West Ninth Street as an ongoing concern. On December 21, 1992—the day that I picked up my second (and last) draw of $21,500 from the City of Cincinnati's Finance Department, I had little way of knowing that the Queen was well into the final delivery of her death blow against me. Of the $45,000 of HUD RRP grant financing that I was federally contracted to receive, only $25,062 was disbursed, leaving a balance of $19,938 that vanished and was never legally accounted for. Fully unaware of my predicament, I had already been swallowed whole by the Queen's culture of racist activity and corruption.

On the same day, as the Ku Klux Klan cross was erected on Fountain Square, Cincinnati became a running local and national news story during the Christmas week of 1992, as angry individuals—both white and black—tried to tear the cross down while the Queen's police and Klan supporters tried to protect it. The year of 1992 ended with late-night comedians making Cincinnati the butt of their jokes. A series of reports by the national media, from NBC's "Today Show" to *The Los Angeles Times*, painted Cincinnati as a racially intolerant city.

At this point, the extent to which the Queen's gimmick had been perpetrated upon me had become painfully clear: I had been flimflammed. As the Queen was unable to eliminate me legally as a highly profiled real estate owner in the central business district, I could see that it had resorted to the illegality of using shadow crimes that were cloaked in secrecy to wrest my property away from me.

As the newly elected and controversial President William Jefferson Clinton named the former mayor of San Antonio, Texas, Henry G. Cisneros, as Secretary of HUD in December of 1992, the year also ended when scandalous circumstances within that federal Department did not bode well for Sandy and I. While Cisneros talked to federal agents during his background check in this month and the next, he allegedly underestimated payments that he made to a former mistress, Linda Medlar (turned Linda Jones). It was these payments, in part, which would cripple this Secretary and, at the same time, significantly contribute to not allowing a scandal-shy Department of HUD to be willing—or able—to take on another criminal wrongdoing such as its illegal involvement at 124 West Ninth Street.

Sandy and I brought in 1993 with a continuation of 1992's events. Due to the overall negative impact of our personal financial position that was brought on by the 124 West Ninth Street fiasco, on January 11, 1993, Sandy and I were forced to sell the first piece of rental property that we bought twelve years earlier in order to pay our mounting bills. On January 12, 1993, George Fulford, Assistant Vice President of Provident Bank, froze the 124 West Ninth Street HUD RRP renovation project due to so-called "cost overruns."

On January 20, 1993, President William Jefferson Clinton became America's 42nd president on by putting his hand on the Bible and swearing an oath to "preserve, protect and defend the Constitution of the United States." At the same time, as the use of the equity in 123 West Ninth Street was my only chance of keeping 124 West Ninth Street alive, I continued to try to initiate dialogues with many lending institutions in the Queen.

Development financing thumbs continued to be illogically turned down to us across the Queen. As all of our financing efforts were futile, Sandy and I felt the pain of being skinned alive as racist municipal attitudes prevailed as operational canons of the Queen. One week later, on January 27, 1993, Cincinnati City Council approved the City Manager's recommendation that $1.25 million in CDBG funds be set aside for Phase II of Garfield housing development, the nearby Milner Hotel site. The plot only thickened in the carrying out of this patently illegal municipal attitude that was responsible for the underappraisals of my Garfield

Place area properties.

When combined with other financial resources that had already been earmarked, these $1.25 million in CDBG funds enabled the Queen to accelerate planning for not only for Phase II of Garfield housing development, but also for Phase III of Garfield housing development, Grofton Lofts. Involving a large seven-story commercial building that would be converted into luxury apartments, Grofton Lofts would be rehabbed at the northeast corner of Seventh and Race Streets, just due east of the Gramercy.

I did not know specifically which laws were being broken against me, but there was one indicator that strongly suggested that things had entered into a much deeper stage of what was criminal: the eyes of the Queen. Just as the famed nineteenth century American sculptor, Hiram Powers, once said, "The eye is the window of the soul," the eyes of the Queen gave its true intentions away. I began to look towards the nation's capital for much needed help.

In Washington, D. C., during a time when the mantle of responsibility was being passed from the recently defeated administration of President George Bush to the new administration of President-elect Bill Clinton, my complaints were fruitless, as HUD was in a state of inanimate suspension. In view of the tidal wave of illegal interference that was deluging me in Cincinnati, Ohio, I could distinctly see why and how 124 West Ninth Street was going under, while the Queen evilly stared down the federal laws that ruled her heinous actions.

I could also see that massive collusion and illegal collaboration was responsible for the sounding of the death knell for my HUD RRP project. Like a flurry of roundhouse punches that walloped us below the belt, Sandy and I were debilitated by the cumulative impact of the Queen's execution of its waylay of 124 West Ninth Street's RRP.

By March 8, 1993, as both Suburban Federal Savings Bank and Provident Bank illegally applied pressure to foreclose on my downtown properties, 124 West Ninth Street ceased to exist as a HUD project and as a viable income stream. Beginning the final stages of their undetected land-grab feeding frenzy, these two mortgage shark lending institutions menacingly circled and closed in for the kill to begin their in camera gorging on the real estate that Sandy and I had lengthily fought to keep afloat.

When Cincinnati's *Downtowner* newspaper printed an article entitled, "City plans to raze Milner [Hotel]" on March 16, 1993, the hidden federal criminal activity that emanated from my HUD RRP project came more sharply into focus as the smoke of the Queen's illusion blew even further away. In this article, the City of Cincinnati announced the go-ahead for the tearing down of the Milner Hotel that stood twenty-five feet away from 123 West Ninth Street's property line. It was also mentioned that the construction of Phase II of the Garfield Place housing project was scheduled to begin two months later, encompassing the area where the Milner stood, and bringing a multi-million dollar project seventy-two inches away from my American dream.

In response to my stinging complaints against the City for the manifold ways in which it artfully injured me—including the conveniently arranged pretense that was intended to make it appear that I was well over budget, I received a tersely written letter from NHC's RRP Manager, Michael Jackson on March 24, 1993. Attempting to deflect attention away from the federally indictable crimes that the City of Cincinnati had committed against the nation and me, he made no mention that the City's architect, Charles Alexander, never gave his federally-required approval of my HUD project in the first place. Instead, NHC's Michael Jackson made a continued attempt to use the City's architect as a construct to federal criminal activity by writing that Alexander had not received any information from me to justify "rehab cost overruns."

The Queen's RRP Manager continued to illegally stumble forward when he wrote, "We have provided you with the maximum funding available under the RRP." Realizing that the Queen had chicaned by stepping dangerously over the line into a federally indictable realm that involved 124 West Ninth Street HUD activities, Jackson attempted to back the Queen out of its contractual federal obligations by feebly attempting to force me into seeking total building financing through the private sector. Jackson showed the Queen's hand by trying to get me to subordinate my original HUD RRP financing to Provident Bank, thereby letting the City off of the hook. As Sandy and I stood in the ruins of our collapsing real estate investment dreams, there was no doubt that our federal HUD RRP contract was our ace in the hole. To that end, we were completely non-receptive to Jackson's obvious ploy.

Knowing that we needed legal help, on April 6, 1993, I met with the lawyer that I had used for years, Cincinnati Attorney John W. Hauck. It was he who had been actively involved with me in overseeing everything from the initial dealings that I had with the City to the eventual 124 West Ninth Street HUD grant closing. On April 22, 1993, I picked up Attorney Hauck and we met Provident Bank at their downtown office on Fourth Street. With Hauck at my side, at length, I told Provident Bank how their actions were illegally hurting me in a variety of ways.

Financially, things continued to get worse for Sandy and I. As heavy negative income burdens surpassed the positive cash flow of our downtown real estate investments, we went further and further under, flailing uselessly as we grasped frantically for straws. The events of the day also prompted the subcontractors and material men, who got needlessly burned at 124 West Ninth Street, to file mechanic's liens en masse against Sandy and I. By May 5, 1993, my downtown gas and electric bills for 123 and 124 West Ninth Street had accumulated to almost $6,500 and my office phone was cut off due to a bill that I could not pay.

By June of 1993, with the Schott and Klan incidents as a backdrop, negative national portrayals by the media against the Queen's ultra-conservative racial attitudes kept surfacing. *Gentlemen's Quarterly* (GQ) magazine portrayed Cincinnati as a "Town Without Pity." In this GQ article, Peter Richmond wrote that Cincinnati is "clean and safe and quiet and repressive, and resolved to keep itself that way" and is the "most enlightened 19th-century city in America."

Meanwhile, on June 4, 1993, as my unswerving pressure forced someone to take the blame, an interesting unraveling of the Queen's shaky cover-up began to occur behind the scenes in Cincinnati's city government. Realizing that he was being blamed and dumped for the RRP project's failure, the City's architect, Charles Alexander, wrote to the City's RRP Manager, Michael Jackson disassociating himself to the legal responsibility that he had to the 124 West Ninth Street cost estimate that was illegally submitted to HUD.

Alexander stated in this letter to Jackson, "I never was given the opportunity to finalize my 124 West Ninth Street estimate in a normally established sequence." Alexander also complained in this June 4, 1993 letter that his estimate for the 124 West Ninth Street HUD RRP project was incomplete, and that the project "was off and running then."

When addressing the suggestion that the Director of NHC, Wayne

Chapman, was planning on dumping him for another architect, Alexander went on further to say to Jackson in this letter, "I find it difficult to understand how another architect could better address this case. So, I respectfully disagree with Wayne's suggestion and ask that he meet with you and I, to further discuss this, if needed." By June 14, 1993, and while Alexander had been furtively replaced, I met with the City of Cincinnati's new consulting architect and Attorney John W. Hauck.

During a time of much duplicity and foot-dragging by Provident Bank and the City of Cincinnati, these two 124 West Ninth Street co-financiers continued to hatch up a plot to cover their complicity in U. S. Treasury theft crimes against America in order to avoid having federal indictments brought down on them. Like two cats that toy with an injured prey before devouring it, I was financially incapacitated and unable to escape the uncaring clasp of an evil Queen that prolonged my agony while illegally controlling my financial fate.

By August 5, 1993, it was a time that was only sixteen days after the controversial suicide of the Deputy Counsel to the White House, Vince Foster, who was deeply enmeshed in the knowledge of President Bill Clinton's Whitewater real estate scandal. It was also a time when I was further cozened by Provident Bank when, in an attempt to appear helpful while continuing to underappraise my 123 West Ninth Street property, it signed and handed me a workout proposal that committed to loaning me an additional $115,000. I found out later that Provident Bank faked this move, as it knew all along that the Queen would continue to drag its feet.

Elsewhere, on August 30, 1993 in the Queen's City Hall, and with local television cameras rolling, I forcefully made sure that the 124 West Ninth Street fiasco came to the fore in an open discussion in the Finance Committee meeting in Cincinnati City Council Chambers. As they faced local elections that were fast approaching on November 3rd of that year, City Council politicians recoiled like Count Dracula to a cross when I exposed them in a true light by publicly calling them on the carpet.

Even though they put a false face forward that was intended to appear to be helpful, their true jig was only designed to deceive, deny and delay in order to illegally eliminate me once and for all as a downtown property owner. The Queen's politicians only wanted me to walk away from my downtown real estate ownership by throwing my hands up in disgust.

But the outward appearance of their actions did not deflect the slings and arrows of the Queen's actual intent. On September 23, 1993, as the Cincinnati Gas and Electric Company came to turn off all of the electricity at 123 West Ninth Street, a last minute payment that Sandy and I had scraped together stayed the power shutoff for the building. On the same day, a water shutoff notice was posted across the street on the front door of 124 West Ninth Street by the Queen's water department, Cincinnati Water Works.

My downtown bills and obligations piled up to the extent of taking on the proportions of an Egyptian pyramid. Sandy and I were financially holding on for dear life. We were being clutched in the Queen's death grip that squeezed us tighter to make the vital economic life signs of our downtown buildings completely disappear. Having no control over ourselves as financial beings, the Queen and its operatives threw us unmercifully about, like overpowering wrestlers in a one-sided tag-team match.

On September 30, 1993, Provident Bank took its turn to castigate Sandy and I by sending us a letter threatening foreclosure on 124 West Ninth Street. This letter indicated that I had fifteen days, until October 15, 1993, to have a work out plan in place with the City of Cincinnati for the completion of 124 West Ninth Street.

I decided to call Mr. William J. Harris in HUD's Cincinnati office on October 4, 1993 and explained to him what had happened to me. As he led me on another wild-goose chase down other dead ends to people who refused to help, Harris said that I should contact John Riordan, State RRP Program Administrator for HUD out of Columbus, Ohio and Wayne Chapman who oversaw the RRP in Cincinnati. As expected, these people did absolutely nothing.

As federal crimes had already been committed by the Queen that were far beyond my possible comprehension, I had entered into a point in my negotiations with the City that was marked by the latest in a series of unpleasant fits and starts, indicating a secretive pattern of delay. After I had applied considerably more pressure on the Queen's handling of its business with me, it was forced into another sloppy attempt of trying to give the appearance that it was coming to my aid.

Not knowing what was really going on, things appeared to me to be moving in a positive direction. It was an encouraging development when the Queen wrote a letter to me on October 12, 1993 committing an additional $124,362 for the completion of 124 West Ninth Street. Likewise, on October 21, 1993, things also began to look promising on the Provident Bank side when a bout of phone tag (occurring on October 19 & 20, 1993 between Sandy Heimann, Carl Lindner's assistant, and myself) ended with a telephone conversation that discussed 124 West Ninth Street's latest developments.

Seemingly, a positive change was in the air. It was as if a refreshing breeze was sweetly wafting through the Queen when Cincinnati's new City Manager, John Shirey, was sworn in replacing acting City Manager, Frank A. Dawson (the former City Director of Finance who signed my HUD contract along with Wayne Chapman) on October 24, 1993.

Desperately gasping for financial breath, I conveniently camped out at Cincinnati City Hall to see to it that the Queen would make good its commitment to loan me the $124,362 that it had promised. In City Council's Finance Committee meeting on October 25, 1993, based upon an outwardly discernible shift in their attitudes, I became more suspect than ever that the City would not deliver on its promises.

The pace quickened. The next day, October 26, 1993, I conclusively found out in the Community Development, Housing and Zoning Committee meeting in City Council Chambers that the Queen had no intentions of delivering on their written word to provide me with the additional 124 West Ninth Street financing. It was at this point that I unequivocally knew that this exercise on their part was nothing more than a continuation of what they had been doing all along. Outraged, I went to City Council meeting on Wednesday, October 27, 1993 and gave them a piece of my mind.

As I got hot under my collar by seeing through their shifty pretenses, any trust that I had for the Queen instantaneously evaporated into thin air. I became steeled in my determination to expose what was going on and decided to get on the offensive for a change.

I went to a professional sign maker, got twenty or so large protest signs made that decried the City's illegal actions and called a group of people who already knew how treacherous the Queen's City government could be. Getting a little help from my friends, I made arrangements for them to meet me in front of City Hall on that upcoming

Friday, October 29, 1993, five days before City Council elections.

As the commencement of my politically timed strategy to the November 3, 1993 Cincinnati City Council elections began in earnest, that Friday, I led an attention-getting picket of Cincinnati's City Hall. Consisting of fifteen to twenty people, damage control was in order for the Queen, as several local television and radio stations covered my politically-embarrassing protest.

Curiously, on the next morning, four days before City Council elections, a newspaper article appeared in *The Cincinnati Post* entitled "City reconsidering another loan to black rehabber." In this article, something was printed that I had known about for quite some time: I was called "downtown's only black large-property owner." As it remained a sad commentary on the stifling real estate discrimination that was ongoing in the Queen, I questioned its timing.

On Monday, November 1, 1993, two days before Election Day, I showed up at the Finance & Labor Committee Hearing in City Council Chambers. As local television cameras rolled while City Council politicians postured nervously for precious votes from a large pre-election audience, I caught the Queen off of its guard when I signed a "Request to speak before Council list." Had City Council politicians known what I was about to say from the reading aloud of a three-page typewritten letter that I had written to Cincinnati Mayor Dwight Tillery on that date, they would not have allowed me to speak.

In a blistering criticism that I leveled at the Queen and Provident Bank for their illegal mishandling of my 124 West Ninth Street HUD RRP, I held back no stops. Being fully aware that this was my long-awaited chance to expose the evil Queen, I took full advantage of the situation to capture the moment. Noticing how the City Councilpeople nervously squirmed in their chairs, I knew—and they knew—that I had the spotlight that gave me the attention of the City.

Speaking of the City's federal chicanery, the gist of my tirade addressed itself to the contemptible nature of the most corrupt, amoral and despicable display of public conduct that I had ever seen. When reading from my letter to Mayor Dwight Tillery, in part, I told a captive city audience "At bottom, laws have been broken and, through deception, lying, and attempted theft, HUD monies have been misused."

Making mention to City Council that I was a U. S. Army veteran who served during the Vietnam era, I continued to lay it on the line by reading from my letter. "Initially", I said, "in my ignorance, not knowing how politics were run in City Hall, I really believed that the solution could be found within the City government. Ha!!...I've seen a prettier picture in the slop at the bottom of a field latrine than in the operation of our City's government."

My appearance in City Council Chambers on this day was one of the worst things that could happen to a city government that was involved in a U. S. Treasury theft cover-up. Boxed into a corner, while television lenses created a public eye which showed that I was an irrefutable argument against many damnable sins of the Queen, City Council publicly attempted to make the 124 West Ninth Street City architect, Charles Alexander the whipping boy for the project's failure.

However, the most disturbing view through the Queen's window came from the ensuing dialogue that followed the reading of my letter in front of a skittish and vote-hungry City Council. Responding to my allegations of criminal wrongdoing by the banks that were involved with my downtown properties, City Councilpeople postured before the citywide cable television broadcast of a pre-election camera.

As they were exposed for the shameful illegalities that occurred under their watch, many image-sensitive Council people fidgeted to say politically correct things while pandering to the desires of a watching populace that was poised to vote within forty-eight hours. Backed into a corner that forced them to confront the lingering U. S. Treasury theft involvement that they were unable to evade, the Queen's City Council openly admitted to the role that the City, Provident Bank and Suburban Federal Savings Bank played in causing my HUD RRP project to fail.

In this November 1, 1993 city council meeting, the Queen was videotaped admitting its role in the federally indictable crimes that were committed at my 124 West Ninth Street HUD RRP project. In the express admission of the illegal mishandling of HUD tax dollars, City Councilwoman Roxanne Qualls spoke to the cameras by saying, "There is obvious complicity between the banks [Provident and Suburban Federal Savings] and the City of Cincinnati regarding Mr. Kiah's buildings." Similarly, it became a disquieting reality when City Councilman Todd Portune said, "There is complicity on the City's part for the 124 West Ninth Street project not being successful."

It was a strange day on the day before the 1993 City Council elections; a day of mixed emotions, stimuli and news. While being badly pummeled by so many, and for so long, I received a telephone call from the new Cincinnati City Manager, John Shirey. He asked me to meet with his subordinate, the Director of NHC, Wayne Chapman, on the morning of the following day. I was informed by Shirey that the purpose of the meeting would be to work out a deal in order for the Queen to give me the $124,362 that it had committed to me.

As the Garfield Place neighborhood was again hit with another gargantuan wave of development excitement, it was also the same day that the City of Cincinnati reached an agreement to purchase the 115 room Milner Hotel for $2.75 million for use in the City's Phase II of the Garfield Development project, Greenwich on the Park. The announcement on that day that the Greenwich on the Park would be a four-story building with about 80 apartments, underneath parking and some limited retail space on the ground level made area property owners become even more eager in anticipation. For me, with an illegal noose around my neck, I did not know quite how to feel.

On Election Day morning, November 3, 1993, I met with Wayne Chapman in his office and left having every indication that a deal had been worked out. In a last ditch effort to put a good face forward before the polls closed, and as it was reeling from the public admission that it had erred, that afternoon Cincinnati City Council passed Emergency Ordinance No. 392-1993, which was to have provided me with $124,362.

As Cincinnatians narrowly voted in first-time mayor Roxanne Qualls on November 3, 1993, a disgruntled and vindictive Dwight Tillery was re-elected but had been knocked out of the highly coveted mayor's seat. Councilmen Nick Vehr, Bobbie Sterne and Tyrone Yates were also returned to City Council.

Councilmen Peter Strauss, John Mirlesena and Nell Surber were defeated. Councilmen Charles Winburn and Phil Heimlich were newly elected, while former Councilmen Tom Luken and David Mann were returned as well. Although Councilman David Mann would resign two months later to do a stint in the U. S. House of Representatives, Councilman Todd Portune replaced him.

Through the painful process of discovery, I found out that the surface politics in the Queen were incomparable to the deeper, darker and more sinister breeding ground that laid fertile in secluded recesses within the federal government. In HUD, by the close of 1993, Henry Cisneros severely compromised his position as Secretary by stopping hidden payments to the irately dismissed woman that he had an extra-marital affair with, Linda Medlar (Jones).

In the White House, knowing that he needed lots of money in facing an expanding three-front war—denying Gennifer Flowers' sexual relationship charges; figuring out a way to stem the flood of negative publicity regarding the gone-bad Whitewater (Arkansas) real estate dealings; and coping with his blind obsession to drastically change the net worth that had made him the least affluent occupant of the White House in 15 years, Bill Clinton was openly for sale. The President was made-to-order grist for the deep pockets of the opportunistic Queen.

Chapter 5

The Emperor Has No Clothes

"Time is precious, but truth is more precious than time."
—Disraeli

The nineteenth-century Danish writer and collector of children's stories and folklore, Hans Christian Andersen (1805-1875), published a fairy tale in 1836, "The Emperor's New Clothes," that told of an emperor who had such a grand opinion and puffed-up image of himself that he believed he had on clothes, when he did not. Due to the trickery and self-delusion that negatively affected this fabled sovereign ruler, over the years, the statement, "The emperor has no clothes," has become synonymous with getting caught lying.

On the day after the City of Cincinnati passed Emergency Ordinance No. 392-1993, extended to me as recompense for its highly embarrassing pre-1993 City Council election admission that it had illegally handled 124 West Ninth Street's HUD RRP, I soon discovered that the Queen, too, had no clothes.

Like an airplane that has gone too far down a runway on takeoff to stop, by November 4, 1993, the Queen had reached a point of no return in its more than one year federally incriminating HUD U. S. Treasury theft cover-up. By this time, the Queen realized that too many of its central people had been involved in the illegal procurement, disbursement and use of federal tax dollars at 124 West Ninth Street. Like flies about a horse's ears in summer, swarms of lies buzzed about the Queen.

I had used the power of television cameras to keep the underhanded Queen at bay before the 1993 Cincinnati City Hall elections. But, once the elections were over and the glare of the public spotlight had dimmed, I was unable to offer an effective public awareness countermove to the pent-up rage of a vindictive Goliath whose hands had been freed.

Like the feeling of a hare that is missed on the first pass of a swooping bird of prey, or the dread of a child with an abusive parent, Sandy and I could feel that the air was tinged with the threat of another attack by the Queen. We did not know where, when or how the Queen would strike, but we did know that it had the wherewithal to hit us again—and to hit us hard. While keeping meticulous documentation of the dates and events surrounding the 124 West Ninth Street criminal cover-up, Sandy and I were defenseless, as we ruefully kept vigil for an attempt at hurt that we knew would surely come again.

As it pursued a conspiratorial defense as its only course from federal prosecution, the Queen attempted to cloud the air of public opinion with falsehoods and ancillary issues that had nothing to do with its admitted complicity in the U. S. Treasury theft at 124 West Ninth Street. In the beginning stages of a preemptive media campaign that was designed to discredit me, I could see one facet of the Queen's power being hastily deployed when I was visciously attacked by a mainstay that it controlled.

Practically before all of the ink had dried on the election results following the 1993 City Council elections, *The Cincinnati Enquirer* printed an article on November 4th entitled, "City OKs new loan to developer." Buried deep within a back section of this particular edition, it was a malicious 244-word obituary page article that unearthed the Queen's latest effort to publicly vilify me. Consistent with the longtime maneuver to openly deny the facts, deceive the public and delay justice for the federal HUD crimes that had occurred at 124 West Ninth Street, a mass media attempt was nakedly made to distort the truth and to rewrite history.

Like an enchantress calling forth spirits from the vastly deep of a seething cauldron of desires, the evil Queen used the power that was at its command to conjure up *The Cincinnati Enquirer's* ability to assist the City's sleight of hand. As the article was concocted from the Queen's crooked sphere of influence, Sandy and I took a profoundly negative hit from our names being widely scandalized in the public domain. Despite the open blow that we took from this newspaper article, again, fuel was only added our fire.

Yet, despite the flexing of muscles by the Queen, a federal trail of incrimination was continuing to be established behind the walls of Cincinnati City Hall. Unknown to me, and on the same day of this scandalous *Cincinnati Enquirer* article, the City's HUD RRP architect, Charles Alexander, wrote a letter to the City of Cincinnati that defended himself from the alleged wrongdoings that the City had accused him of in the mishandling of 124 West Ninth Street's HUD RRP.

Distancing himself from being the fall guy for the City's failure to draft a federally required Scope of Work that was necessary for the lawful release of U. S. Treasury grant financing at 124 West Ninth Street's HUD RRP, Alexander said in this letter "I had always maintained serious reservations about the feasibility of his [Kiah's] development package." The letter came after Alexander had reviewed a videotape of the City's November 1, 1993 Finance and Labor Committee Hearing where the Queen's City Council used him as a scapegoat for the failure of my federal building renovation project.

After I had met all of the set of requirements that were preconditions of the City's Emergency Ordinance, a rapid succession of events signaled the Queen's wholesale onslaught to make quick work of me. In a well-coordinated effort, like great white sharks rising from the abyss to hit its helpless prey on the surface of the sea, Suburban Federal Savings Bank struck first on November 8, 1993, moving to file a Complaint in Hamilton County Common Pleas Court to foreclose on 123 West Ninth Street.

As this bank knew all along that they were part of an illegal financial subterfuge against Sandy and I, in that 123 West Ninth Street could have been used as collateral for the additional funding at 124 West Ninth Street, this submerged bank predator rose out of the dark to render us powerless. With Suburban Federal's move, the actual feeding frenzy on our downtown property began in earnest.

I wrote a joint letter to Jack Rubenbauer, Senior Vice President of Provident Bank, and Wayne Chapman, Director of NHC reiterating the difficult financial position that they had put me in due to the delays in my project. I told them that time was extremely of the essence and that further delay was not in our best interests. Elsewhere, the means that the Queen illegally used to deprive me of access to the equity in my West Ninth Street properties became even more apparent.

Pain was added to injury when, on November 9, 1993, the *Downtowner* newspaper printed an article that announced the City of Cincinnati's plan for Phase III of the Garfield Development plan, Grofton Lofts. As it was made public that this multi-million dollar project was to have included about 36 loft apartments—with high ceilings and large windows in a restored building located approximately 300 feet away from 123 West Ninth Street, I saw money being ripped from my hands and thrown out of a window.

The emotional pain and agony that Sandy and I went through was akin to preparing oneself for impact with a brick wall when skidding on ice in a car: It is bad enough hitting the wall, but it is the sheer experience of terror that one experiences before hitting it which can be equally as bad. The predicament for Sandy and I, however, was not like a brief skid, but like an elongated slide that produced intermittent intensities of stress, as we slid uncontrollably into an illegally erected wall of financial disaster.

Coincidentally, we began to receive incessant and intimidating phone calls in my downtown office and at home. Some of the telephone calls hung up immediately; some of the telephone calls waited for several seconds before hanging up; and some of the prank calls delivered racial epithets or obscenities. Whenever voices were heard, the phone receiver button was quietly depressed on the other end to disconnect the line, bringing on an eerie dial tone that would otherwise be normal sounding.

On November 15, 1993, Suburban Federal Saving Bank rendered me financially impotent when it told me that it was going to enforce the Assignment of Rents clause in my 123 West Ninth Street mortgage. This contractual provision allowed them to collect any and all of the downtown rents that I was collecting at 123 West Ninth Street. From this point forward, as absolutely no rental income was being generated at 124 West Ninth Street, in effect, I was out of business.

On this same day, I talked to a stressed out Wayne Chapman who was aware that his federally incriminating HUD activities at 124 West Ninth Street were being increasingly exposed by me. Sensing panic in his voice, I soon received a letter from him which mandated that I accomplish a completely different set of requirements from the City's Emergency Ordinance, an illegal municipal move within its own right.

Yet, the jittery Chapman went one further. In order to make it appear that the continued HUD RRP project's failure would have been of my making, he sloppily changed the language in the Emergency Ordinance by significantly increasing my debt, by significantly reducing my equity and by, otherwise, attempting to throw a monkey wrench into the works.

After all, just as surely as this letter that was from the top City department that received federal money from HUD's RRP, it was conclusive evidence to me that the Queen's Emergency Ordinance was never legitimate. As the pieces of the puzzle began to fall into place, I wondered how many others were being victimized by the same modus operandi. I knew that a person only needs to see a single cockroach to know that there are others.

After staying up all night, on the following day, November 16, 1993, I hand-delivered a 35-page document to Wayne Chapman with the caption, "The Elimination of African-American Real Estate Ownership in the Central Business District of Downtown Cincinnati, Ohio." In summary, this document expanded upon the reasons for and causes of the 124 West Ninth Street debacle. Addressing how NHC always used excuses in answer to dealing with my easily solved building renovation problems, I called a spade a spade when I accused the shifty-eyed Chapman of always looking the other way.

Speaking of how he never answered questions, I also wrote in the letter how there was a code of silence, why the demise of my real estate holdings fell on deaf ears and why there was a cover-up. Even though I did not exactly know which laws had been violated, I spoke of documents, evidence, facts and proof that federal laws had been broken. That night, my downtown office was broken into.

The same familiarity that one gets through repetition—i.e., the feel of handling a long-owned car, the touch of a favorite fishing reel, the running of the fingers over one's head—was the same touch and feel that I had for opening my office door. As I had personally installed it in 1983, and was at my office on the average of six days per week for ten years, I had an intimate awareness of its feel, as it relates to the specific efforts that were required to open it.

Due to the fact that my office contained valuables, e.g., computer system, color television, stereo components, microwave oven, petty cash box, etc., I had reinforced the doors to my office with single pieces of angle iron that were affixed to the inside of the door jambs, where the latches of the lock sets hit the strike plates. This prevented my office doors from being kicked in.

My rear office door could not be opened from the outside because I kept it barred from the inside. However, in order to open my front office door, two things had to happen: first, the key had to be roughly jiggled into the exterior doorknob; and secondly, the door had to be simultaneously pulled up by the outside knob while still jiggling the key and twisting the knob in a clockwise direction. That was the personality of my office door. With no exceptions, that was the way that my office door was religiously opened for ten years.

On the morning of November 17, 1993, I knew something was different when my front office door key slipped into the doorknob like a hot knife through butter. Upon immediately pulling the key out of the doorknob and inspecting it, I noticed an oily graphite type of substance glistening on the neck of the key. Once I reinserted it and the door opened effortlessly after I lightly turned the key, I knew that someone had broken into my office.

Even though I could not tell if anything had been taken, I cautiously inspected the contents of my place of business. As I had anticipated such a possibility, it gave me great comfort to know that I had removed all of the evidentiary 124 West Ninth Street documentation from my office.

I was incensed. On that Wednesday afternoon, I stormed a block and a half from 123 West Ninth Street to Cincinnati City Hall, where I barged into a 2:00 meeting in City Council Chambers that was attended by most of the Queen's City Councilpeople. After I announced to them what had happened at my office, I was greeted with blank stares and obviously disingenuous responses. Again, their eyes said it all by confirming to me that they knew that there was something very sinister happening behind the scenes.

Although I could not definitively prove it, there was a reasonable degree of certitude on my part that my office, indeed, had been broken into. While a solid crack in the Queen's cover-up dam had been revealed to me, at that point, the perspective of my fighting stance was altered radically. From my perspective, it was the beginning of the next phase of a wartime strategy for me.

Figuring that, if they could break into my office, they could break into my home, I began dispersing the incriminating copies and originals of all critical evidence that I had earlier moved to my residence to trusted friends and relatives outside of the State of Ohio. Sandy and I also actively began to watch what we said in our home, at our 123 West Ninth Street office and on the telephone. We had reason to believe that big brother was alive and well.

Whenever we talked about what we were thinking or doing with respect to our fight with the Queen, and as we did not feel comfortable talking in our cars, we either walked into the yard outside of our home or we carefully whispered over our pillows while in bed. More significantly, I began to look more observantly over my shoulder. Like a rape victim after being violated, from that point on, I lost the comfort level that I had in my buildings, as I knew that they had been illegally invaded.

A line had been drawn in the sand. The Queen had openly become my nemesis. As the financial resources that I should have had access to had been illegally tied up under a veil of legality, getting help from an attorney requiring remuneration for his or her services was beyond my ability to pay. Facing a choice between two alternatives, Sandy and I had to decide whether to yield or to fight against the crushing power of the Queen.

I could see that this was a perfect crime in the making for the Queen, replete with a system of camouflaged political conduits that made its illegal behavior virtually impossible to detect. It became more obvious that what was going on around me was part of an intentionally coordinated campaign of fraud and deceit. I knew that if I did not stand up in opposition to the Queen, 124 West Ninth Street's crimes against my family and America would have been deeply buried out of sight and forever.

Not hesitating because of our relative size to the Queen, the decision boiled down to being a no-brainer for us to fight. Overnight, Sandy and I became self-appointed, standard-bearing witnesses who stood in opposition to a type of U. S. Treasury theft that was being covered-up right in front of our eyes. We began to actively lay out a strategy against a far superior foe while anticipating getting the legal help that we desperately needed.

Help certainly did not come from Provident Bank when I had an appointment with their Vice President and Community Affairs Officer, Amin Akbar on December 2, 1993. Instead, Akbar got greatly perturbed after I showed him a copy of a newspaper article from the preceding day, "Banks under pressure over lending bias" by John E. Jacob.

The article reported how the Federal Reserve Board, a federal institution that governed banks like Provident, was treating lender discrimination investigations as major offenses that would prevent banks from implementing such strategic business plans as mergers or acquisitions. When I departed from the appointment, Akbar was so upset that he yelled physical threats at me across the wide-open floor of Provident Bank's downtown headquarters office.

As an underdog, I did not lose sight of the forest for the trees. I was able to see that, as Akbar was an inferior in the scheme of things, his frustration was only indicative of the pressure that was put on him from superiors who had a much greater risk of having 124 West Ninth Street's U. S. Treasury theft crimes detected. It only stood to reason that Akbar was only a pawn, an underling for those out of sight individuals at the top where the real decisions of Provident Bank were made.

Even after I wrote separate letters detailing complaints about the treatment that I had received to Allen L. Davis, President of Provident Bank and Jack Rubenbauer, Senior Vice President of Provident Bank, 1993 ended with the Queen's tightening of the screws by a powerful entity that was under its influence: the government of Hamilton County, Ohio. On December 6, 1993, Hamilton County Treasurer, Robert A. Goering, filed foreclosure complaint against Sandy and I for delinquent taxes on 123 West Ninth Street. By January 10, 1994, Provident Bank initiated a foreclosure action on 124 West Ninth Street in the Hamilton County Court of Common Pleas.

As I tried to make politicians outside of Cincinnati aware of the hidden U. S. Treasury theft that I was aware of, on January 12, 1994, I wrote to Ohio Governor George Voinovich and U. S. President Bill Clinton. On this same day, I not only wrote to U. S. Congressmen from Ohio David Mann and Rob Portman, but to U. S. Senators from Ohio John Glenn and Howard Metzenbaum. By January 31, 1994, Senator Howard Metzenbaum's responded to me saying that he "will be glad to contact the appropriate officials regarding the situation that I mentioned." He further stated that he would be in touch with me as soon as he received a report.

During this timeframe, a news story hit the press that captured America's attention. In *The New York Times*, on February 12, 1994, Paula Jones said that U. S. President Bill Clinton, when he was the Governor of Arkansas, made a sexual advance to her in a hotel room during a conference in 1991. Although the White House denied the charge, Paula Jones appeared at a news conference with two state troopers and Cliff Jackson, a childhood friend of President Clinton's, who had made various accusations about Clinton's past.

I had developed this thing about looking deeply into people's eyes in measuring sincerity levels. As I gauged the eyes of those that I came into contact with at NHC, City Council, Suburban Federal Savings Bank and Provident Bank, it was my gut sense that they were only front people who were following orders from a more weighty and unseen source. Although I previously had a working hypothesis of how lower-leveled City and Provident Bank employees were ultimately involved in the 124 West Ninth Street cover-up, I found out that the more that I dug into the matter, the more serendipitous and upward ranging my discoveries would be.

For the sake of myself and my country, I knew that I would have to take this fight wherever it would lead me. As a concerned American, I knew that if it could happen to me in the Queen City, these same U. S. Treasury theft crimes could happen anywhere in this country.

Seeing how Cincinnati's politicians treated the cover-up of 124 West Ninth Street as business as usual, I had a burning desire to delve deeper into this shameful activity to figure out how these major federal crimes were being covered-up, and who was responsible. I was convinced that these were the types of illegal government activities that were part and parcel of the decline of morality in American society.

As determining the depth of the Queen's cover-up was difficult to measure, I set out on a journey to provide answers to profound questions that I had. Why wasn't anyone doing anything about the bureaucratic bungling of federal tax dollars that was causing people like me—and my country—so much harm? Which specific laws were broken at 124 West Ninth Street? Who was ultimately responsible? In pursuit thereof, I became a detective who began to make contacts with any- and everyone I could think of that had anything to do with 124 West Ninth Street's HUD RRP.

In getting to the bottom of 124 West Ninth Street's criminal cover-up, I followed the HUD RRP dollar trail while using the corporate sales questioning techniques that I had used successfully in the past to make sales and close orders. Thereupon, I began a fact-finding mission by asking questions and making follow-up statements that were used as feelers to narrow the circle of people and organizations that I suspected were involved in the Queen's U. S. Treasury theft crimes. Through the process of elimination, I was able to weed out those who I believed were not involved and focus deeper on those who I identified were involved.

In the intervening time, the steady accumulation of punishing haymakers that were thrown on me by the Queen took a mounting toll upon my ability to fight. As if I needed something else to go against me, on February 17, 1994, the local electrical utility provider, Cincinnati Gas & Electric Company, transferred the final bills from 123 and 124 West Ninth Street, totaling close to $2,000, to my residential account at 12066 Hitchcock Drive. With everything else happening the way that it was, I needed that to happen to me just like I needed another hole in my head.

Although our commitment to fight never wavered, an intense period of shared introspection accompanied the psychological and financial pummeling that Sandy and I took. But, even as we were battered, bloodied, bruised, rubber legged, and holding on to the ropes with one eye swollen shut, we could still see that the Queen was attempting to get away with federal foul play. Plainly put, it was axiomatic that Sandy and I were dealing with a bunch of crooks.

In the Queen's self-serving attempt to benefit from this federally financed sham on American taxpayers, Sandy and I could also see that the City, Provident Bank and Suburban Federal Savings Bank had the maximum amount of confidence that their stratagem was working, and that it was foolproof. We observed that NHC's Wayne Chapman, a career bureaucrat, was their trusted point man who was already in place and was heading an integral part of a well-oiled and corrupt political machine. With the clear inside view of corruption that we had, we could not help but to notice that the Queen's Chapman was being considerably relied upon to cover the telling tracts of the federal crimes that had been left behind.

Just as classical mythology's Atlas (a Titan; son of Iapetus; and brother of Prometheus) was condemned to bear a heavy burden by supporting the sky on his shoulders, the Queen had initially assigned Chapman to carry the burdensome weight of hiding its 124 West Ninth Street's Treasury theft crimes. Due to the wide latitude that was afforded him in his position of public trust within both HUD and the Queen, the utmost reliance was placed in Chapman's ability to support the federally indictable cover-up that was being used against me. Besides, as the Queen's fail-safe stratagem went, Chapman was dispensable and could be used as a fall guy or a patsy who could be sacrificed, if things went awry. Sandy and I were determined not to let the Queen's ploy succeed.

In that most people would have chosen not to fight the Queen due to its out-and-out power, Sandy and I, understanding that we were cut from a different cloth, respected—but did not fear—its ability to have its way. With our standing in the way of the concealment of federally prosecutable white-collar criminal activity, which carried prison terms and hefty fines for many powerful and influential individuals involved in 124 West Ninth Street's cover-up, we also realized the danger that was involved. It did not take much for us to figure out that the corrupt Queen was completely capable of placing a price on our heads that could range from the payment of a measly amount to a strung-out crackhead to that of paying many thousands of dollars for a professional hit man.

As the word spread about what was happening to Sandy and I, we were astutely aware of how the Queen's whip hand was controlling the press and was negatively affecting many of those who were close to us. Watching how the news media tore us apart in reporting only what the Queen wanted to be reported, nothing drove this realization home more than our seeing many of the people who we thought were friends of ours disassociating themselves from us. We could see that they were either incapable or unwilling to understand the oppressive difficulties that we faced.

Worse still, as some of our close relatives perceived our opposition to the power of the Queen as being folly, it was exceedingly more painful to watch them distance themselves from us. Had it not been for our continuous process of shared introspection, centering on growing religious and societal perspectives, we would not have reached a cogent rationale for standing up to the vile nature of the Queen.

The danger that surrounded me from the stiff resistance that I mounted against the Queen's guarded secret at 124 West Ninth Street engendered a spiritual perspective from within me that was matched to the occasion. As I did not view earth as being my everlasting home, the fear of death did not discourage me: I saw myself as being a mere sojourner who is between eternities with a temporary human body.

As I saw it as a fight of good versus evil, nothing typified my resolution to stand in opposition to the Queen more than many of the words from Ephesians 6: 10-17 in the Bible. Words like, "Finally, my brethren, be strong in the Lord, and in the power of his might. Put on the whole armor of God, that ye may be able to stand against the wiles of the devil. For we wrestle not against flesh and blood, but against principalities, against powers, against the rulers of the darkness of this world, against spiritual wickedness in high places."

"Wherefore take unto you the whole armour of God, that ye may be able to withstand in the evil day, and having done all, to stand. Stand therefore, having your loins girt about with truth, and having on the breastplate of righteousness; And your feet shod with the preparation of the gospel of peace; Above all, taking the shield of faith, wherewith ye shall be able to quench all the fiery darts of the wicked. And take the helmet of salvation, and the sword of the Spirit, which is the word of God: Praying always with all prayer and supplication in the Spirit, and watching thereunto with all perseverance and supplication for all saints."

Boy, did I pray. The melding of my spiritual beliefs with my societal concerns only buttressed my overall abhorrence to the thievery that was being kept buttoned up. Since the Queen was going to take everything that I owned any way (totaling $641,000), I was not going to let them take it without my fighting to the end.

I did not feel the way that I did because I saw myself as an idealist who was defending the nation against all fraud, corruption and malfeasance. Nor did I see myself as the consummate bearer of truth, who could right all sins within American society. No, I simply realized that such endeavors were well beyond my capabilities as an individual and that, instead, I was spurred into action because these crimes were plainly about right versus wrong. From this vista, instead of witnessing the development of my buildings, I was witnessing the development of a better part of myself.

In that I had become a muckraker in the classic sense of the word, I knew that I was exposing real misconduct by prominent individuals in the Queen. Even though I did not have the necessary evidence in hand to convincingly prove U. S. Treasury theft at my HUD project, all of the signs of higher rot were there: the lying, the dead giveaway eyes, the arrogance, etc. Up to this time, I was only able to develop my case of incrimination against the Queen only as far as I could see from the shadow that was made from 124 West Ninth Street. I knew that the telling tracks of federal incrimination were there, but vanished into a horizon that was intentionally made cloudy.

Outside of a piece of paper (the federal contract between HUD, the City of Cincinnati and myself), a videotape (showing the Queen incriminating itself) and a few other incidentals, I fell short of having the type of blockbuster legal evidence that I needed to support my assertions. Disadvantaged by fighting in the dark, I had no specific knowledge of which laws were broken to expose the treasonous Queen for what it really was.

There was one thing that I did know, however. I could see through the smoke screen that the successful execution of the 124 West Ninth Street cover-up had been entrusted into the care, custody and control of Chapman. As it was within his ability to set, spring and hide my HUD RRP project, it was Chapman who was being heavily counted on to carry out the Queen's hidden graft job.

However, something went wrong with Chapman's HUD fraud scheme, as things did not go quite the way that the Queen had hoped. Due to a plethora of bureaucratic sloppiness that was associated with the City's bungled 124 West Ninth Street heist, a trail of federally incriminating evidence was left behind by Chapman. As I shot the Queen's cleverly contrived scheme full of holes, it became apparent that it had grossly miscalculated, while its stratagem fell apart right in front of its eyes. What should have been hidden became naked and exposed to view.

Up varying lines of authority, many financially and politically powerful people became exposed to the 124 West Ninth Street HUD Treasury theft scheme by me. Down the tubes went Chapman's washed-up conspiracy. As cover-up efforts took on a whole new dimension outside of my purview, the use of local and national judicial influences escalated, as the Queen attempted to save face at all costs.

While they attempted to muscle the burying of the federal crimes by the Queen under the guise of state court foreclosure proceedings on our downtown buildings, Sandy and I, increasingly, felt the hot breath of Suburban Federal Savings Bank and Provident Bank on our necks. Thankfully, we were cognizant of a profound steeling process that was occurring between the two of us. Thence, we rededicated ourselves to the fight of our choosing.

The gripping pressure caused us to think more critically, more analytically. As it walked in lockstep with the powerful Queen, the Hamilton County, Ohio State court revealed how it was the latest weapon of choice to get rid of us as a threat to the Queen. Even though the Hamilton County, Ohio state judges were sworn to uphold the Constitution of the United States, Sandy and I saw that the chances of our getting a proper adjudication there for the damage that was being done to us was slim and next to none.

In the middle of the donnybrook, it only stood to reason that the proper adjudication of these white-collar crimes should have been placed squarely in the jurisdictional lap of the federal government: it had original jurisdiction of all offenses against the laws of the United States. Therefore, we analyzed, if federal courtrooms had to be entered into, they should have rightfully been the U. S. Sixth Circuit District Court for the Southern District of Ohio, Western Division, that is located in the Queen's downtown central business district.

To justify our entrance into the federal court, however, the gargantuan task before us was finding a way to definitively prove the Queen's robbery of the U. S. Treasury. As have-nots, who were outgunned but not outguessed, and with legal help that was no where to be found, Sandy and I, began to call into play a strategy that we were familiar with: freezing the Queen in place by publicly exposing it. Following the advice of an old adage, we believed that the truth did not have to be defended, only revealed.

Feeling that we had come up with a winning battle plan that was conceived like those that come out of the free world's most deliberative corporate boardrooms, Sandy and I believed that we would make headway. In defense of ourselves and our nation, we intrepidly implemented an attack plan that purposely raised the stakes which, in turn, countered the Queen's attempt to railroad us through her more easily controlled State court system of Ohio.

The running of the sand and the striking of the clock made March of 1994 a month to remember. With the Queen's Hamilton County Court system closing in for the kill, and because we found it impossible to get an attorney, Sandy and I, having no other known choices, made a bold move to go it alone in the federal realm.

On March 2, 1994, we filed a federal lawsuit against the City of Cincinnati, et al. (and others) in the U. S. Sixth Circuit District Court, also known as the trial court. United States District Judge S. Arthur Spiegel was assigned to rule over our lawsuit, U. S. Case No. C-1-94-150. As we represented ourselves in our own behalf without the aid of counsel, we were classified as *pro se* litigants.

Positioned two steps down from the United States Supreme Court (the highest court in the land), the only other federal courts that ranked higher than the U. S. District Courts are the U. S. Courts of Appeals. Cincinnati's U. S. District Court, a.k.a. the U. S. Sixth Circuit Court, lower court or trial court, had original jurisdiction to consider and decide federal cases, exclusive of courts of the individual states, for all offenses against laws of the United States. Sandy and I knew that we had justification for our federal action because there were offenses against laws of the United States when the City of Cincinnati stole and attempted to cover-up its misuse of HUD RRP U. S. Treasury tax dollars.

On seven pages of fill-in-the-blank, poorly photocopied forms that were nastily dished out me by the Clerk's office of the U. S. Sixth Circuit lower trial Court, I completed the forms, paid the filing fee and fearlessly submitted a total of seventeen pieces of paper to a federal court clerk. As these little sheets of paper brought the full weight of the federal government into the fray, beginning at that point, the Queen's plans for a quick kill went into a nose-dive.

Our lawsuit did not have all of the specifics, nonetheless—as our investigation was continuing, it contained carefully worded allegations. These facts without overwhelming proof were sufficient enough to get the attention of those who were listed as defendants in the lawsuit by either legally locking them into U. S. Treasury theft participation charges or illegal lending discrimination involvement at 123 and/or 124 West Ninth Street.

Referred to as a Complaint, our right to file suit was something that Sandy and I did not take lightly. However, as American citizens, who tenaciously held onto our right to be in the federal court, our highly qualified legal opposition viewed us as total aliens, pariahs and trespassers. Their perception of us changed from that of being a bothersome gadfly, to that of being a dangerous threat to the Queen. As the stage was set for a new level of legal fighting, Sandy and I entered into a new phase of legal involvement that was dramatically different from the feel of the state court.

Our lawsuit was straightforward. Twenty-five defendants, their titles, their places of employment, how they were involved with the federal HUD crimes at 124 West Ninth Street, and the dates of their involvement were painstakingly listed in detail.

The following defendants were listed: Cincinnati Mayor Roxanne Qualls; Cincinnati City Manager John Shirey; CEO of Provident Bank (and Chiquita Bananas), Cincinnati billionaire, Carl H. Lindner, Jr.; NHC's Director, Wayne Chapman; NHC's Supervisor, Charles Bronson; NHC's RRP Manager, Michael Jackson; and Cincinnati City Councilpeople Dwight Tillery, Tyrone Yates, Charles Winburn, Todd Portune, Bobbie Sterne, Tom Luken, Nick Vehr, and Phil Heimlich (the son of the world-famous Dr. Henry Heimlich who invented the lifesaving "Heimlich maneuver" for choking and drowning victims).

Also listed were former Cincinnati City Councilpeople Peter Strauss and John Mirlesena; Provident Bank's Allen Davis, Jack Rubenbauer, George Fulford and Amin Akbar; Suburban Federal Savings Bank's John Buchheid and Randy Fields; Attorney John W. Hauck; and, from the Federal government, HUD's John Riordan and The Federal Reserve Bank's Stephen Ong.

In a ten-page chronology of events that was attached to this complaint, Sandy and I called attention to the main occurrences that transpired. Wherein the City of Cincinnati used tactics of deception, excessive red tape, extensive delays, and inordinately cumbersome and complicated procedural requirements, we alleged that it had a net result of causing us significant injury and overall harm. We also alleged that the City of Cincinnati, Ohio operated its HUD RRP illegally under the laws of the United States of America.

On the same day the Complaint was filed, I issued a news release to all of the local television and radio stations announcing this federal lawsuit. After the bright television interview camera lights had slowed down traffic by shining out of the windows of 123 and 124 West Ninth Street onto news coverage trucks parked on the street, I received press coverage on Cincinnati television that evening.

All of the precise procedural requirements that are attendant to moving within the federal court system was a new dimension for me. The unforgiving landscape contained many pitfalls of legal death, where the bones of countless thousands of ill-prepared pro se litigants laid, as they had tread alone, just like Sandy and I were beginning to do.

Like a lost man crossing a desert on foot and alone, we cautiously felt our way around, took risks to gain our bearings, and depended on our hunches. We had no idea, though, that the U. S. Sixth Circuit Court would prove to be a doorway, a portal into a secret way of existence for the American elite, where a privileged class could routinely conceal U. S. Treasury theft at it's discretion.

After Sandy and I filed our federal lawsuit pro se, we painted on a poker face, shut-up, did not blink, sat back, watched attentively for a reaction and waited for more favorable developments to unfold. Until we went against convention by slapping a giant with our federal legal countermeasure, the sneering obstinacy that the Queen kept well-hidden in its closet could no longer be held back from public view, as the blood began to boil in its veins. Its wrath was immediately unleashed upon us.

Sandy and I soon realized that we had struck a virtual hornet's nest of opposing legal resources when phalanxes of high-powered lawyers came out of the woodwork. We were dizzied by endless waves of never before seen court documents that either asked judges for our case to be dismissed or for summary judgments (without a trial) to be made against us. It was the beginning of a deluge of paperwork, as legal motion after legal motion was filed into federal court by the skilled lawyers of all of the defendants that Sandy and I had named in our lawsuit.

While waiting for someone to come to our aid, Sandy and I had become self-styled legal wanna-bes with no legs. Like legal pipsqueaks with popguns at an OK Corral type of courtroom shoot-out, we stood facing a broad front line of well-armed and steely-eyed "hired gun" Philadelphia lawyers with winning reputations.

For Provident Bank, there was Attorney J. Michael Debbeler of Lerner, Sampson & Rothfuss, and Attorney John R. Wirthlin; for Suburban Federal Savings Bank, there was Attorney Bruce K. Gilster; and from the City of Cincinnati's Solicitor's office, there was the City Solicitor and the Assistant City Solicitor, Attorneys Fay D. Dupuis and Mark C. Vollman, respectively.

When viewing this cluster of opposing legal practitioners who stood shoulder-to-shoulder and had over 100 years of court advocacy experience, one did not have to be a brain surgeon to figure out that the probability of my legal success against them was somewhere in or around the domain of the impossible. Regardless, we readied ourselves for whatever they were going to fire at us, knowing full well that they had to whip us into submission to hide the guarded U. S. HUD Treasury theft that we knew about. Only later would we find out that this line of attorneys paled in comparison to the army of attorneys that the Queen had in reserve.

As if our actions did not bring enough damaging attention to the illegal activities of the Queen, there was another event that happened during this same month where the City of Cincinnati cast a bright light upon itself by revealing the inherent contradictions, the incriminating wrongs and the hidden agendas that were part of its 124 West Ninth Street HUD fraud conspiracy.

Just as it was well within spitting distance of my property line at 123 West Ninth Street, a wrecking ball began the demolition of the Milner Hotel in March of 1994 to make way for the $12 million Phase II of the Garfield Place housing project, The Greenwich on the Park. Even as the Milner Hotel wrecking ball swung, the Queen was hard-pressed to leave standing its defense for the financial demise of Sandy and I, as it was forced to call forward more expensive reserves to maintain its growing laundry list of crimes against the national government.

On March 14, 1994, while 124 West Ninth Street-related garnishment proceedings were going on in the Hamilton County Court against us for $4,251.84, another local newspaper brought more unwanted attention upon the Queen. Though ineffectual, *The Cincinnati Business Courier* printed an article about my legal fight entitled, "City property owner alleges racism."

Sandy continued to teach school full-time and I devoted my full-time to fighting the Queen as a pro se litigant. In effect, I had willingly put myself into the unenviable position of practicing law with no law degree. Just as ignorance of the law is no excuse, I had no excuse in not understanding the rules of the court and how the game was played, especially since it was me who had boldly initiated stepping up to the plate by filing a federal lawsuit.

I soon learned that, for the ill prepared, the courtroom is a very implacable place. I could imagine hearing the raucous laughter of the learned scores of trained legal professionals who were arrayed against me, as they belly laughed over the legal minefield that I had entered into—blindfolded!

As a non-legal practitioner who was buried to the top of his eyebrows in federal court legal requirements, there were many things that I had to understand. With the sudden stress of having to understand the legalese of court documents that had to be responded to in a timely fashion; that had to be formatted and captioned in a specific way; that had to be sent to the right people; at the right place; within specific guidelines; with the right usage of terminology; under the appropriate application of law; and everything else that requires a lengthy legal education to fully comprehend, I had my work cut out for me.

I had become a bona fide jackleg lawyer. Groping in the dark, I did not have the foggiest idea as to how to practice law. Operating in this foreign environment, I did not know the difference between the intricacies of a motion and the man in the moon. Yet, two of my biggest assets were that I knew how to read and comprehend.

As a born tinkerer around my buildings and my home, I initially found it to be a natural extension of my inquisitive nature when I bought do-it-yourself law manuals and "how-to" legal books in order to be able to fight without the aid of an attorney in federal court. Try as I did, however, I discovered that these meager reading materials were not sufficient enough resources for my heavy legal informational needs.

There is much truth to the oft-repeated phrase of the Irish dramatist, George Farquhar (1678-1707), who popularized the maxim "Necessity is the mother of invention." In having to come up with something (anything!) that would have allowed me to gain an effective initial toehold inside of the unyielding U. S. court system—with all of its stringent legal requirements and deadlines, I improvised a truly jackleg solution that was born of necessity. This solution was born from what I remembered of my trip to Bamako, Mali, West Africa, during July of 1989.

Arriving in Mali as a welcomed guest of my Muslim Malian host, Lamine Mademba Sy (pronounced "See"), I was honored to be invited to attend a Islamic religious ceremony at a large Bamako mosque on the morning of a holiday that was a national day of feast. As I had never been in a mosque before, the blending-into-the-mosque-crowd concern that I had was not attributable to what I was wearing; Sy saw to it that I did not stick out like a sore thumb. He provided me with a dress outfit of fine African men's garb that made me indistinguishable from the locals.

Rather, as a ceremonial participant, I felt uncomfortable due to my unfamiliarity with the timing of the physical movements that required me to kneel, bow, bend-over or stand at specific intervals in the Muslim ritual while in front of the religious leader, the Imam. Sensing my discomfort as he stood next to me in the prayer line, Sy reassuringly whispered in my direction, "Follow me."

I inconspicuously focused all of my peripheral vision on him during the prayers that were offered up to Allah in the jam-packed mosque. When Sy kneeled, I kneeled; when Sy bowed, I bowed; when Sy bent over, I bent over; and when Sy stood, I stood. Although my moves were a brief nanosecond behind Sy's every move, I was able to blend in amongst a throng of many praying Muslims that knew what they were doing. By following Sy, I was able to effectively participate in an environment that was totally unfamiliar to me.

Likewise, by mimicking the written legal format that the opposing defense lawyers in my case were attempting to use against me, I merely followed what they were doing in Cincinnati's U. S. Sixth Circuit federal court. By closely imitating the basic wording (almost verbatim) in the federal court documents that were submitted in response to my charges against their clients who were defendants—and then reversing the wording, I was able to effectively hit the legal ball back into their court. By following these defense attorneys in the federal court, I was able to participate in a structured legal environment that was totally unfamiliar to me.

When the defense lawyers responded to my response of their response to my charges, I knew that this tactic had worked. In so doing, I bought much needed time by vehemently refuting everything that they said, while keeping on the front burner the fact that federal HUD and banking laws had been broken and covered-up. I moved forward on my own prayerfully.

Somewhere in my reading about what I should have been doing as a pro se litigant, I came across a reference that made mention of the United States Sixth Circuit Legal Library, a little-spoken of place that I later found to be obscurely tucked away on an upper floor of downtown Cincinnati's Federal Building. With its impressive size, extensive collection of legal books, reference materials, microfilm readers, copying facilities and nationally connected computer data banks, I found out that the Sixth Circuit Library contained an abundance of legal knowledge—the type of information that I was searching for.

Although it is open to—and paid for by— the public, I found it to be a sterile, insular and occupationally prejudicial type of place where, typically, federal judges and lawyers frequent and roam in pursuit of legal excellence. I also quickly learned that it was a strange and cold place where lawyers did their thing, and where one is non-verbally shunned—almost like wearing a scarlet letter—for violating the non-written decorum of asking more than a few questions about how to access information there.

In order to appear as lawyeresque as possible, I made every attempt not to stand out as an ordinary John Q. Public in the stuffy and generally pompous U. S. Sixth Circuit Library. With a library penetration game plan that was designed to not draw attention to who I was, what I was doing and why I was there, I always went there dressed incognito; in a suit and tie.

Outside of an initial cordial greeting of the day to the front desk receptionists, I made it a point to not maintain eye contact with library workers on my way to and from voluminous book stacks. A confusing library indexing system provided me limited legal help. I did most of my reading at the out of view back wall desks that are located in the far recesses of the library.

After countless hours of reading ad nauseam, I came across a federal law pertaining to the HUD infractions that occurred at 124 West Ninth Street, 42 U.S.C. (United States Code), Section 3612(b), which made the possibility of Sandy and I getting an attorney that much greater. The gist of the law reads, "Upon application by the plaintiff [me], and in such circumstances as the court may deem just, a court of the United States in which a civil action under this section has been brought may appoint an attorney for the plaintiff and may authorize the commencement of a civil action upon proper showing without the payment of fees, costs, or security…"

With this knowledge, on March 15, 1994, Sandy and I forced the hand of the trial court of the Sixth Circuit by appropriately filing a motion that was captioned "Plaintiff's Request for Assistance in Obtaining an Attorney," referred to as our "Motion for the Appointment of Counsel." Sandy and I submitted paperwork to the court truthfully arguing that we were not financially able to assume attorney's fees due to the wrongdoings of the defendants.

Besides, in light of the fact that no attorney would touch our politically sensitive case, we also argued that it was the responsibility of the U. S. Sixth Circuit District Court to step in to appoint a lawyer for us. Moreover, because money was stolen and being covered-up from the U. S. Treasury via Cincinnati's HUD RRP, we emphatically pointed out that the federal court should be in the position of protecting its parent, the Federal government of the United States of America.

Based upon federal law, this was my rationale and strategy. Based upon fundamental fairness and what was right, that is what the federal court was beholden to do. Though, based upon the hidden strings that the Queen pulled into the highest levels of the American government, my eyes would be opened like they never were opened before.

With my motion to have an attorney appointed to me, I initiated a potent piece of legal ammunition that was used to fire back at the Queen, who was increasingly feeling threatened. As its ruse came a step closer to being exposed, behind the scenes, the Queen consulted with secreted reserves that were available to its call and whim, as it still had a considerable number of unplayed cards up its sleeve. Remembering that my office had been illegally broken into, I bought a puppy to be my ears while I slept.

Sandy and I had already established that the City of Cincinnati and the State of Ohio were deeply involved in covering-up the theft of HUD money from the U. S. government because my HUD money flowed through these entities. But, strangely enough, the trail of incrimination became conspicuously erased at the threshold of the federal government, as it was muddied beyond recognition and shrouded with devices.

As a result of the suppressive railroading of 124 West Ninth Street's HUD RRP through the Queen's willing Hamilton County, Ohio Court system, on March 17, 1994, Sandy and I received more bad financial news. On this day, a nationwide collection agency for public utilities threatened possible legal action against Sandy and I if the balances that were transferred from 123 and 124 West Ninth Street to our residence were not paid in full within 10 days.

Outside of the time that we bought from our weakling—but efficacious—legal efforts, nothing seemed to be going right for us. Though I was awash in the legal resources of the Sixth Circuit Library, I could not figure out how to interconnect the pieces of what was legally required of me to what was available to me.

The frustration over not knowing how to give adequate service to my federal civil action was made greater by knowing that I had access to the tools of legal information but no working knowledge of how to use them. As an island, still, I read on, searching for just enough of a legal practitioner's knowledge that would allow me to contend with the Queen's illegal ploy.

In my concentrated attempts to uncover an incriminating connection establishing a verifiable link between what happened at 124 West Ninth Street and HUD's knowledge of it, I finally hit pay dirt while digging deeper into the confines of some of the federal government's archives. I ascertained that, at least, HUDs' outer fringes were actively involved in the Queen's cover-up.

I unearthed pertinent information on HUD's Office of Fair Housing and Equal Opportunity whose charter was to enforce federal laws which prohibit the type of lending discrimination, underappraising of property and intimidation that was used against Sandy and I. With respect to the way in which federal Fair Housing laws are written, the submission of a Fair Housing complaint by Sandy and I should have exposed the criminality at 124 West Ninth Street and forced HUD attorneys to litigate a federal case on our behalf.

I read that the filing of a complaint (HUD form 903) at the Fair Housing office could have forced the Queen to compensate us for actual damages, including humiliation, pain and suffering. As a Fair Housing complaint was the ticket to providing Sandy and I with injunctive or other equitable relief, it was also a powerful federal weapon that was designed to force the Queen to pay the Federal Government a civil penalty to vindicate the public's interest.

In pursuing the full compliance of the Federal Fair Housing Law, on April 18, 1994, Sandy and I met with HUD's Fair Housing representative, Charles Jung, in his Cincinnati, Ohio Federal Building office. What we discovered at this meeting let us know that we foiled an attempted federal ambush of our efforts to exercise our Fair Housing rights against the City of Cincinnati, Provident Bank and Suburban Federal Savings Bank.

As per federal Fair Housing procedures, we came to Jung's office to file a request for prompt judicial action, legal representation and a temporary restraining order. When Jung nervously and awkwardly attempted to get us to detrimentally change the wording of our Fair Housing discrimination complaints, thereby letting these defendants off of the legal hook, it was plain as the nose on one's face that this career bureaucrat had received marching orders from someone higher than himself.

As his mishandled pressure technique went well-beyond ineptitude and into being characteristic of the cover-up activity that we had become familiar with, Sandy and I only had to look at each other in his office, like two longtime card-playing partners, to nonverbally acknowledge what we were seeing. It was Jung's behavior that allowed Sandy and I to definitively put in place the first piece of federal criminal activity into the 124 West Ninth Street cover-up puzzle.

As the war for my economic survival raged all around me, I could not help but to chuckle at the City's hypocrisy in the April 21, 1994 printing of an out of town newspaper article in the *Richmond (Virginia) Free Press*. Living upon the notoriety that it received as being "North America's Most Livable City", the Greater Cincinnati Chamber of Commerce sponsored a visit to the Queen City by a 59-member delegation of government, business and civic organizations from the Richmond, Virginia area.

When speaking to this group, Mayor Roxanne Qualls was quoted in this newspaper to say, "We no longer can afford to be at odds with each other. The door of opportunity must be open to all." In the same article, Cincinnati City Manager, John Shirey, was quoted to say, "We're promoting the idea that everyone ought to think of Downtown as everybody's neighborhood." I wondered if anyone in the group had the foggiest idea that they were being lied to by Qualls and Shirey.

On April 28, 1994, a day that revealed a higher level of HUD connectivity to the crime scene at 124 West Ninth Street, U. S. Congressman David Mann responded to my January 12, 1994 letter. As a former Democratic Mayor and City Councilman who hailed from the Queen, Democratic Congressman Mann had resigned from Cincinnati City Council on January 2nd of the previous year to assume his elected federal position in the U. S. House of Representatives.

Included in this correspondence to me was a copy of a March 17, 1994 letter that had been sent to Congressman Mann from William J. Gilmartin, HUD's Assistant Secretary for Congressional and Intergovernmental Relations in Washington, D. C. I could see that Gilmartin had written to Congressman Mann telling him to contact one of my defendants, John E. Riordan, HUD's Ohio Director of Community Planning and Development in Ohio's capital, Columbus. Forasmuch as Gilmartin's letter to Mann was noticeably filled with untruths, distortions of facts and statements that were grossly misleading, it went well beyond being criminally connective to 124 West Ninth Street, although it did not give me the convincing knockout evidence that I was looking for.

The good news was that I had written confirmation that there was high-level HUD awareness of the HUD problem at 124 West Ninth Street. In any event, as the ball was in HUD's court at that point, whether or not they would right the wrong remained to be seen. I would later find out that Gilmartin was only buying time for HUD in this letter, leaving a way out for the Department, by writing to Congressman Mann that an investigation was being conducted and that HUD "will make its determination which will be provided to you and Mr. Kiah."

Masterminding a plan to get us to yield to its crushing power from a remote helm, the Queen applied mounting pressure on many fronts which greatly compounded the troubles that Sandy and I experienced. From just the motioning of its hand, the Queen caused the creation of wave after wave of nocuous events that, cumulatively, were designed to defeat us by beating us into submission.

It was during this time that the wretchedness of the Queen's unbridled use of its power again surfaced to expose the vast arsenal of tools that were at its command. In order to render us null in the federal court, the Queen had a malevolent two-pronged strategy that, first, entailed impaling us in the politically controlled Hamilton County, Ohio state court with foreclosure proceedings for 123 and 124 West Ninth Street.

Then, once we were ruled against in the state court, the Queen's plan was, secondly, to finish us off by using a legal maneuver known as the doctrine of *res judicata*. The legal policy underlying this doctrine would have barred us from proceeding in the federal court, as the case would have already been decided in a state court of competent jurisdiction, thereby barring any subsequent litigation involving the same cause of action.

The Queen's Hamilton County, Ohio state court strategy was to make sure that we were helpless and on our knees before we were drawn and quartered. As far as the Queen's logic went, regardless of cost, it was imperative for Sandy and I to have been countered in the State court by being rendered legally impotent under the doctrine of *res judicata*, lest we were able to obtain an effective federal court attorney first.

But, we had been set up for the kill. As quick as a wink, Sandy's checking account was hit and drained by a local bank, due to rulings that were made against us through state garnishment proceedings that were initiated by one of 124 West Ninth Street's unpaid building material suppliers. Concurrently, Suburban Federal Savings Bank was conveniently granted a state court summary judgment, which was a legal device designed to effect a prompt disposition of controversies without resort to a lengthy trial, thereby initiating the doctrine of *res judicata.*

Having us where it wanted us, the Queen's tenacious legal blockade had eliminated our access to a counselor-at-law to effectively present our case in the courts. Caught in a withering hail of crossfire from the state and federal courts under the Queen's control, Sandy and I were pelted with an unrelenting barrage of confusing legal papers, memorandums, motions, judgments, reports, recommendations, addenda and court orders that required timely and accurate legal responses.

On April 29, 1994, the Queen handed the ball off to a hot-tempered, obstinate and junior United States Magistrate Judge, Robert A. Steinberg, who stepped up to the federal courtroom plate hoping to mop up for the Queen and to be recognized within political circles for a clean defeat of my law suit. In a same-day, one-two punch that left us spinning and not knowing where we were, Magistrate Judge Steinberg issued two visciously punishing court orders that legally cut Sandy and I off at the knees.

The first order denied our "Motion for the Appointment of Counsel," stating that the "plaintiffs have not demonstrated that exceptional circumstances exist or that this is the type of case where they will be unable to represent themselves." Magistrate Judge Steinberg went on further to proclaim in his first order that appointment of counsel "is not appropriate when a pro se litigant's claims are frivolous…, or when the chances of success are extremely slim."

Attempting to throw Sandy and I a curve ball of legal mumbo jumbo, U. S. Magistrate Judge Steinberg's second order was equally another way for him to carry out an inside job from within the federal court system. By underhandedly fabricating grounds for the dismissal of our politically sensitive federal lawsuit, Steinberg's second order gave lengthy and complicatedly detailed legal instructions that set forth the requirement that Sandy and I "file a document entitled 'Response to Show Cause Order'" within thirty days. As it was to show why our complaint should not have been dismissed, Steinberg's second order was a crafty federal court instrument that set forth knowingly unattainable legal requirements which necessitated the filing of intricate and complex legal documentation by Sandy and I.

As an avid fisherman who was raised at the mouth of the Chesapeake Bay in the seaside resort town of Virginia Beach, Virginia, I am familiar with the helpless feeling that one can experience while being in a small boat at sea during a tempest. As the howling courtroom winds of U. S. Magistrate Judge Steinberg's orders stormed all around us and threatened to legally sink our federal lawsuit, Sandy and I felt completely powerless. At a time like this, when it appeared that we would go down in legal defeat and be lost forever, providence once again smiled upon us, and gave us a much wished for reprieve from the Queen's hostile intentions.

One day, while in the U. S. Sixth Circuit library, I was vainly attempting to make heads or tails of the legal confusion that had inundated me. I happened to notice a gentleman that did not fit the mold of the types of personages that I typically found there: he did not have on a suit and tie, he looked like a bodybuilder, his head was shaven and he was an African-American.

Seeing that he was busy transcribing information from volumes of legal research books that he had piled atop a table that he was working from, he looked like he knew what he was doing. I did not want to take up too much of his time so, out of desperation, I took the liberty of interrupting him by briefly introducing myself and asking him for assistance.

Maybe it was because of the look of legal confusion that he saw written all across my face that led this gentleman to see that I was legally in trouble. Or maybe it was because of the logical progression of rapid-fire questions that I posed to him, which let him know that I was legally lacking, even though he could see that I had done some legal research homework. Or even yet, maybe he saw that I was hungry to find answers and was not that far away, procedurally, from having a firm grasp on what I was trying to do in a federal court of law.

Although he did not have a Juris Doctor degree, I found out that this fellow was an ex-convict who had been a jailhouse lawyer, an inmate who, through self-study of law, assisted fellow inmates in the preparation of their appeals, but was not licensed to practice law. In any case, miraculously, he related to my torment and began to freely impart to me just enough necessary legal procedural understanding for me to become dangerous.

Like a godsend, the former jailhouse lawyer gave me the much required focus and understanding that I needed in a theretofore confusing place. In the brief period of time that we talked, he was like an angel to me, listening and understanding my plight. Figuring that I was worth salvaging, he placed me under his tutorial wing by walking me through the U. S. Sixth Circuit library while introducing me to some of the potent legal weapons that were available to me.

While I could tell that his time was precious to him, and as those moments were purely golden to me, he reassuringly bolstered my belief that I could represent myself. He did not let me lose focus of the fact that the weight of my federal legal fight was on my shoulders—and my shoulders alone. Accordingly, he stressed that I was the only means by which I could be assured of access to the federal courts. As a result, I began to funnel my efforts exclusively in the federal court and did not worry about the state court's actions.

The jailhouse lawyer gave me vision in a place that I could not see; the know-how of using federal laws against the unlawfulness of the Queen; and the legs to defend my country and myself by using the rules governing the basic aspects of a court proceeding. Because of a brief and chance bookshelf encounter with a mentor, I, too, became a self-taught and very serious student of finding and understanding applicable federal laws—laws that the Queen was trying to keep me away from using against it.

Armed with newfound knowledge, I became a regular fixture in Cincinnati's U. S. Sixth Circuit library. Strengthened, I continued to go forth, much more prepared to do battle against the jigs of the Queen. Strangely, I never saw the nameless former jailhouse lawyer again. From that point forward, it was no longer problematic for me make inroads into the discovery of which specific federal laws were broken at 124 West Ninth Street.

The real problem that I faced was the Queen's ability to hide the individual participants in its cover-up. I could only go but so far before doors were slammed shut in my face through red tape, delay, passing the buck, and other shields that were raised in cloaking exactly how the Queen did its duperies. Sandy and I were steadfastly forced into a labyrinth of complex legal dead ends.

For me, it was a given that the named defendants in my federal lawsuit participated in U.S. Treasury theft crimes. As I could also see that individual participation in 124 West Ninth Street's criminal activity kept getting covered-up in higher and higher organizational hierarchies, I pressed forward with an invigorated legal strategy that would allow me to reveal the named Treasury theft plotters by increasingly following the HUD money trail.

It was not until I analyzed the surveillance results of my deeper reconnaissance efforts into federal operations that I was able to see that I had opened the doors to a much wider level of federal government corruption than I had originally anticipated. I began to witness the depth of the Queen's power and how it was able to use its resources to illegally influence the outcome of its Treasury theft crimes.

In a mix of emotions, I was, in one way, saddened from knowing that the federal government itself—on at least this level—was involved in the 124 West Ninth Street criminal cover-up. In another way, I was heartened that I was on the right track for tracing down the enigmatic power source behind these crimes.

My efforts to smoke out the 124 West Ninth Street Treasury theft plotters thickened appreciably when I began to surveil a higher HUD echelon through the writing of a letter of complaint to one of Charles Jung's superiors, Ms. Barbara Knox, Deputy Director of Fair Housing and Equal Opportunity in HUD's Chicago Regional office. I waited for a response from her.

Inasmuch as U. S. Treasury tax dollars had been misappropriated, secretly funneled into my HUD RRP, and systematically lied about in a multi-layered scheme, it increasingly appeared that the HUD was involved in the defrauding of the federal government itself. As such, I began to camp out ad infinitum at the U. S. Sixth Circuit Court library in search of legal weapons that could be used against the Queen. Knowing full well that there were federal laws somewhere in the library that proscribed the Queen's hidden crimes, my digging finally paid off when I discovered the laws that were contained in sections 1001, 1010 and 1012 of Title 18 of United States Code.

Being quite unambiguous in spelling out the length of prison sentences and fines for transgressors thereof, typical phraseology from these federal laws included: "Whoever, in any matter within the jurisdiction of any department or agency of the United States knowingly and willfully falsifies, conceals or covers up by any trick, scheme, or device a material fact, or makes any false, fictitious or fraudulent statements or representations, or makes or used any false writing or document knowing the same to contain any false, fictitious or fraudulent statement or entry, shall be fined...or imprisoned..., or both."

Other apropos wording from these federal laws included: "Whoever...makes, passes, utters, or publishes any statement, knowing the same to be false, or alters, forges, or counterfeits any instrument, paper, or document, or utters, publishes, or passes as true any instrument, paper, or document, knowing it to have been altered, forged or counterfeited,...shall be fined...or imprisoned.., or both."

It was quite encouraging for me to see that no one—from HUD on down the criminal cover-up ladder—was immune from federal prosecution. Logically deducing that the 124 West Ninth Street U. S. Treasury theft cover-up had to be much deeper inside of HUD, I sensed that HUD's William J. Gilmartin was merely a lower-echelon bureaucrat shield, who was insulating a higher-up from federal incrimination. Like a hound dog following a scent, it gnawed at me to not know who in HUD was to blame. Other incriminating pieces of the puzzle fell into place that dealt with the identification of the U. S. Treasury theft conspirators who laid hidden within the HUD hierarchy.

By May of 1994, I felt increasingly denied by watching Phase II of the Garfield Place housing project begin. In Washington, D. C., President Bill Clinton had similar sentiments when he worried that Democrats were not keeping up with Republicans in the money chase. Harold Ickes, former White House deputy chief of staff was quoted as saying, "Bill Clinton questioned about our lack of fundraising...compared to Republicans."

On May 2, 1994, a letter was written to me from the boss of Fair Housings' Barbara Knox and Charles Jung, Thomas Higginbothan, Director of HUD's Chicago Regional Office (Region 5), Office of Fair Housing and Equal Opportunity. This letter informed me that my complaints had been accepted for processing through HUD pursuant to the Fair Housing Act, as found in 42 U.S.C. 3600-3620. Although this brief letter was inconclusive, it did not put an end to the unethical and criminal activity that Sandy and I brought to the attention of his federal purview. As far as Sandy and I were concerned, it was HUD's last chance to convince us that it could effectively police itself in its regional structure, as its city, state and national levels had already demonstrated complicity in the shadow robbery of our national government.

As my basic legal application knowledge had grown, on the same day, Provident Bank dug a deeper hole for itself when it committed an additional felony by lying to a federal department, the U. S. Sixth Circuit Court. Just as surely as it felt the inescapable pressure for federal indictments that I was able to construct against it, Provident Bank was backed into a corner because the efficacy of the federal court papers that I filed had improved.

In a signed and sworn affidavit submitted to U. S. Judge S. Arthur Spiegel on May 2, 1994, Provident Bank's George Fulford prevaricated in a legally flawed courtroom attempt to break free of federal incrimination. On this date, and beyond question, George Fulford committed a cardinal sin of perjury (a felony) against the U. S. government, which states that you cannot lie to a U. S. Judge.

In part, George Fulford quoted the following to Judge Spiegel in his May 2nd affidavit: "The loan made by The Provident Bank to William Kiah and Sandra W. Kiah, which is the subject of their Complaint, was not part of, or approved by, any federally assisted or sponsored program. Said loan was solely between The Provident Bank and William R. Kiah and Sandra W. Kiah and was not subject to any requirement by any federally assisted or sponsored program." Like an escaped convict who hears the sound of barking bloodhounds on his trail for the first time, this was a time when I first saw Provident Bank running scared.

Coincidentally, very serious problems were developing for Bill Clinton in Washington. On May 5, 1994, *The New York Times* reported that President Clinton hired lawyer Robert S. Bennett to defend him against Paula Corbin Jones's lawsuit. By the next day, the former Arkansas State worker, Paula Corbin Jones, filed a civil lawsuit against Bill Clinton accusing him of making unwanted sexual advances in a Little Rock, Arkansas hotel room during a state-sponsored conference while he was Arkansas Governor in 1991. Jones described the episode as "repugnant" and said she spurned Clinton's advance and was later transferred to another state job as punishment.

Events surrounding a developing presidential sex scandal in the America's capital and a developing U. S. Treasury theft HUD cover-up scheme in the Queen moved inexorably closer towards a confluence of similar legal problems for the nation's Chief Executive. Time would show that both of these legal predicaments were threats to Bill Clinton's presidency.

The criminal plot thickened on May 6, 1994 when U. S. Senator Howard Metzenbaum responded to my January 12, 1994 letter urging him to conduct a formal investigation into the HUD funding of my federal building renovation project. In this letter, the name of HUD's Washington, D. C. based William J. Gilmartin conspicuously popped-up again into the foreground of the 124 West Ninth Street cover-up. This time, as his lies went beyond the vague HUD fraud cover-up pattern that he established on April 28, 1994 when he intentionally misled U. S. Congressman David Mann, Gilmartin's opened HUD up to felony indictments.

As U. S. Senator Howard Metzenbaum sent me an attached copy of Gilmartin's May 3, 1994 letter from HUD's Washington, D. C. national headquarters that was addressed to him, I immediately recognized that HUD's 124 West Ninth Street criminal cover-up was being orchestrated from there. When I saw that Gilmartin wrote to Metzenbaum, "Mr. Kiah received $45,000 of RRP funds from the City of Cincinnati in September [of] 1992…", the evidence was in front of me that Gilmartin had committed a felony and was part of 124 West Ninth Street's HUD cover-up. HUD was fully aware that I had only received $25,000 of the $45,000 that had been federally contracted to me.

I cried "Eureka!" as this letter provided me with my initial evidentiary glimpse of the incriminating role that HUD's headquarters was playing in the 124 West Ninth Street cover-up. Convinced that someone in HUD central was responsible for the 124 West Ninth Street Treasury theft ruse, I felt compelled to find out how federal money could be stolen and covered-up so easily from America's national government. I began to plan a mission of discovery to Washington, D. C. to find out how deep the cover-up was, and how these HUD tax dollars were capable of being stolen.

On another connective front in Washington, D. C., then-White House deputy chief of staff Harold Ickes this time wrote in notes of a May 9, 1994 meeting regarding President Bill Clinton, "BC will have breakfast – to raise $." In his earliest known use of the White House for fund-raising, President Clinton hosted a series of private breakfasts with wealthy Democrats to help raise money in 1994 for the party's health care fund.

At least ten breakfasts or lunches hosted by President and Mrs. Clinton in 1994 in the executive mansion were specifically designed to generate "both political and financial support" for the Democratic Party's ad campaign on behalf of their ill-fated health care initiative. Several of the donors who attended the 1994 breakfasts gave five- and six-figure donations in the days after their visits.

The White House defended the breakfasts as legal, saying the Clintons' goal was not to raise money for their own political use but rather to air ads to repel special interest attacks against their plan seeking universal health care. Internal White House documents show, however, that presidential aides viewed the breakfasts as fund-raisers.

For instance, Ickes addressed the issue to then-Chief of Staff Mack McLarty in a May 7, 1994 memo entitled "scheduling fund-raising events." "We need to schedule several additional breakfasts with the President to facilitate the additional fund-raising for the health care media campaign," Ickes told his boss. I later found out that White House special counsel Lanny Davis said the President attended at least eight fund-raising breakfasts, the first on May 5, 1994 and the last on Aug. 23, 1994.

Back in the Queen, on May 10, 1994, I received a written response from Thomas Higginbothan, Director of HUD's Chicago Regional Office. This letter further confirmed my suspicions that there was an intricate cover-up web that was already in place which allowed the unauthorized siphoning of federal tax dollars from the place where America's public revenues are deposited, kept and disbursed. As surely as the sun rose every morning, the certainty of a deeply entrenched federal Treasury theft cover-up was increasing steadily with time.

Instead of appropriately dealing with the HUD U. S. Treasury theft dollar trail that came through his federal office, Higginbothan informed me that my complaints had been waived back to the state milieu, into the Ohio Civil Rights Commission. Contrarily, on May 13, 1994, HUD in D. C. wrote to me telling me to direct my complaints and inquiries to Higginbothan's Chicago Regional Office. In slick bureaucratic moves that had been conveniently designed to cause frustration and confusion—and used to deflect public scrutiny away from HUD's federal criminal cover-up involvement at 124 West Ninth Street, higher-up criminal insulation thickened along with an odorous plot.

The national press began to intensify its dissemination of relevant presidential information that shed light on President Bill Clinton's growing inclination to turn his office into a cash cow at all costs. On

May 18, 1994, *The New York Times* printed an article regarding the 1993 financial disclosure form of President Bill Clinton and wife, Hillary. As the article went on to reveal that most of their wealth was in her name, the Clintons' net worth was estimated at between $633,015 and $1,620,000, thereby verifying them as being the least affluent occupants of White House in 15 years.

More and more everyday, I knew that the shots against me were being called somewhere in the HUD stratosphere. On May 20, 1994, I received a letter from Suburban Federal Savings Bank's lawyer, Bruce Gilster, stating "We have been notified by HUD that your complaint for housing violations against Suburban has been dismissed." Even though it was bad news, in a sense, I felt that I was making progress, as through the process of elimination, I was on the road towards finding out who was pulling the illegal strings from HUD's top.

With no legal help in sight, Sandy and I ran an advertisement in the Business Section of *The Cincinnati Enquirer* for a lawyer on May 22, 1994, desperately hoping that we could procure legal help from any source. As our buildings were scheduled to be taken away from us at a Hamilton County, Ohio Sheriff's Sale that was scheduled thirty days away, pressure built on us to do more. Unfortunately for us, we could not see that powerful people high in the federal government were methodically, systematically, and increasingly laying the groundwork for an attempted burying of the 124 West Ninth Street HUD crimes.

On June 1, 1994, HUD's Chicago Regional representative, Thomas Higginbothan, wrote to me again. This time, he was vigorously defending HUD's Fair Housing representative in Cincinnati, Charles Jung, by providing him with an additional layer of cover for his felonious activity from inside of HUD. Seeing the handwriting on the wall that had become commonplace, I could only surmise that I was seeing business as usual at HUD's regional level.

As the date to sell my buildings neared, my talking to the U. S. Attorney General's office in Washington proved to be fruitless; my appeals to Cincinnati City Council continued to have no effect; and I could see that the Ohio Civil Rights Commission was picking up where HUD left off by attempting to water-down my complaint within the State by radically changing its wording. No matter how much better I was becoming in using the tools of the courts in fighting the Queen, my appeals in the Hamilton County, Ohio courts continued to fall on deaf ears.

As if my life had become a great big punching bag, I was on the receiving end of castigating blows from the Queen. From the left and from the right, a devastating financial toll was continuing to be exacted upon me, as my life seemed to fall apart. To a certain extent, I felt discombobulated, like the character Olivia de Havilland played in the 1948 Twentieth Century Fox psychological film drama, *The Snake Pit*. Unlike the character, I was not mentally deranged. Like the character, I was able to keep my feet on the ground by fully understanding why I felt the way that I did. I fully comprehended that the Queen was using its raw political power against Sandy and I to keep its U. S. Treasury theft crimes under wraps.

In order to allay the growing federally incriminating pressure that I was applying against a cabal of individuals who had conspired to cheat the American government, the Queen remained steadfast in its pattern of increasingly pulling out bigger guns to sway public opinion. On Sunday, June 19, 1994, *The Cincinnati Enquirer* printed the second of two negatively slanted newspaper articles against me, while attempting to maintain the illusion of the Queen's 124 West Ninth Street legitimacy.

In a news item that spanned more than the top halves of the first two pages of the attention-getting Business section of this Sunday edition, *The Cincinnati Enquirer* used large and bold one-inch headline letters at the top of the front page that read "Ninth Street story" when it should have read "Ninth Street lies." In seeing the shameful journalistic reporting that guilefully fixed the blame of 124 West Ninth Street's failure on me, it was appalling, but not surprising, for Sandy and I to see the depth of *The Cincinnati Enquirer's* involvement in secreting the Queen's U. S. Treasury theft crimes.

Well-written to misinform, the article craftily deluded its readers through the interplay of carefully chosen photographic images and text. Absolutely none of the relevant HUD Treasury theft information that I provided to *The Cincinnati Enquirer* at its interview was reported. It was all too evident to Sandy and I that I was portrayed as a total incompetent in this hatchet job of an article. Just as a large 13 x 6 inch photograph was printed on the front page showing me standing amidst the disarray of half-opened bags of cement, chunks of plaster board, unfinished walls and exposed wiring, *The Cincinnati Enquirer* wrongly depicted me as being disordered and responsible for the HUD project failure at 124 West Ninth Street.

In contrast, while two of the defendants in my lawsuit, Cincinnati politicians Dwight Tillery and Peter Strauss, were photographically and verbally portrayed in a favorable light, *The Cincinnati Enquirer* aided these two U. S. Treasury theft conspirators in the commission of crimes against the American people. Regardless of the role that this biased newspaper played in smearing me, I became even more steeled instead of becoming more discouraged.

In the revulsion of being largely ineffectual against a united front of crooked politicians, shady bankers, seedy bureaucrats and others, I had my fill of seeing how U. S. Treasury theft crimes were being successfully committed through the exertion of power and influence. I could see that the whole cover-up process had far greater national ramifications than that of my localized situation. Having every indication to lead me to believe that my demise had been intentionally orchestrated from Washington, D. C., I began to make final arrangements to embark upon an eagerly anticipated fishing expedition to the national headquarters of HUD itself.

My lofty objective was simple and clear: to penetrate the insularity of a crooked Cabinet Department of the President of the United States of America. In so doing, my goal was to personally talk to the President's Cabinet appointee, HUD Secretary Henry G. Cisneros. My strategy was to go unannounced. My plan was to get past screens that would, otherwise, screen me out.

I realized that most people would have deemed that such a move would be bordering on the verge of the absurd and virtually impossible to accomplish. But, the unique circumstances of my life were the driving forces that compelled me to go outside of the boundaries of typical behavior and into the realm of taking on such a monumental undertaking. In a move that had to have been considered abstract by some, I was directly driven into action by an obsession to get to the bottom of the hidden U. S. Treasury theft criminal activity that occurred at 124 West Ninth Street. Contrary to what others thought, I viewed my behavior as good citizenship.

It did not matter that this move on my part could have been viewed as ludicrous by some. I felt good about it. Jousting at windmills? Farfetched? I thought not! It was my singular, go for broke attempt to identify hidden U. S. Treasury thieves within an almost $30 billion federal bureaucracy by using tactics of irregular warfare against an entrenched federal Department of the President of the United States—while operating on a shoestring budget, I might add. Improbable? Maybe. But, I thought, if not me, then, who?

Since America had labeled its war against Iraq's Saddam Hussein as Operation Desert Storm in response to his repulsive actions in the Gulf War, I labeled my personal mission as Operation Capitol Storm in response to HUD's repulsive actions in D. C. I intrepidly purchased a cheap round trip airline ticket on a discount carrier for $116 and packed my bags in preparation for a three-day visit to HUD's national headquarters in the nation's capital to see if I could make a dent in the cover-up efforts that I would surely face.

In making last minute preparations on the day before beginning my ambitious trip to a place that I could only envision in my imagination, the money chase intensified for President Bill Clinton. On June 20, 1994, Harold Ickes, former White House deputy chief of staff, wrote to Mack McLarty, then the White House chief of staff, noting that the DNC (Democratic National Committee, the fundraising and finance wing of the National Democratic Party) was "hard pressed" for cash.

On June 21, 1994, I flew to Washington, D. C. to pay a visit to HUD on the first leg of Operation Capital Storm. I was faced with the types of formidable tactical barriers that were brought on by having a war chest that was insufficient for completely financing my incursion into HUD's national seat of power. Like a patriot guerrilla fighter who was forced to do with what was available to him to stage an essential offensive, I depended on sympathetic family members who lived in and around the immediate Washington, D. C. area for transportation, food and lodging.

After arriving in Washington, I was picked up at the airport by one of my first cousins and later bivouacked at a very dear aunt's house, who would have it no other way. I set up my base camp of operations there. As far as food was concerned, I came to Washington fully prepared to rough it out at the likes of Mickey D's. However, instead of wolfing down bites to eat at fast food joints, as I had anticipated, my aunt awakened me in the mornings to sumptuous breakfasts, and laid out lavish spreads for me at dinnertime, even though I had pleaded with her not to. She even provided crabs and beer to boot.

Instead of my using taxicabs for transportation, she insisted that I use her car. On top of everything else, she gave me a key to her house, thereby allowing me to make maximum use of her telephone, which provided me with the utmost of convenience. I was only looking for a place to lay my head. Instead, under the circumstances, I was provided with every creature comfort that one could ask for. Moreover, as a godsend, her words of encouragement and support in the face of an unmistakable mismatch were just the spark needed to sufficiently animate me.

Upon arriving at HUD's massive and sprawling ten-story national headquarters very early on the next day (with a stomach full of bacon, sausage, eggs, fresh biscuits, strawberry preserves, orange juice and coffee, I might add), I didn't have a clue as to how I would get to see HUD Secretary Henry G. Cisneros at 451 Seventh Street, S. W. It was not until I actually laid eyes on HUD's mountainous headquarters that I first began to lay out a strategy as to how I was going to get into the building unannounced and past the armed security guards at the main entrance.

Like a rock climber beginning to lay out a plan of ascension from a mountain's foot to its summit, I was facing an obstacle that was just as formidable. Captured by the moment of feeling involved in a real undercover operation, I felt like a cross between Sylvester Stallone's big screen portrayal of the fictional John Rambo, in his 1982 movie *First Blood,* and one of the espionage agents on the hit television show that was first telecast on September 17, 1966, "Mission Impossible."

Unlike the role that Stallone played of Rambo, I was not a fanatically militant and violently aggressive person whose behavior was marked by excessive enthusiasm and intense uncritical devotion. To a positive degree, like a big screen spy who had to come up with answers to a seemingly unattainable mission, I saw myself as being militantly engaged against those who were involved in covering-up the U. S. Treasury theft that occurred at 124 West Ninth Street.

The immediate challenge that I faced was getting inside of a U. S. government headquarters fortification of a presidential Cabinet Department that loomed in front of me. Since close parking in front of most federal buildings was severely restricted due to terrorist considerations, I was initially only able to snatch brief glimpses of HUD's entranceway while repeatedly circling the block in busy Washington traffic.

Being that I could not see what I had hoped that I could, plan "B" provided me with a much closer inspection of HUD's main entrance, as I feigned automobile trouble by pulling into a taxi stand directly in front of HUD's headquarters. In this pretext, while peering underneath the upraised hood of my aunt's car, I was able to adequately surveil the yawning front entranceway of the building to see how a great number of armed security guards and counter attendants handled the heavy stream of America's incoming HUD pedestrian traffic.

In analyzing what was going on by looking across the top of my aunt's perfectly running car engine, I quickly caught on as to how the people without security badges were ushered in through metal detectors, and how they were required to sign in at a long hotel-looking registration counter. In planning my approach, I went through the motions of doing insignificant things like moving my aunt's oil dipstick in and out and flicking on her air filter cover wing nut to make it spin up and down. I knew that I was truly on the battlefield when I felt the pressure to come up with a feasible building entrance strategy that would allow me to breach the well-fortified perimeter of HUD's bureaucracy of bureaucracies.

The launching of my personal D day arrived when I parked several blocks away and walked towards HUD completely immersed in attempting to plan for the next move that I would have to make, but to no avail: I drew only blanks. One block away, and still unable to work out specifically in my head what I was going to do upon entering 451 Seventh Street, S. W., the only personal directive that I could come up with was that I had to think on my feet. Within seconds before entering HUD's headquarters, I said two things to myself: "Act like you're here on official business" and "It's too late to turn back now."

Like the uneasiness one often experiences when following confusing directions while traveling down an unfamiliar road, I was slightly on edge upon entering HUD's portal. Not knowing what environs would confront me thereafter, I did not want to make the wrong move, or say the wrong thing, that would lead me right back out of the door that I had just come through.

As I walked between HUD's forward detachment of observant security guards, and then passed uneventfully through their metal detectors, it was quite comforting to know that my generic American-on-official-business facade was working well in successfully hiding the true Rambo that was inside of me. Approaching the long counter, I still did not have a clue as to what was next.

Under the watchful gaze of a stone-faced uniformed HUD security guard behind the counter, a much-used clipboard was routinely pushed to the edge of the counter to meet my approach. It was probably because of my corporate sales and marketing experience that I had in handling objections in order to get around sales-killing screens that caused me not to shrink away from the do or die HUD mission pressures that I then faced.

In acting as if I had been there many times before, I scanned the columnar headings of a sign in sheet on the clipboard and became immediately aware that there was a space on a line that had to be completed which required the name of the person that I had an appointment with. For my plan to work, I had to be creative and think quickly on my feet, because, of course, that person that I had an appointment with just simply did not exist.

While the professionally trained HUD security guard's hand remained on the clipboard that held the sign in sheet that I was filling out, and while the eyes on his unsmiling face gave me the once-over, I realized that I had everything riding on whose name I would write down on the form. I immediately thought of Mrs. Velma Thomas, an employee there that I had talked to at least one hundred occasions on the toll-free HUD Waste and Fraud Hotline. Having developed somewhat of a love/hate relationship with her from my persistent calling, I recalled that I had, at some point in the past, said that I would like to meet her someday. It was a long shot, but it worked as the busy security guard's finger pointed towards a waiting area in the cavernous headquarters lobby where I was instructed to have a seat.

While sitting on pins and needles, I did not know if they were going to ask me to leave, or what. Knowing that I had come too far to be turned back at that point, I planned my next unauthorized move to penetrate deeper into the building, as I was determined not to be defeated sitting down. I was obsessed with getting upstairs to find out who was responsible for trying to steal my future and money from the American government at the same time.

Glancing over the top of a magazine in a feint (just as I did with my aunt's well-tuned car engine), I looked for weaknesses in HUD's security and noticed how engrossed the guards were in handling the large volume of incoming traffic. My heart raced as none of the guards were paying attention to me. I knew that I had to make my move: it was then or never.

At the count of three, I stood up, pretended to impatiently glance at my wristwatch, and, while frowning my face at an extraneous piece of paper that I was moving my pointed index finger across, I began to make a not too fast paced beeline towards the elevators across the spacious lobby floor. I knew that I was trespassing on U. S. government property, but my transgressions paled in comparison to the bureaucratically covered-up U. S. Treasury theft that I was attempting to reveal.

It seemed like it took an eternity for me to get across the wide HUD lobby. Midway across, I instinctively tilted my head downwards as if I was looking at my shoes and rubbed my forehead while simultaneously peering through my separated fingers to see if I was being watched—and I was not. I shifted my pace up a gear. Looking back towards the guards was not even a consideration until I had gotten on an up elevator and turned around to face outward. As the doors closed and I saw that I was still undetected, I said an inaudible "Yes!" to myself and thought, "So, this is the land of the evil HUD Empire where America is getting bilked."

On my way up to a floor—any floor, I chuckled internally when I reflected that this Treasury theft identification mission that I was on was somewhat akin to the live machine gun fire that I crawled under while in U. S. Army basic training back in 1969. During this combat training, had I stood up from the protection of my cover, I would have been shot. Similarly, while at HUD, I had every intention of staying down.

Like a true guerrilla fighter, the secretive and camouflaged Rambo that resided deep within my ego came to the fore and was fully operational as I stepped off of the elevator onto a center-building floor. As I commenced my blending into the HUD headquarters building's surroundings, I was on the ready to shuffle through the papers that I was carrying in order to look like many of the machine-like federal bureaucrats (HUD-bots, as I called them) that were all around me. After walking miles of hallways reconnoitering, more so than at any other time that had preceded it, I genuinely felt like a solitary soldier.

I had to rely on my creative ability to buy the much-needed thinking time that was required to plan my next moves from within HUD's headquarters. As my mainstay feints of shuffling through papers and hiding around corners became old very fast, I took full advantage of the building's natural resources that were available to me for additional camouflage.

Making my way to a succession of available men's restrooms that were located throughout the building, I falsely sat down on numerous occasions in the privacy of available toilet stalls and planned how I would attempt to get to see HUD Secretary Henry Cisneros on the 10th floor. After I had stressfully gotten past the front entrance security guards; had evasively slipped on and off of elevators; and had actively blended into the crowds within HUD's headquarters, it was both anti-climactic and atypical for me to have staged the next phase of Operation Capital Storm while sitting on the seats of federal privies.

Even though it was somewhat of a risky move, I decided to make my way back downstairs to the only fairly secluded recess of pay telephones that I had seen which was on the far side of the first floor elevators. Using another resource from the lay of the land, this pay telephone area provided me with a modicum of cover from being detected while I faked telephone calls and contemplated concurrently. It was at this bank of phones that I decided to place a long distance toll-free telephone call ten floors above where I was to Mrs. Velma Thomas at the HUD Waste and Fraud Hotline.

As luck and timing had it, I reached her, told her that I was in the building on business and that I would very briefly like to meet her. I was surprised that she agreed to meet me. I was even more surprised when I saw her face for the first time as she walked past the armed security guard that protected the tenth floor entranceway to Secretary Cisneros' Cabinet office. She sent me to see one person that was a dead end, who sent me to see another person that was also a dead end, who sent me to see someone else with likewise results, et cetera, et cetera, et cetera. The word began to spread that I was in the building.

Having wasted precious time, I made myself invisible again by blending back into my surroundings. After figuring out what I was going to do after attending a large departmental meeting and sitting in on an awards presentation in HUD's cafeteria, I decided to pursue my own agenda inside of HUD by following 124 West Ninth Street's dollar trail.

As speaking to HUD Secretary Henry Cisneros was at the top of the list of my goals, I made my way up to the tenth floor armed guard vestibule area outside of Cisneros' office. Using a similar surveillance technique of the Secretary's entranceway that I had used earlier in the downstairs lobby, I pulled out my notepad and began scribbling over and over again the first part of the Gettysburg Address, while pretending that I was writing something that pertained to authorized HUD business.

I could not help but to notice a very attractive lady who got a lot of smiles and attention from the admiring guards upon her entrance and departure from the area where the Secretary's office was. In the process of her walking directly in front of me as she was leaving, I blurted out, "Excuse me,..." and then proceeded to tell her who I was, where I was from and why I was there.

Introducing herself as Sylvia Arce-Garcia, she graciously told me to see Frank Wing, who was a special assistant to Secretary Cisneros. I could tell by the way that she carried herself and the way that people reacted to her that she pulled some kind of weight there. When we parted, I immediately made my way back downstairs to my telephone bank cover area and called Frank Wing's office, using Sylvia Arce-Garcia as a reference to get to see him. Although Wing was not in, his secretary set an appointment for me to meet him in his office at 10:30 A.M. on the following morning. Little did I realize how significant Sylvia Arce-Garcia was to Cisneros' overall operation; on unrelated charges to mine, she was later indicted with him.

Immediately following the telephone call to Wing's office, I decided to take full advantage of my time by moving further down the 124 West Ninth Street HUD dollar flow ladder. I spent a great deal of time in the office of Deputy Secretary Terrance Duvernay's office in Room 10100. Since a division of HUD, known as Community Planning and Development (CPD), was responsible for 124 West Ninth Street's money being lawfully allocated and spent, I was fortunate to have been able to get into the office of CPD's Assistant Secretary, Andrew Cuomo (who would later replace Secretary Henry Cisneros) in Room 7100. Once there, I explained in detail to his secretary, Terri Nicolosi, what had happened to me.

At the very time that I tried to remain objective, once more, things just did not feel right. As her body language—especially her eyes—did not jibe with her recommended solution to my problem, I found that it was a little strange that a meeting was hastily called by her between Marsha Dodge of CPD and Richard Burk, who was the Director of the Program Operations Division in HUD's Office of Affordable Housing. In the middle of that afternoon's meeting, I soon realized why my hunches were right.

In the battle royale that ensued, this HUD headquarters duo tried to convince me through intimidation that I had not seen what I had seen at my RRP rehab project. Immediately, it became clear to me that I had just been ambushed again in an attempt to hide the truth.

That was the bad news; the good news was that I had established a telling trail of HUD incrimination by working my way up the HUD hierarchy and establishing, at least, CPD's culpability in 124 West Ninth Street's illegal cover-up. My efforts to smoke out HUD blame continued to bear fruit.

Inspired from my discoveries of the previous day, on the morning of June 23, 1994, I self-assuredly walked past the armed security guards at HUD's lobby entrance and signed both my name and Frank Wing's name on the clipboard that a counter attendant handed me. Not showing my excitement from the progress that I was making, I mentally pinched myself when I walked past the Secretary's security guard station on the tenth floor when Wing's secretary led me in.

Upon entering Frank Wing's office in Room 10226, I realized that HUD Secretary Cisneros' office in Room 10000 was so close, but yet so far away. Getting right down to business, in my opening statements to him, I fully explained to Wing what had happened to me in Cincinnati and showed him relevant 124 West Ninth Street evidence and documentation of foul play.

As expected, things did not smell right. During our entire conversation, Wing sternly stared at me through thick eyeglasses. I never fully completed articulating my thoughts to him before he cut me off. He also sat on the edge of his seat with a case of the jitters. All of a sudden, Wing abruptly stood up to let me know that our brief meeting was over. He then dubitably told me that foreclosure on my downtown property would be stopped and that I should call him on the following Monday when I was back in Cincinnati.

But it was his final gesture to me that took the cake; Wing hurriedly sent me to the downstairs lobby to meet with (of all people) Marsha Dodge of CPD, who finally showed up after I waited for over an hour and a half. As this meeting with her had the unmistakable feel of a HUD headquarters that was in denial, I could tell that she had been sent to handle me.

By Friday, June 24, 1994, I knew that I was not going to see HUD Secretary Henry Cisneros. Based upon a telephone conversation that I had with Sandy the night before, we did not feel comfortable with the events of the previous day, having nothing more to go on than Frank Wing's word. In an attempt to get something in writing that would verify that the foreclosure on my downtown property would be stopped, I again reentered HUD unannounced.

I could not reach Frank Wing from the haunt of my pay telephone hideout, nor could I reach him past the armed security guard outside of his office on the tenth floor. Sensing that my welcome had been thoroughly exhausted, I shot down to Andrew Cuomo's office in Room 7100 and asked his secretary, Terri Nicolosi, to sign a statement that I had prepared acknowledging that my buildings would not be foreclosed upon, as Frank Wing had told me.

I knew that my cover was blown and my HUD penetration goose was cooked when Nicolosi frantically whispered inaudible words into her desk telephone after she had nervously said to me, "Stay where you are and do not go anywhere." Like something out of a movie, next came the growing-louder-by-the-second running jackboot sound of fast footsteps that reverberated in HUD's stone hallways. I was not going to be tolerated any longer. I had become a problem and was escorted downstairs to the front entranceway of HUD's headquarters by unpleasant, large and armed security guards. One of them looked like the former Pittsburgh Steeler football player, Mean Joe Green and, in that he could have broken my neck by tightly clinching his hand, I did not resist.

I felt as though I was being banished from a military fort, like the character of Jason McCord (played by actor Chuck Connors) on NBC's 1965-66 television show "Branded." Saying nothing to me, the guards only stared me down. Walking away from HUD's headquarters, I knew that the eyes of the people that I saw inside said it all. Even though I did not meet my goal of talking directly to HUD Secretary Henry Cisneros, I learned a lot inside of his building. Accordingly, I placed little stock in Frank Wing's words that he would provide me with relief for what his operation was ultimately responsible for.

I called Frank Wing from Cincinnati on Monday, June 27, 1994 as he had instructed. Sandy and I were not as much surprised as we were disappointed when he reversed himself by telling me that he could not stop the foreclosure of 123 and 124 West Ninth Street, which was scheduled to be held three days later. I was not surprised when he was later subpoenaed by a federal grand jury looking into financial help given to Cisneros' former mistress.

In visualizing the heights to which the 124 West Ninth Street HUD Treasury theft cover-up crimes had gone to that point, I only had to look at my hand to visualize the criminality that was going on. By holding my hand out in front of me (palm in, fingers together and thumb up), I used my fingers in an analogy that demonstrated the quandary that faced me in sorting out the known from the unknown in the 124 West Ninth Street HUD trail of federal incrimination. I knew that my pinkie finger, representing the City of Cincinnati, Ohio and Provident Bank, was involved at the bottom of these HUD crimes. Next, moving up to my ring finger, representing the State of Ohio's HUD office in Columbus, Ohio, I knew that illegal HUD money had flowed through there as well.

In this same vein, my middle finger represented the known criminal involvement of HUD's Regional office in Chicago, Illinois. Advancing further, and knowing that I could doubtlessly trace 124 West Ninth Street's stolen HUD tax dollars to at least this level, my index finger represented the hidden federally indictable activities that were being conducted from HUD's Washington, D. C. headquarters.

Whether Henry Cisneros was aware that his special assistant, Frank Wing, knew about 124 West Ninth Street was not of importance to me at the time. No one knew better than I did that the Queen's poison had tainted the political structure from Cincinnati City Hall to HUD's highest level, a plane all too close to the White House.

In stark contrast, however, it was the mystery of my thumb, the unknown entity positioned on top of all of the fingers of my outstretched hand, that left me guessing. I asked myself, "Did 124 West Ninth Street's cover-up really stretch beyond the confines of HUD into the dominion of the President of the United States?" Although the trail of incrimination then stopped abruptly at HUD, and while I did not have evidence of direct White House involvement at the completely bogus HUD RRP building renovation project at one of my downtown properties in the Queen, with the nose that I have, Bill Clinton's odor was everywhere. As the only one who was standing in the way of a perfect U. S. Treasury theft crime, I was more determined than ever to continue to see how far the illegal trail went.

Webster's New Collegiate Dictionary defines a syndrome as "a group of signs and symptoms that occur together and characterize a particular abnormality" and "a set of concurrent things (as emotions or actions) that usually form an identifiable pattern." After I visited HUD in D. C., I could not find any words that described the pattern of illegal U. S. Treasury theft occurrences in Cincinnati, Ohio better than the *Queen syndrome*.

As the Queen syndrome represented an identifiable link between the larger scourge of American racism and the disastrous Treasury theft evil that was happening to Sandy and I in the Cincinnati microcosm, some of Martin Luther King, Jr.'s words came into my mind. King once said, "The disease of racism poisons and permeates the whole body politic." From my federal government experiences with HUD, I was seeing how his words rang true.

On the day before our downtown building were scheduled to be forcefully sold away from us, Sandy and I met with the American Civil Liberties Union's attorney on June 29, 1994. After turning us down, we later found out that he represented the Ku Klux Klan.

On June 30, 1994, 123 and 124 West Ninth Street were foreclosed upon at a sheriff's sale in the Hamilton County Courthouse in Cincinnati's central business district. Despite our vehement protestations, the foreclosure actions against Sandy and I were for (get this) "failure to make payments upon loans." Adding insult to injury, what made this sheriff's sale indicative of the area's racial intolerance was the way in which the Queen employed the Gestapo tactics of its Hamilton County Sheriffs.

Sandy and I wanted to see who was going to buy our buildings. While we were waiting for the public bidding of the sheriff's sale to begin, a lieutenant in the Hamilton County Sheriff's Department (along with three other sheriff's deputies) walked up in front of me and asked me if my name was William Kiah. Upon my responding in the affirmative, I was told that they needed to talk to me in the nearby Sheriff's office. Puzzled, I looked at Sandy and asked if she could go along, and they, in turn, responded in the affirmative.

We were escorted from the building auction area and into a separate room inside of the Sheriff's adjacent office space where the lieutenant informed me that he had reason to believe that I was carrying a concealed weapon (a gun) and wanted to search me. My eyes met Sandy's and we immediately knew what was going on: more intimidation. Sandy could not hold back her rage and angrily snapped back at them, "Well, do you want to search me too?" The Hamilton County lieutenant responded in the negative.

Up against the wall I went, spread-eagled, where I was disrespectfully frisked. I was determined not to let them derive pleasure from their intimidation tactics, so I smiled back at them to let them non-verbally know that their exercise in futility did not work on me. Sandy, on the other hand, seeing what they were doing to her man, had smoke coming from her ears behind her silent scowl.

More interesting developments occurred in the sloppy trail of federal incrimination that the Queen could not cover. On July 11, 1994, as he put forth an effort to distance himself from being incriminated, the Queen's architect in charge of the 124 West Ninth Street HUD building renovation project, Charles Alexander, gave me a signed affidavit that, instead, incriminated the Queen. Pointing the finger of blame at the City of Cincinnati, he said that NHC had approved the HUD RRP financing for 124 West Ninth Street before he did what federal law required him to do.

Regarding 124 West Ninth Street, Alexander therein attested, "I further state that I was not allowed the opportunity to fulfill my standard duties, sequentially, to a logical and typically expected completeness level. Because of this lack of proper procedures, I never felt comfortable with the rapid series of events that eventually lead to a "loan closing" on this case, and had verbally stated such more than once." As this latest development was evidentiary proof that the evil Queen had callously broken federal law and wronged me in the process, just like I had been saying all along, within three days, I filed in the U. S. Sixth Circuit District Court a "Motion to Review."

Despite the unquestionable federally indictable evidence of 124 West Ninth Street criminal activity that I had presented to the proper authorities, the Queen remained secretly involved in the repressive march against me. It continued to ruthlessly dispense hurt and injury on my family when, on July 25, 1994, two officers, Meincke and Fishesser, from the Hamilton County, Ohio Sheriff's Office, hand delivered to me an official notice to vacate my Hitchcock Drive home of sixteen years.

Elsewhere, events occurred with rapidity. During the week July 26, 1994, after I had applied unceasing federally indictable pressure against him for his role in stealing and hiding HUD financing from the U. S. Treasury at 124 West Ninth Street, the Queen's housing director, Wayne Chapman, ended his control of NHC with a surprise resignation. In Washington, D. C., HUD's leader sank deeper into a debilitating scandal when a former mistress of Henry Cisneros, Linda Medlar-Jones, sued him on July 29, 1994 alleging breach of contract and fraud. Cisneros sank even more when he denied that he had agreed to make regular payments to her. On this same day, having no other logical path to follow, Sandy and I filed for bankruptcy.

Further indications of the criminal underappraisals of my Ninth Street properties and the Queen's corrupt nature abounded. On July 30, 1994, a *Cincinnati Enquirer* front page headline read: "Library Ready to Skip Across Ninth Street." The article announced a $31 million expansion of the Public Library of Cincinnati and Hamilton County. This public library was only a block and a half away from 123 and 124 West Ninth Street.

On the next day, Sunday morning, July 31, 1994, an article was printed on the top of the front page in this same newspaper entitled, "Housing Department Wasted Millions." This two-page article led off by talking about how NHC's Wayne Chapman "left behind a troubled department and a failed strategy to provide decent housing throughout Cincinnati's neighborhoods."

A troubled presidency continued to be spotlighted during August of 1994 when Kenneth W. Starr was appointed by a three-judge U. S. Court of Appeals panel to replace Robert B. Fiske, Jr. as independent counsel. Starr, a former Federal appeals judge and Solicitor General, began examining Bill and Hillary Clinton's Whitewater land deals and related issues.

By August 2, 1994, the stubborn legal examinations that I had been pursuing produced explosively catastrophic results against the Queen. As the shaky 124 West Ninth Street HUD fraud plot caved even more, a legal collapse of the cover-up commenced in earnest that pancaked from HUD Secretary Henry Cisneros all the way down to the Queen. On this date, I struck the mother lode of incriminating evidence when I got my hands on a copy of the federal regulations and guidelines included in 24 CFR (Code of Federal Regulations) Part 511.

As these federal regulations unambiguously spelled out what should and should not have happened at 124 West Ninth Street, the true magnitude of the abuse of power by HUD and the Queen came sharply into focus. Due to the breadth and the depth of the cover-up that I had previously revealed, the addition of these federal rules and regulations to my arsenal against the Queen was the timely boost that I needed. It became increasingly clear to me that the concealment of my HUD building renovation project was an underplot in a much larger story.

Immediately after I began to read the thick federal manual that contained 24 CFR Part 511, I could not put it down, as my eyes were glued to its pages. Uncovering one specific violation after another, I revealed a veritable cornucopia of federally indictable white-collar criminal activity that was just what I had been searching for. I put on a pot of coffee, burned the midnight oil and stayed up all night deciphering these federal regulations that had been kept hidden by many shadowy people with power and influence.

In stitching the pieces together from this lengthy federal manual, I came up with eighteen specific federal violations that were very easy to see. When I catalogued and realized the magnitude of the federal crimes that were committed against me, it was no wonder why such a massive HUD fraud cover-up scheme had been thrown into high gear for such a long period of time. This is when I knew that the emperor had no clothes.

As far as my having hard evidence against the criminal HUD/Queen connection, I had already proven the existence of a long laundry list of federal criminal activity that was used against me. I had already shown that HUD's William J. Gilmartin committed a felony against me and the United States by intentionally misleading U. S. Congressman David Mann in his letter to him on April 28, 1994. I had already shown that Provident Bank's George Fulford committed a felony against me and the United States by intentionally lying to a federal department (the U. S. Sixth Circuit Court) via a false affidavit on May 2, 1994.

Similarly, I had already shown that HUD's Gilmartin committed another felony against the United States and me by intentionally lying to U. S. Senator Howard Metzenbaum on May 3, 1994. But it was my discovery of one specific federal regulation, in particular, that was included in 24 CFR Part 511 that made the July 11, 1994 affidavit of the Queen's architect, Charles Alexander, a nuclear bombshell of incrimination. It was my finding of this federal law that completely vaporized any logical defense that the HUD/Queen stratagem attempted to use.

There was one key federally mandatory HUD document that was instrumental in the determination of whether or not my HUD project should have been approved: HUD's Pre-Rehabilitation Inspection Report, federal form number HUD-40014. In order for the Queen to have legally received grant financing from the U. S. Treasury via HUD's RRP for 124 West Ninth Street, federal law strictly mandated that accurate information should have been submitted to the government. Pre-Rehabilitation Inspection Reports to HUD RRP projects are like directions to a journey: without them, the federal government will have a very difficult time in knowing up front how the project looks, or where it will be going.

The Bible of HUD's RRP, the RRP Handbook (federal handbook No. 7360.01), states, "Once a project is set up and assigned a project number [which was the case at 124 West Ninth Street], grantees or State recipients [in my case, the City of Cincinnati or the State of Ohio respectively] must immediately forward Pre-Rehabilitation Inspection Reports to HUD in Washington, D. C....If Pre-Rehabilitation Inspection Reports are not received by HUD or the information is incomplete or inadequate, the project will remain in a suspended status and no funds for the project will be available to the grantee [or State recipient]."

The more I read, the more I found out how extremely illegitimate my HUD project was; how it was used against me in a designed plot; and why it was covered-up. HUD's RRP Pre-Rehabilitation Inspection report is required by federal law to describe the deficiencies, the total costs of the rehabilitation—including both RRP (HUD) and non-RRP funds (Provident Bank), and evidence that proposed building rehabilitation undertakings do meet the specific grant and project program requirements.

By reading 24 CFR Part 511, I discovered that 124 West Ninth Street's deficiencies were not described. The Queen's architect, Charles Alexander stated in his signed July 11, 1994 affidavit that the City did not allow him to do the inspections, cost estimating, evaluations, recommendations and bid pricing work that HUD deemed to be compulsory.

By reading 24 CFR Part 511, I ascertained that 124 West Ninth Street's total costs were not determined. At the time the Pre-Rehabilitation Inspection Report was submitted to HUD (if it was ever submitted at all), the Queen made a guarantee to the federal government that the total costs for the RRP project at 124 West Ninth Street would be $91,000 in order to receive HUD financing. Based upon the federal laws contained in 24 CFR Part 511, when my HUD project went over the $91,000 that was contracted for, it was incumbent upon the Queen to have made up the difference. But, as the Queen illegally caused my total costs to go over $329,000, froze the project, blocked substantive refinancing efforts, and left Sandy and I high and dry, our two valuable pieces of real estate were dubiously foreclosed upon.

By reading 24 CFR Part 511, I also found out that 124 West Ninth Street's RRP requirements were not met. As my Pre-Rehabilitation Inspection Report was incomplete and inadequate, the federal grant and program requirements of 24 CFR Part 511 were criminally violated. Consequently, U. S. government grant financing for 124 West Ninth Street was wrongfully disbursed to the Queen and illegally used.

The fallout from the Queen's awareness of my discovery of 24 CFR Part 511 was considerable and immediate. Just as NHC's Wayne Chapman resigned from the Queen's employment one week earlier, due to the unceasing federally indictable pressure that I applied against him, on August 6, 1994, NHC's RRP Manager, Michael Jackson, was conspicuously separated from the employ of the City of Cincinnati. The Queen was left smarting because I was tenacious of my constitutional rights.

In the nation's capital, negative political pressure continued to build on a President Bill Clinton. In September of 1994, *The Washington Post* reported that Linda Medlar-Jones sold secretly taped conversations with Clinton's Department of HUD Secretary, Henry Cisneros, to "Inside Edition" and said on that television program that Cisneros lied in his federal background checks. Also in September, Independent Counsel Donald C. Smaltz was appointed to "investigate to the maximum extent" authorized by law Clinton's Department of Agriculture Secretary Espy's dealings with large agricultural interests. Increasingly, Bill Clinton needed 124 West Ninth Street's cover-up to surface like he needed another hole in his tricksy head.

On September 18, 1994, I wrote President Bill Clinton a certified letter captioned "HUD Fraud Forcing A Veteran Into Bankruptcy." With this correspondence, I also sent him a copy of document that I had also presented to the U. S. Sixth Circuit Court that listed the eighteen specific HUD infractions at 124 West Ninth Street. Although I could not specifically see it at the time, my words were being purposefully disregarded, as the Clinton administration had another agenda on its mind.

With a plethora of nationally broadcast investigations and scandals going on in and around his presidency, widely-ranging cover-up decisions were being made near to and by Bill Clinton that kept my 124 West Ninth Street victimization in place. Already up to his neck in alligators, conventional White House wisdom was that it could ill-afford another scandalous hit like the one that I could deliver. Thusly, 124 West Ninth Street's illegal political cover-up became a top priority for the President that was a former governor of Arkansas.

President Clinton's twin needs for generating lots of money and hiding his Cabinet's HUD crimes wickedly coupled with the Queen's need to keep the 124 West Ninth Street HUD crimes hidden. In the process, a perfect marriage was formed that was born of mutual criminal necessity, as the historically corrupt and intolerant Queen willingly availed itself to go in league with a rapidly emerging form of unlawful Clinton White House prostitution.

By repeatedly filing federal court papers citing the federal law that necessitated the appointment of an attorney to represent me, I applied mounting and unavoidable legal pressure on U. S. Sixth Circuit District Court Judge S. Arthur Spiegel for lawful compliance. Concurrently, extensive efforts in the nation's capitol had been largely unsuccessful in dismantling my federal case that stood a strong probability of being extremely embarrassing—if not terminal—to the Bill Clinton administration. As sure as death and taxes, unseen criminal powers deep from within the heart and soul of the unethical Clinton White House made further calculated decisions to get rid of my legal threat once and for all.

Continuing to pursue a malevolent strategy of denial, deceit and delay, the White House pulled out of its hat an abuse of power orchestration that stretched down from the President through U. S. Attorney General Janet Reno's Justice Department and into Cincinnati's U. S. Sixth Circuit District Court. On October 24, 1994, U. S. District Court Judge S. Arthur Spiegel clandestinely appointed internationally renowned Attorney Stanley M. Chesley of the Queen's Waite, Schneider, Bayless & Chesley Co., L.P.A. to represent Sandy and I.

Not knowing what was going on behind our backs, Sandy and I were cautiously encouraged to know that, at last, we had triumphed in getting legal representation. We knew that, by law, it was an attorney's legal responsibility to ethically represent us. However, as 124 West

Ninth Street criminal activity had reached new heights, there was no way for us to see that the cover-up ante had been considerably upped. Under the color of law, Chesley personified the big guns being called out, as he was the much-needed Clinton cover-up reinforcement that was quickly busied to be the secret weapon, the agent provocateur, the shill and the plant. As a result of this appointment, the emperor having no clothes gained new meaning.

Stan Chesley was not just any lawyer. As one of the most prominent plaintiff's attorneys in America, the context in which he was appointed to us reveals the presidential scheme. Unbeknownst to Sandy and I, he was a trusted confidant and a close, personal friend of President Bill Clinton; he was one of the largest campaign contributors to President Bill Clinton and The National Democratic Party; he traveled on Air Force One with President Clinton; he was purported to be a representative of the Israeli government; and he was a personal friend to the famous defense attorney F. Lee Bailey.

With a case history that reads like the Who's Who of American lawyers, Chesley also was the Plaintiffs' attorney in the June, 1977 Beverly Hills (Kentucky) Supper Club fire case, the Dow Chemical Breast Implant case, the Union Carbide vs. Bhopal, India case and many other cases of note. From January 1, 1994 to December 31, 1995, Stan Chesley was the powerful Chairman of the Board of Commissioners on Grievance and Discipline for the Supreme Court of Ohio. There, Chesley was in charge of this adjudicative body that held hearings which dealt with the wrongdoing of attorneys and judges in Ohio when formal complaints against them were made.

Like a large and unsightly pimple on the tip of one's nose, Chesley's legal conflicts made his appointment to Sandy and I an ugly and messy thing to behold. At the time of Chesley's appointment to us, a defendant in our lawsuit, Dwight Tillery (the person who was the Mayor of Cincinnati when the City defrauded the U. S. government at 124 West Ninth Street), was a member of Attorney Stanley M. Chesley's law firm. A greater indication of the glaring conflict of interest that existed when Stan Chesley was appointed to represent us was in the fact that he was appointed to prosecute the Bill Clinton HUD Cabinet for Treasury theft at the same time.

Try as I did, Chesley could not be reached to set up our initial meeting. On October 27, 1994, only three days after he was appointed to represent me, I found out that Chesley was in Israel with President Bill Clinton.

In November of 1994, the Democratic Party suffered a terrible loss in the off-year elections. U. S. Congressman Newt Gingrich and the Republicans swept into Washington and took control of both houses of Congress. It was President Bill Clinton's biggest and most conspicuous failure and the Republicans made the 1994 mid-term elections a referendum on Bill Clinton. It was the worst mid-term loss in more than 50 years for the National Democratic Party. Republican U. S. Senator from Ohio, Mike DeWine, was elected, succeeding U. S. Sen. Howard Metzenbaum.

It was seventeen days before Stan Chesley gave me a chance to talk with him. I initially met him in his office at 5:30 P.M. on November 9, 1994 and immediately knew that something was not right when the always arrogant attorney opened up his conversation by cursing at me like a sailor. "I know your goddamned kind. You just want to use me because of who I am…#@+∂*#!!!" were his first words to me.

While continuing to glower, he only tried to belittle and dissuade me and, otherwise, tried to make me think that I did not have a case. Behind the closed doors of his fifteenth floor conference room, I first felt that Chesley had been appointed to resort to subterfuge in helping politically and financially powerful people evade the federal laws that proscribe the theft, misuse and cover-up of HUD Treasury financing. Nevertheless, I gave him the benefit of the doubt because, after all, he was my federally appointed attorney. As he was leaning back in his chair with his feet on top of the long conference table while giving me the evil eye, I smelled that the extinguishment of 124 West Ninth Street's crimes had been given precedence by someone whose power was greater than Chesley's.

Sitting eyeball to eyeball at Chesley's long conference table, a serious bout of mental wrestling had begun. By this time, it was all a game—but, it was the only game in town, and I had to play. Wasting no time, Chesley let me know, nonverbally, that he was not there for me. I did not actually know if he was testing me or not to see if I had the mental toughness for this type of fight, but I was determined to let him know that I was up for the challenge.

Having no fear of him in the umbra of his apparent crookedness, I said to him, "I'm going to win my fight with or without you."

Immediately following the initial exchange, we sat there for at least one minute in complete silence, staring into each other's eyes. I did not blink.

In a very pushy way that was marked by impulsiveness, Chesley resumed pressing forward with his discouragement by attempting to lure me into a verbal trap that was characteristically designed to intimidate. Insisting that I hurry up to give him the names of three people that could have corroborated my allegations of 124 West Ninth Street RRP misdeeds, I immediately obliged his request, while he impatiently, loudly strummed his fingers on the conference table.

I gave him the names of the City's architect, my personal architect, and my electrician. I realized that, although they were not as knowledgeable of the specifics of the 124 West Ninth Street HUD project details as I was, they knew enough to shed meaningful light onto the Queen's farce.

In an obvious blurt of fibbery, he instantaneously barked back at me, "I've already talked to them and they can't help you to prove your case." Then, in a heartbeat, before he could finish one breath, Chesley quickly bellowed, "Who else, who else can corroborate your allegations? Give me the names of three more people." In the midst of the battlefield fray at the table, I began to peer behind the mask of deception that Chesley had been hiding behind. Down went the face of a grumpy old gasbag of an attorney and up came the visage of a wolf in lambs clothing who had been commissioned as a big-time player in a U. S. Treasury theft presidential cover-up scheme.

The ball was back in my court. In seeing that Chesley was looking for a way to get my case dismissed by receiving the names of three more people who did not know enough about the entirety of my HUD RRP, I remembered an old IBM marketing technique that checked his bushwhack. To increase the probability of my past sales successes, I knew that my efforts had to be focused at top decision making levels, instead of at bottom end-user levels. Being that he wanted the names of people who could corroborate my story of 124 West Ninth Street RRP misdeeds, I was not going to give him the names of any more locals that he could use to try to kill my legal thrust. I took away his effort to steer me into a trap by giving him the names of top employees of HUD who had responsibility for what happened at 124 West Ninth Street.

Playing my more than strong hunch that the HUD Secretary was somehow aware of what happened at my HUD project, instead of being played, I decided to play Chesley in a way that I knew he could not handle. I told Chesley to contact Henry Cisneros to corroborate my allegations, and that I wanted to have a written confirmation given to me from him of all of the names that I was giving to him.

I realized that I was putting Chesley in an impossible position because, if Cisneros would have been contacted regarding what I said had happened, the Secretary would have lost the tactical legal advantage of distancing himself from 124 West Ninth Street's illegal failure. Moreover, Chesley would have incurred significant condemnation from those at the top of the HUD fraud plot by establishing a clear trail of incrimination leading into the Cabinet of the President of the United States. If he was the crook that I thought that he was, I knew that Chesley could not have had such a monkey wrench thrown into his cover-up gears.

Under the legal rules of the game that we were playing, I let Chesley know, without saying it, that I was driving him, not the other way around. He wanted names, so I gave him more, many more. I leaned forward, looked through Chesley's eyes and told him to pick from any of the following people at HUD headquarters: Frank Wing, Terrance Duvernay, Andrew Cuomo, Terri Nicolosi, Marsha Dodge or Richard Burk. After that meeting, I never saw Chesley again.

The events in Washington made for strange bedfellows between Bill Clinton and Stan Chesley. As long as Stan Chesley remained active in his federal appointment as my lawyer, the liability that he created on an already scandal-laden presidency was too much to bear for the White House. When the plan for Chesley to eliminate me as a legal threat backfired due to an original oversight that he was just too close to the President to be effective, the Clinton/Chesley camp also realized that they had greatly underestimated the resolve that Sandy and I had to fight.

On December 8, 1994, after a crucial forty-six day window of damage that stagnated my case in an unforgiving federal court setting, U. S. District Court Judge S. Arthur Spiegel ordered the granting of a motion to rescind Stan Chesley's appointment as the counsel of record for Sandy and I. By this time, a distinct pattern had arisen in the federal court: we were systematically being denied due process and equal protection under the law, as crucial evidence was avoided and suppressed.

Also in December of 1994, more pressure was exerted on a Clinton administration that was coming increasingly under question. During this month, Webster Hubbell, former U. S. Assistant Attorney General and law partner of Hillary Rodham Clinton, (an early focus of special prosecutor Kenneth Starr's Whitewater investigation) pleaded guilty to embezzling $400,000 from his former law partners in Arkansas and overbilling their clients.

Just as surely as evidence of the President's frequent crookedness was surfacing nationally with sickening regularity, my wife and I knew that the total shutdown of help to us from duly notified federal, state and local politicians, agencies, departments and bureaus was too complete, and too total, to be merely coincidental.

Chapter 6

The Chopping Off Of "Kunta Kiah's" Foot

"When a man is pushed, tormented, defeated, he has a chance to learn something; he has been put on his wits; on his manhood; he has gained the facts; learns his ignorance; is cured of the insanity of conceit; has got moderation and real skill."

—Ralph Waldo Emerson

In Alex Haley's book *Roots*, and the 1977 television miniseries made from it, a portion of Kunta Kinte's foot was callously chopped off in an attempt to break the spirited zest for freedom of this early American slave. Similarly, by the start of 1995, as an attempt was made to teach Sandy and I a lesson not to buck the repressive system that enslaved us, we continued to face a series of crippling unconstitutional traumas.

By keeping our lawsuit alive, we kept boxing the President and the Queen into a corner. As a result of not yielding to threatening demands to drop our lawsuit against those who participated in the theft of U. S. government HUD financing at 124 West Ninth Street, floodgates of retaliatory measures were maliciously unleashed against my immediate family. However, between the scathing court evidence that we had against them and our dogged determination to not let them stand, the HUD fraud plotters were not able to completely eliminate us.

Even as we were financially trounced and steamrollered by them, they were in the uncontrollable position of not being able to rewrite history. It was bad enough that I strongly regarded what they did to me with aversion, but, again, seeing what they were doing to all Americans by robbing our Treasury made me redouble my commitment to fight.

124 West Ninth Street was a sloppily kept secret that had become an embarrassment to many of the power elite. To their chagrin, Sandy

and I had become an exacerbating pea in the shoe of those who were part of the Queen syndrome. Our unyielding resistance to the completely bogus HUD building renovation project that we had been illegally lured into remained the last line of America's constitutional defense opposing these U. S. Treasury theft crimes.

Like the ominous threat of a deadly gathering storm, the clandestine federal government effort arrayed against us intensified, revealing well-coordinated White House winds that blew roughshod over the American landscape in an attempt to conceal presidential criminal involvement at 124 West Ninth Street. As the target for stopping us remained our soft legal advocacy underbelly in the Queen's U. S. Sixth Circuit Court, illegal government operatives converged, institutionally bent on getting us good, once and for all.

The waters had already been significantly bloodied from the financial and emotional hemorrhaging that left Sandy and I critically injured, incapacitated and flailing defenselessly in the water. As they had circled in the protective wake of the politically powerful Queen, the two predatory mortgage sharks, Provident Bank and Suburban Federal Savings Bank, thought that they had craftily devised the perfect plan that allowed them to operate above the federal laws that they were governed by. In their expediency, they reasoned that politically powerful friends were providing them with the perfect alibi for purloining the very valuable real estate that they had stalked and snatched from Sandy and I.

In January of 1995, at the nadir of his first term, there was a tone of urgency verging on desperation in one of President Bill Clinton's notes, two months after his party's defeat in the congressional elections. Not only did he approve the plan for inviting big donors to coffees at the White House, but he also instructed aides to get the program under way "right away" and supply more names of contributors in the $100,000 range.

As political contributions have always been made with the understanding that favors could be expected to follow, President Clinton pushed the donor envelope to the limit. In the Clinton White House, the nature of those favors was made far more specific than before. The linkage was made more explicit when, for $50,000 to $100,000, some political donors were promised an invitation to a White House coffee or even to spend the night in the Lincoln Bedroom.

Unmistakably, the coffees were Bill Clinton's handiwork, an outgrowth of his belief that he could win a second term only by pursuing what his adviser Dick Morris called "the permanent campaign," fueled by television spending, which required large amounts of cash. Bill Clinton learned early that money was power and that it was political oxygen.

Two events in Clinton's past shaped his views when it came to money in politics. He was stunned by his Republican challenger's deep pockets in his most devastating political defeat, when Frank White ejected him from the Arkansas governor's mansion in 1980. He also watched opponents of the premier legislative proposal of his first term as president, the health-care overhaul, seize the debate with clever "Harry and Louise" commercials.

Facing the 1996 elections, he embraced a re-election strategy that depended on spending millions of dollars on early TV advertisements. Outspent by the Republicans during his 1992 presidential race, and clobbered when the GOP won control of Congress in 1994, Bill Clinton went into the race determined to raise money early, quickly and at all costs. The urgency of Bill Clinton's fundraising orders that huge sums of money must be raised criminally drowned out his willingness to adhere to the federal laws contained in the guidelines and regulations of HUD's 24 CFR Part 511.

The arcane curtain of a legal vacuum was stealthily kept in place, further denying Sandy and I the federal court appointed representation that we were entitled to. On January 31, 1995, at a status conference in Room 838 at Cincinnati's U. S. Courthouse Building, U. S. District Judge S. Arthur Spiegel surreptitiously told me that another attorney could not be appointed to us. Even though I objected vigorously, the strangest observation about the whole status conference, however, was that, for the first time, an attorney from the U. S. Attorney's office, Jerry Kamiski, showed up on the side of the bad guys, the defendants in our lawsuit.

At a second status conference in U. S. District Judge S. Arthur Spiegel's chambers on February 28, 1995, I walked into a room where a broad front of austere legal antagonists sat on one side of a long conference table. In addition to Judge Spiegel, also in attendance were four defense attorneys: Jerry Kamiski, who showed up again representing the U. S. Attorney for the Southern District of Ohio, Edmund

Sargus; Attorney Mark Vollman from the City of Cincinnati; Attorney John R. Wirthlin from Provident Bank; and Attorney Bruce Gilster from Suburban Federal Savings Bank.

Five sets of eyes stared at me when Judge Spiegel opened the status conference by saying that he was accepting U. S. Magistrate Judge Steinberg's finding to dismiss my case. Deceit mixed with hypocritical flattery when Judge Spiegel then said that the time frame for my getting another lawyer had expired, and that he was dismissing my case in such a way that I could file an appeal—an appeal that he knew would also be doomed in a politically controlled U. S. Sixth Circuit Appeals Court.

I intensely continued to express opposition to his decision, whereupon a seven-minute exchange between us took place. Abruptly interrupting me, he told me that a jury had just been seated in his courtroom and that the status conference had to be ended. In a heartbeat, determined to capture the moment and not waste my time, I held my ground and told him that I had come prepared to discuss some pressing issues and requested that he, at least, hear me out. He concurred and I made my points known to all who were there.

I succinctly told Judge Spiegel that my case was about principle; the principles that were included in the eighteen specific violations of federal law that I had brought to his attention in my "Addendum To Motion To Review" (Document 30) on September 16, 1994. I reiterated by telling him that my case was very easy to prove and that one did not have to dig to find the evidence, as all of it laid plainly on the surface, clearly in view.

After telling him that I would have needed O. J. Simpson's lawyers and money to win a legal fight that was based on race, I, again, told him that my argument was based on the federal infractions of 24 CFR Part 511. I made it a point to inform him that there were many victims at my HUD project, that there was tremendous stress on my family, that money was illegally taken from America, and that I had over five hundred signatures on a petition that was ready to be sent to U. S. Attorney General Janet Reno.

Continuing, I made sure that he understood that I needed an effective court appointed attorney, thereby going on record as having said such. From my insistence on not letting him shut down the status conference when he initially wanted to, I was able to put procedural pressure back into the Judge's court. Later on that day, as he really had no other choice in his U. S. Treasury theft cover-up role, Judge Spiegel again surreptitiously made the appointment of my second federal lawyer, Attorney Marc Mezibov.

By March 1, 1995, the volcanic dome against the White House swelled even more. Under increasing political pressure, the U. S. Justice Department began an initial review to determine whether an independent prosecutor should investigate Clinton Transportation Secretary Federico F. Pena in connection with a contract awarded in 1993 to an investment firm he had just left.

March 3, 1995 was a day that I faxed a "Petition and Call to Action" to U. S. Attorney General Janet Reno that had over 500 signatures on it. The petition called for an investigation into the U. S. Treasury theft infractions at 124 West Ninth Street that were characteristic of a pattern of disparate treatment towards African-Americans by the Hamilton County, Ohio court system and the Queen. On the same day, I sent, via certified mail, the same petition that I had faxed to her. Although Reno's office received this petition, I never heard back from anyone there.

On the morning of March 9, 1995, the day that I was first allowed to meet with my second federally appointed lawyer, I filed another motion to Judge Spiegel before the meeting, knowing how shenanigans had been previously played in the Sixth Circuit. As part of my strategy that was designed to not allow any of my antagonists to legally defeat me because they could say that they did not understand what I was saying in federal court, I came up with a nontypical—but completely acceptable—front page caption on my latest motion that even a nincompoop could have fathomed. The motion was captioned, "Request for Clarification of the February 28, 1995 Federal Court Status Conference; A Statement of Concerns; and A Call for Help to the United States Judicial System to Expose HUD Fraud by the City of Cincinnati, Including the Illegal Cover-up Which Has Ensued." This federal court document brought even more unwanted pressure on the Clinton administration.

It was more of the same thing with Attorney Mezibov when I initially met with him. His eyes, too, gave him away, as he did a very bad job a trying to get me to follow his agenda of not pursuing the Queen and the other HUD fraud plotters. I quickly deduced that he, like

Chesley, was a plant who continuously did absolutely nothing that I asked him to do. Each successive day under his legal care brought accruing attention to my maltreatment.

The final straw was when he sat back like a bump on a log after I asked him to file an injunction that would have stopped the fast approaching eviction from my home by the Hamilton County Court. Like Chesley, all outward indications glassed Mezibov's ill intentions that he had me under his control.

The match in the powder barrel was when I deliberately overstepped his role as my only voice to the court by filing a stinging motion captioned "Request For Injunction" in U. S. District Court on the morning of March 14, 1995. It was a legal move on my part that, if granted, would have turned over the HUD fraud plot apple cart by exposing it to unwanted scrutiny, thereby delaying the punishment that had been designed to force me into submission. I knew that I had caused an explosion when, by the afternoon of the same day, Mary from U. S. Magistrate Judge Steinberg's office telephoned notifying me of an injunction hearing that had been hastily scheduled less than 24 hours away.

I knew what I was walking into when I saw that U. S. Magistrate Judge Steinberg's March 15, 1995 injunction hearing was a stepped-up exercise to both corral and cement me into federal imposition. From the outset, Judge Steinberg made it a point to let me know that he was the big enchilada, the top dog in his federal courtroom who was representing the federal government. In the mental wrestling match that followed, the obstinate Steinberg got increasingly irritated, as all of the questions and statements that I responded to and made kept my unreported U. S. Treasury theft agenda on the front burner.

As my being at the injunction hearing was indicative of Mezibov's inability to control me, unwanted pressure was brought upon him by his crooked legal peers. In putting forth a feeble attempt at looking like he was ethically representing me, his sycophantic showing exacerbated the fact that he was there with egg on his face and that he had blown his hidden charter to lead me to an easy slaughter.

With no one in the courtroom but federal court employees and lawyers of the defendants, Steinberg stepped in to save the day for the federal HUD plot by predictably and illogically ruling against my injunction. While Mezibov sat back and did nothing, I expressed my overall objections to the pontificating magistrate judge.

After the injunction hearing, and when hardly no one was around in the hallway by the elevators outside of Steinberg's seventh floor courtroom, a fistfight almost erupted between myself and Ted L. Wills, an embarrassed attorney from Mezibov's law firm of Sirkin, Pinales, Mezibov & Schwartz. Without provocation, Wills instigated the confrontation by angrily jumping in front of me and invading my very close private space.

I knew from the start that his violent displeasure was actually a direct result of the pent-up frustration that he and Mezibov felt in their conspiratorial inability to keep the 124 West Ninth Street HUD crimes out of my federal injunction hearing setting—a hearing that they had been charged with suppressing. Wills angrily shook his finger within several inches of my eyes and vociferated, "Shut up and listen." That was strike one.

Soon thereafter, due to my unwillingness to go along with what was obviously bad advice to acquiesce, without any justification whatsoever, the pressure on my second federally appointed court attorney reached a boiling point. All of a sudden, Mezibov heatedly snatched Wills from in front of me and, while shaking his finger in my face, put his face within inches of mine and began yelling loudly at me with train-smoke breath. "Listen, you…" were the first words out of Mezibov's mouth.

But, before he could get in another word edgewise, I calmly said to him, "Get out of my face!" At bottom, I was being double-teamed in the name of hiding HUD's and the Queen's U. S. Treasury theft involvement. Even more than Mezibov's hot and pungent breath, that was strike two.

Knowing that I still could deliver the formidable quick-draw right hand punch of my Army days, I waited with bated breath, deceivingly coiled in anticipation of strike three. Mezibov was no fool: he saw the raging fire that was beyond my calm face and into my unblinking eyes. In issuing a firm warning to him, Mezibov became astutely aware of the physical harm that he and his cohort were subjecting themselves to, and immediately backed away, removing his person from my private space.

A break in the action occurred when the nearby elevator doors opened at the height of this ruckus, wherein one of Mezibov's legal acquaintances made an egression from it. Mezibov quickly, awkwardly changed the tone and substance of the confrontation to make it appear that he was in control of a conversation that did not have anything to do with the argument at hand. As Mezibov's extreme measures bubbled up from the abyss of a multi-leveled HUD fraud plot designed to eliminate my presence in the U. S. Sixth Circuit Court, the opening of elevator doors staunched my raison d'être for punching my second planted federal lawyer squarely in the nose.

As I took an elevator down to the ground floor, it was all too obvious to me what was really going on: the U. S. Sixth Circuit Court was nothing more than a tool of 124 West Ninth Street cover-up conspirators. The certainty of a broad cover-up grew greater when I exited the Queen's Federal Building and approached attorneys Mezibov and Wills who had just joined a receptive huddle that had gathered on the building's exterior stone steps, consisting mostly of the defense lawyers in my case.

Like a group of teenagers who were unsuccessful in playing a hidden practical joke, the Queen's cartel of powerful lawyers were so brazen that they nakedly chuckled uncontrollably in public upon hearing Mezibov's opening words to them. As I began to pass them, and with all eyes on me, Mezibov quickly wheeled his head away from the parley, said to me in a contemptuously sarcastic way, "Call me", and then turned back into a smiling group of faces with a poorly hidden smirk on his face.

This incident was nothing more than the latest in a continuing series of events that let me know that an impenetrable wall had been erected against me to hide something well beyond the HUD/Queen façade. From that point on, even though Mezibov tried to put a positive spin on a very negative situation by continuing to maintain the illusion that there was a legitimate basis for a lawyer-client relationship, everything else between us went further downhill.

In many ways, my home was like Kunta Kinte's foot: it was rightfully mine, I was emotionally attached to it and it was forcibly held into harm's way as punishment for going against a repressive rule. Words cannot possibly convey the agonizing feeling of being held down by the U. S. Sixth Circuit Court, unable to move, while seeing this type of crippling blow coming at me. On March 16, 1995, as we had been left vulnerable to the retribution and retaliation of the U. S. Sixth Circuit Court, the punishing ax came down on my family as my home of sixteen years was also wrongfully foreclosed upon at the Hamilton County Sheriff's Sale.

Like the unpreparedness that one goes through when trying to imagine how it feels to lose one's mother prior to her death, imagining the loss of our home was nothing like losing it: the actual loss was far greater than the thought. Though I saw it coming, this designed draconian event ushered in a negative sea change in my emotional, spiritual, and future outlook. I had a little over sixty days to move out of a house that I had treasured, my wife had adored and my three girls had formed larger-than-life images of.

Unable to buy another house because my credit had wrongly been ruined, it was truly a life-altering experience that was fraught with all of the demoralizing end results that stunned and stupefied my family. To an overwhelming degree, my young daughters felt comforted by the explanations that Sandy and I gave to them regarding what was going on, but they did not fully comprehend the full enormity of what had transpired. Like the dormant nightmares of torture victims, only time would reveal the latent fears and scars that were hidden within my precious girls.

In particular, this juncture of my punishment reminded me of the threatening warning that was given to Sandy and I by the attorneys of Provident Bank and Suburban Federal Savings Bank, Michael Debbeler and Bruce Gilster, at our bankruptcy hearing six months prior. Like American slave masters of yesteryear who warned their slaves not to escape under the threat of severe punishment, these legal cogs on the rim of the Queen's wheel had told us that they would let us keep our residence if we dropped our federal lawsuit against them. Having not taken their terribly illegal advice, I was seeing how their threat had become manifest.

As the federal government's money and power was thrown at us in an effort to intimidate, this last of a continuous succession of blows was indicative of the inordinate amount of resources that had been brought to bear on Sandy and I. From the way that we thought, our resistance was only stiffened because the U. S. government was being used illegally against us.

Becoming further steeled, I went into a defensive psychological metamorphosis that caused my withdrawal into a state of mind that I refer to as the *wilderness*. Similar to the lone Rambo mentality that totally consumed me when I penetrated HUD, I removed myself from the social and civic involvements of my past and entered into a more solitary form of existence because I did not feel comfortable in trusting anyone but my immediate family. The reality of my legal fight had dictated that my world had changed significantly around me, and that it was a new day. With the stakes being so high, I had learned that illegal resources from high within America's federal government were too vast and omnipotent for me to foolishly disregard in mounting my opposition.

I kept punching back. On March 24, 1995, I filed a "Negligence and Legal Malpractice lawsuit against Attorneys Stanley M. Chesley and Marc D. Mezibov with a jury demand." U. S. District Judge Carl B. Rubin was assigned to case. On another front, as I had already sent him a certified letter on September 18, 1994 in an attempt to see if he was involved with my cover-up, by April 1,1995, I sent another letter to the White House via certified mail entitled, "A Letter to President Bill Clinton from a Victim of HUD Fraud."

Like a starter's gun to a large marathon race, a stampede of additional cover-up activities commenced, as it became even more obvious to Sandy and I that we had set into motion a new series of shady events. On April 4th, 1995, Judge S. Arthur Spiegel withdrew from our federal case via an "Order of Transfer." U. S. Judge Herman J. Weber replaced him in U. S. Sixth Circuit to District Court.

The tit for tat continued with serious infighting between the HUD cover-up antagonists and myself. As he was not able to withstand the pressure that was exerted upon him, on April 7, 1995, Marc Mezibov petitioned the U. S. Sixth Circuit District Court to withdraw him from being my trial counsel. By April 18, 1995, I was hit with a letter from the Sheriff of Hamilton County, Ohio, Simon L. Leis, Jr., ordering us to vacate our home by midnight, May 19, 1995 to avoid our belongings being set out on the street.

Several ongoing events occurred that exhibited the Queen's cockiness in believing that it could hide its HUD theft crimes. The first event happened on April 23, 1995 when NHC's former RRP Manager Michael Jackson, was returned to the employ of Cincinnati's NHC after leaving suspiciously on August 6, 1994. Even though I fired back at the U. S. Sixth Circuit District Court on May 1, 1995 with a motion that was captioned, "Request For Injunction To Eliminate Being Made

Homeless Due To HUD Fraud," the Queen moved brazenly forward by combining NHC and its Department of Human Services to form the Department of Neighborhood Services. Effectively, this evasively calculated move shutdown the public's ability to view the incriminating evidence that was in the public NHC files for 124 West Ninth Street.

Soon after a motion was granted allowing Marc Mezibov's withdrawal as my federal Attorney, and as Sandy and I faced much difficulty in finding a new place to live, on May 19,1995, I signed a three-month rental agreement in the eleventh hour with the new owner of the house that had been brutally chopped away from me.

At this point, I was up to my neck in alligators while actively fighting in two federal courts of law. With respect to my legal malpractice lawsuit, on June 2, 1995, I filed my "Plaintiffs' Response To Show Cause Order" (in response to U. S. District Judge Walter Rubin's May 24, 1995 "Order To Show Cause") along with my "Plaintiffs' Memorandum In Opposition To Defendant Chesley's Motion To Dismiss."

By June 13, 1995, the day before O. J. Simpson put on a pair of gloves in his criminal trial for the murders of Nicole Brown Simpson and Ronald Goldman, I filed a federal court document that left 124 West Ninth Street's conspirators scratching their heads. On this date, I filed a "Response To Memoranda Of Defendants In Opposition To Plaintiffs' Motion For Affirmative Relief And Provisional Remedy Due To HUD Fraud and Plaintiffs' Request For an Effective Court Appointed Attorney" (Document 55) in U. S. District Judge Weber's court.

Document 55 was an almost complete package of U. S. Sixth Circuit Court evidence that torpedoed the HUD/Queen strategy to procedurally render my court presence moot. With my filing of it, I forcefully refocused the legal debate on the HUD Treasury theft issue, and sank any hope that my case could be dissolved into a successful and crafty diversion by high-priced schemers. As it was full of evidentiary proof of my charges, it left no question as to what happened at 124 West Ninth Street.

The following evidence was included in Document 55: a flowchart showing how the defendants participated; copies of letters showing perjury to the U. S. Senate, Congress and Sixth Circuit Court; the City's architect's affidavit that implicated the Queen; the HUD contract that proved that money had been illegally taken from the U. S. Treasury; canceled City of Cincinnati checks showing that all of 124 West Ninth Street's money was not disbursed to me as had been reported to the Senate, Congress and federal court; and the eighteen specific violations of federal law that were contained in 24 CFR Part 511.

Usually, when evidence is compelling, the court moves. However, the gross inaction by the U. S. Sixth Circuit Court on the evidence that I presented to it made it abundantly clear that it was acting in collusion with the Queen and Provident Bank.

All of the cover-up pieces interconnected. There was no puzzle to solve. The problem for me was that the U. S. Sixth Circuit Court illegally chose not to acknowledge the Treasury theft that it saw. The high criminal activity that I witnessed underscored the far-reaching effects of how powerful political, financial and judicial forces could circumvent the law in a cover-up scheme—even if Uncle Sam was robbed.

All of my objections to the U. S. Sixth Circuit Court's findings were firmly established in the illogical nature of its decisions, especially since the rulings were inimical to the prosecution of those who committed or participated in 124 West Ninth Street's HUD fraud. As we continued to increasingly expose a massive HUD fraud cover-up network, Sandy and I remained resolute in our burning desire to fight a cancer that was illegally phlebotomizing the coffers of the United States of America.

The sum of it all was that I was getting too close to the powerful people who were deeply involved in the 124 West Ninth Street HUD cover-up. As growing efforts from deep within the federal government were illegally being made to shut down my threat in the federal court system, it became clear that the burying ground for my politically embarrassing HUD project had been designated as the headquarters of HUD itself. Sandy and I increasingly saw how HUD's policing of its unregulated receipt of U. S. Treasury tax dollars was like the fox watching the chicken coop.

On June 16, 1995, I received a letter from Robert G. Damus, General Counsel in the Executive Office of the President's Office of Management and Budget (OMB), saying that he had referred my letter to him to HUD's Inspector General's office. He made it a point to also say that I might contact HUD through their Hotline and that "She (Mrs. Velma Thomas) will take further action as she deems appropriate."

When I called and talked to her—for well over the hundredth time—with Damus' recommendation, as always, she did nothing. By then, it had become a foregone conclusion that the HUD Hotline was only a screen that was being used to figure out which federal HUD crimes were to be covered-up.

In continuing to apply pressure on the federal government to enforce the laws of the land, I kept on fighting, digging and scratching in both of my federal lawsuits, as my legal prowess became more sharpened. On the legal malpractice lawsuit front, it increasingly became more self-evident that I had backed U. S. Judge Carl B. Rubin into a legal corner. Having no other choice in his highly illegal role to eliminate my threat by concealing the evidence and the articulation of the federal infractions that I presented to his court, on June 26, 1995, he was forced to relent. On this date, he had no other choice but to issue a court order in my favor because I showed appropriate cause why my case against Chesley and Mezibov should not have been dismissed.

Later, political events in Washington tended to establish the unmistakable HUD fraud connective motive between the nation's White House and the Queen. Exactly fifteen days after Judge Rubin's pressured ruling, negative news stories about plans to give big donors special perks prompted DNC Chairman Don Fowler to suggest limiting donations to $2,000. But that would "substantially reduce the ability of the DNC to raise funds and compete" with the Republican Party, Harold Ickes wrote in a memo to President Clinton. So, "The 'practice' of raising large amounts of money from individuals, who in turn, will be invited to meet with the president, the vice president and others...will continue," Ickes wrote.

Like America's punitive chattel slave system, the wrongful use of the federal court system had long been prohibited. With all of the infractions that had been committed by Chesley and Mezibov in their federal court appointments to maintain the 124 West Ninth Street HUD cover-up front, extraordinary methods were needed by them for protection against the federal incriminations that were knocking on their doors.

Federal Court cover-up activities went from being blatantly bogus to bizarre on July 31, 1995 when U. S. District Judge Carl B. Rubin lamely dismissed my case against attorneys Chesley and Mezibov at 4:22 P.M. A little over fifty and one-half hours after his dismissal of my lawsuit that erroneously absolved these corrupt attorneys from federal prosecution, U. S. District Judge Carl B. Rubin died from excruciatingly painful cancer, just after 7 p.m. on August 2, 1995. On top of the implausibility of his dismissal, the decision was made that much more suspect when I considered the amount of mind-altering drugs that are typically administered to dying cancer patients.

Sandy and I knew that the truth of the matter was that Judge Rubin attempted to erase the telling trail of federal incrimination that led from his personal friend and synagogue member, Stan Chesley, to the doorstep of President Bill Clinton. We also knew that, as Chesley's ruse had been exposed, and as Chesley had no other way out, Judge Rubin attempted to rescue Chesley from the jaws of certain federal prosecution by making an ultimate deathbed decision that was unapproachable, thereby letting Chesley off of the hook. What made this dismissal even more questionable was that his last signature differed drastically from his previous signatures—if it was his signature at all!

During the same month that a little-known-of woman, Monica Lewinsky, held President Bill Clinton's hand at his birthday party, I made a tactical legal move to smoke over the feds to see if they would come to my aid. On August 2, 1995, I released the only two federal defendants from my lawsuit by filing a "Motion to Voluntarily Dismiss Defendants John Riordan and Stephen Ong," who worked as federal employees for HUD and the Federal Reserve Bank, respectively.

With this move, I eliminated the possible conflict of prosecution by the U. S. Sixth Circuit Court against any other feds. Giving them one last chance to exonerate themselves, this was a trial run on my part to see if the Sixth Circuit Court would have come to my aid when all possible barriers were eliminated. Since they did not, their actions confirmed what I had known all along.

However, on August 9, 1995, I made an interesting observation. On this date, two powerful federal government attorneys, U. S. Attorney for the Southern District of Ohio, Edmund A. Sargus, Jr., and his inferior, Gerald F. Kaminski, filed a motion in U. S. Judge Weber's court expressing their interest in releasing the federal employees from my lawsuit. The motion was captioned "Federal Defendants' Response To Plaintiffs' Motion To Dismiss Defendants John Riordan and Stephen Ong."

When they filed this motion, one did not have to be a brain surgeon to figure out that this should have been the point where the federal government's U. S. Attorney's office should have also been interested in the eye-catching U. S. Treasury theft issues that were attendant to my lawsuit. As I was also aware that Edmund A. Sargus Jr. had written to me more than eight months prior to this date informing me that he had forwarded my information to the FBI, the silence from the FBI and the U. S. Attorney's office was made that much more deafening.

On the same date of August 9, 1995, I made it absolutely plain to U. S. Judge Weber that there was no legal reasoning for the 124 West Ninth Street federal crimes to be left unpunished. It was on this date that I filed a "Motion to Indict Defendants City of Cincinnati and Provident Bank." With all of the incriminating evidence of U. S. Treasury theft involvement that I had filed in his court against these two defendants, I drove home the point that clear nexuses of complicity existed not only between those two, but between the remaining Defendants as well.

Leaving the federal court no quarter to hide, I put forth no-nonsense legal arguments that justified the indictments of all of the defendants. Even more, through reiteration, I enumerated the federal laws that are contained in sections 1001, 1010 and 1012 of Title 18, U.S.C., which prohibit Fraud upon the federal government and HUD. In part, I said to U. S. Judge Weber, "... as this Court should be four square against allowing the misappropriation, misuse and cover-up of federal tax dollars by these Defendants to go on unimpeded, there is a directed legal imperative here: this Court should hand down indictments to the City of Cincinnati and Provident Bank, as specified under Article V of the U. S. Constitution."

In making my point crystal clear, I told U. S. Judge Weber that, "instead of federal legal efforts continuing to be directed against the Plaintiffs [Sandy and I], the efforts of the U. S. Attorney's office and this Court should now be more appropriately directed against the City of Cincinnati and Provident Bank. Accordingly, as per the aforementioned sections of Title 18, U.S.C., they should be indicted on the following counts: tricking, scheming against, falsifying records to, and making fraudulent statements to the government of the United States. As well, they should be indicted for illegally influencing the actions of HUD and making, passing, uttering a and publishing false statements to federal departments."

The inability of the U. S. Sixth Circuit Court to publicly lay a false scent to befog its flagrant duplicity became more unmistakable. Also on August 9, 1995, I kept hammering away at the federal court's weakness in hiding the truth by filing the latest in a continuing succession of motions captioned, "Fourth Request For Motion For Affirmative Relief and Provisional Remedy Due To HUD Fraud and Motion For An Effective Court Appointed Attorney." The first three of these pressure-generating motions were filed on May 19, July 24, and August 2, 1995.

Try as it did, the U. S. Sixth Circuit Court was not able to outflank Sandy and I because we kept giving them different looks that they could not handle. Armed with incriminating evidence that allowed us to remain dynamic as moving targets, we kept hitting them back with incriminating evidence that exposed their criminality. Our strategy was that the best defense was a good offense. On the heels of the national public frenzy surrounding the O. J. Simpson trial, my financial status made me legally null and void, but my evidence was substantive and beyond reproach.

As September of 1995 rolled around, the White House way of thinking began to visibly parallel the 124 West Ninth Street cover-up motives when President Bill Clinton said, "I can't focus on a thing but the next fund-raiser. Hillary can't, Al can't—we're all getting sick and crazy because of it."

In spite of the unidentified U. S. Department of Justice source that was continuing to disregard the incriminating evidence that I had properly presented, unlike Clinton, I did not become sick and crazy because of the invigorating successes that I was having in exposing the U. S. Sixth Circuit Court's misdeeds. However, the federal government-wide shutdown against me continued unabated.

By September 7, 1995, and after a prolonged six-month response time, the U. S. Justice Department responded to me saying, "there was no basis for action" by them. As was typical of the Queen syndrome cover-up paradigm, my complaint was, again, suspiciously funneled back into HUD.

Like a guillotine lopping off my right arm, the hidden controls of the U. S. Sixth Circuit Court continued to sever my efforts to obtain fair jurisprudence by maintaining its criminal grip into the State of Ohio. On September 14, 1995, the Ohio Civil Rights Commission reached the following conclusion: "Based on the evidence obtained during the investigation, the Commission has determined that probable cause does not exist to believe that a discriminatory housing practice has occurred."

While the HUD/Queen Treasury theft plotters rallied to exact revenge upon us, and even though they had hobbled our ability to fight, they could not vanquish our fighting spirit. However, as scars from repetitive federal hacks to our minds and bodies revealed a group of battle-impaired individuals that limped through a multiplicity of attempts to legally butcher them, my immediate family struggled to come to terms with the lengthy traumas that we had to wearily withstand. All that we could do was to endure.

The destruction of our downtown real estate business took a toll on all of our psyches, as a hard-earned record of successful real estate development was expunged under the great weight of the Queen. As we had been forced into bankruptcy, not only did I have to hand over to the U. S. Bankruptcy Court $10,000 that I had recently inherited from a dearly departed relative, but the debilitating effects of a wrongly superimposed bad credit standing had a pernicious effect on our ability to move forward.

Nothing drove this point home more than the circumstances surrounding an instance where Sandy and I attempted to buy an automobile. In going to a friend of ours who sold new cars, we were not surprised when we found out that we were being financially blackballed by Cincinnati's lending institutions. At the same time, as my name became mud in the Queen, I faced a double whammy in not being able to land decent employment opportunities.

The federal government legal shutdown only intensified against me. As the White House put pressure on HUD's headquarters to silence me, on October 27, 1995, Patrick J. Neri, HUD Assistant Inspector General for Investigation, wrote to me regarding my most recent letter to President Bill Clinton. Neri said, "After the evaluations of HUD and the U. S. Attorney's office, we have not found any substantiation to support an investigative effort into your allegations." He also lied by saying that the City of Cincinnati's RRP had been terminated.

The stress and emotional hardship on my family became an all-consuming trudge through very difficult circumstances. In our agonizing search for a place to live, we humiliatingly paid rent in a place that we knew should have been ours. With a steady cadence, the cruel clock ticked menacingly against us in a trial and tribulation that tested the mettle of our souls. While we were holed-up in limbo as transient victims of socio-economic foul play, the day of punishment speedily arrived when our home was amputated from us, thereby, putting us out into the streets.

On October 28, 1995, I was forced to move my family out of our Hitchcock Drive residence into a rotten and stale smelling rental house that left a lot to be desired. On top of having to contend with a putridity of smells, our new place of residence had an infestation of roaches and spiders in the house and, as we would later find out, noisy and stinky raccoons, opossums and barn owls in the attic.

It wasn't until the inside of our new place of residence was beset with hundreds upon hundreds of swarming flies that we discovered the source of the rotten smell that was driving us insane. We found out that the flies were entering into the house through collapsed heating ducts after leaving from the rotting carcasses deposited by the large wildlife that had inhabited the attic. But, it was the death-grip knocking and banging combined with the guttural noises of struggle and death—at all hours of the night—that made the sounds coming from the attic extremely annoying at best, and eerily unsettling at worst.

By November 3, 1995, the FBI sent a letter to me in response to a letter that I had sent to FBI Director Louis Freeh on August 24, 1995. In this letter, the FBI said, regarding my 124 West Ninth Street HUD project, "there is no indication that a violation of federal law falling within the investigative purview of the FBI." In typical bureaucratic form, they told me to "furnish pertinent details to a representative of our Cincinnati Office." Too, like everyone else who was involved in 124 West Ninth Street's cover-up, the FBI conveniently said that it was sending a copy of my correspondence to HUD's Inspector General's Office in Washington, D. C.

On November 6, 1995, having no place else to run with his shaky conspiratorial defense, U. S. District Judge Herman J. Weber ordered the dismissal of my 124 West Ninth Street HUD Treasury theft federal lawsuit, thereby denying me a trial in open court and violating my constitutional right to a fair trial. As it was a specious decision, Judge Weber framed an incorrect basis in ruling against me.

His trick was in his technique. First, he hoodwinked the American taxpayers by totally avoiding the federal laws that were designated to handle the type of Treasury theft that occurred at 124 West Ninth

Street. Secondly, he misled the public by attempting to establish a bogus basis of legal justification that was designed to appear to be correct. Not to be defeated, Sandy and I licked our wounds, prayed for strength and calculated our next move, as we had developed a strong penchant for fighting the bevy of crooks that existed in the U. S. Sixth Circuit Court.

On the next day, Cincinnati City Hall elections made Roxanne Qualls the Mayor again. The other City Councilpeople were as follows: Bobbie Sterne; Nick Vehr; Dwight Tillery; Tyrone Yates; Charles Winburn; Todd Portune; Phil Heimlich; and Minette Cooper.

On December 5, 1995, Sandy and I appealed to the U. S. Court of Appeals for the Sixth Circuit in Cincinnati. As decisions from this court can overrule decisions from the lower district court and affect cases from Ohio, Kentucky, Michigan and Tennessee, this court is one of 13 federal circuit courts, the second-highest system in the land. Its rulings usually stand because the United States Supreme Court reviews so few cases.

In January of 1996, Phase II of the Garfield Place housing project, Greenwich on the Park, was completed on the old Milner Hotel site. Resting only seventy-two inches from 123 West Ninth Street's property line, and smaller than Phase I, The Gramercy on the Park, and four stories high, Phase II occupied the smaller site on the opposite side of Garfield Place, from Elm Street to the east side of the old Milner Hotel site. The long, narrow and almost entire half-block on which it rests fronts on Piatt Park while its back was treated as a mews giving onto the brick alley that separated it from 123 West Ninth Street known as Weaver Place.

Also, by early 1996, people close to the President continued to give closer indications of his affiliation to 124 West Ninth Street's HUD Treasury theft crimes. It was during this time that Clinton deputy chief of staff Evelyn Lieberman recommended that White House aides shorten Oval Office briefings with Clinton so he'd have time for more coffees with donors and prospective donors. "Political fund-raising is critical," she wrote. During the same time, Hillary Clinton testified before a grand jury about missing Rose law firm billing records.

The stark contrast of our new residence was too much for my youngest daughter to quietly take. On January 9, 1996, the emotional stress on Stephanie, my baby, surfaced when she could not sleep and cried because she missed the old home place. Seeing the effect that it had or her was a hammer to my heart that hit hard. My Hitchcock Drive residence was the only home that my girls had ever known.

In their childlike perceptions, they had intimate relationships with their swing set, their sandbox, the fenced-in yard that their puppy and cat ran around in, and knew practically every rock, tree, nook and cranny on that property. As our Hitchcock Drive home symbolized love to them, the forceful removal of us from it was their first experience in life were love was not only stolen, but was taken away without them ever having a chance to properly say goodbye.

Even though I had a strong feeling that President Clinton was somehow involved with the 124 West Ninth Street cover-up, it was very difficult for me to directly tie him into these federal crimes. When I saw his January 23, 1996, State of the Union Address, I stared into his eyes through my television set and did not like what I was seeing. I saw a ruthless politician whose primary concern—even before the elimination of U. S. Treasury theft—was fund-raising. That was not a good sign for America.

When March arrived and the firing of the White House travel employees was added to a federal probe, that situation did not look good for the nation either. But when President Bill Clinton met with one of my former federally appointed court attorneys, Stan Chesley, for a private fund-raiser lunch at Cincinnati's premier restaurant, the Maisonette, on March 26, 1996, things looked even worse for the country in view of the fact that Bill Clinton had just recently appointed Stan Chesley's wife, Susan Dlott, as a federal judge in the U. S. Sixth Circuit Court.

In sheer defiance, I kept on swinging back against a more clearly defined conspiracy. In the beginning of April, 1996, I filed an appeal of the Sixth Circuit's lower court ruling in the Sixth Circuit Court of Appeals. In May, I filed an "Appellant's Brief and Motion for a Court Appointed Attorney" in the same court.

May was also a month where cash and corruption problems continued to plague the Clinton White House. Even the DNC was irritated about competing with Clinton's money-hungry fundraising campaign. DNC official Faith Brown complained, "There is only so much money we can raise from the same people. If the president wants more money from DNC donors, the DNC will raise less." Also during the same month, there were fraud and conspiracy convictions of former Arkansas Governor Jim Guy Tucker and former Clinton business partners Jim and Susan McDougal.

In June of 1996, there was more of the same, as an investigation expanded into how 700 background files of former White House employees ended up with Clinton aides. It was also during this month that Susan McDougal was jailed for contempt because she would not answer grand jury questions.

Sandy and I were not chastened because our attempts for getting justice were forced to a screaming halt by suffocating impediments. Instead, we were trouble-plagued because of our occlusion from the jurisprudence of the American Constitution.

Like the awareness that one can have when seeing the rippling wake from a circling protuberance made by a large underwater creature in a mirrored sea, Sandy and I knew that something hidden and of substantial size was moving out there, denying us the protective harbor of federal protection. In fishing for an answer as to who was ultimately responsible for causing us so much pain and agony, Sandy and I attentively analyzed the churning factual horizons that were all around us, while studying the political currents of the day.

In so doing, we definitively identified the underlying reason that was the sole cause of our illegally calculated demise. By establishing an unquestionable 124 West Ninth Street criminal link directly to the doorstep of the White House, Sandy and I found out that we were being severely punished because of the threat that we posed to the most powerful man in America. After we had presented to the federal court volumes of incriminating evidence that implicated him, like the stealthy striking of tuna bait by an ascending deep sea predator, it became plain to us that we were being hit and crippled by the bite of United States President Bill Clinton.

The Queen's 123 West Ninth Street

The Queen's 124 West Ninth Street

Contract No: 25X0130

Property Address: 124 West Ninth Street

U.S. DEPARTMENT OF HOUSING
AND URBAN DEVELOPMENT

AND

CITY OF CINCINNATI

PART I

OF

RENTAL REHABILITATION PROGRAM
FUNDING AGREEMENT
FOR THE REHABILITATION OF ELEVEN OR FEWER
DWELLING UNITS
BETWEEN
THE CITY OF CINCINNATI

AND

William R. and Sandra W. Kiah

OWNERS

The front page of the federally-binding HUD Rental Rehabilitation Program contract which serves as an evidentiary base to show that the Bill Clinton White House illegally used its power to protect Provident Bank's billionaire Lincoln Bedroom-contributing owner, Carl Lindner, Jr., from federal prosecution.

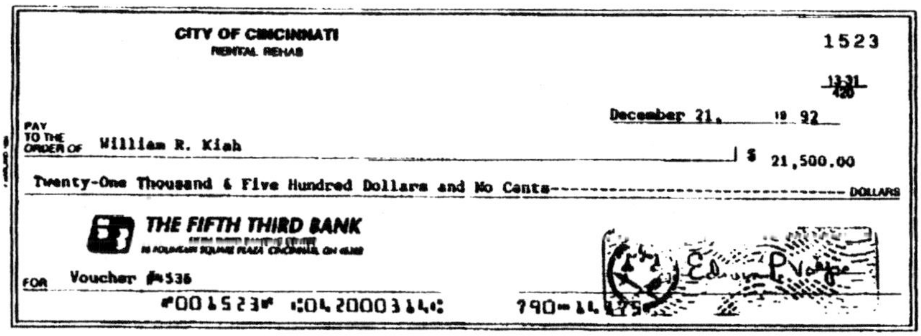

CITY OF CINCINNATI
RENTAL REHAB
1523
13-31/420
December 21, 19 92
PAY TO THE ORDER OF William R. Kiah $ 21,500.00
Twenty-One Thousand & Five Hundred Dollars and No Cents DOLLARS
THE FIFTH THIRD BANK
FOR Voucher #536
⑈001523⑈ ⑆042000314⑆ 790-14375⑈

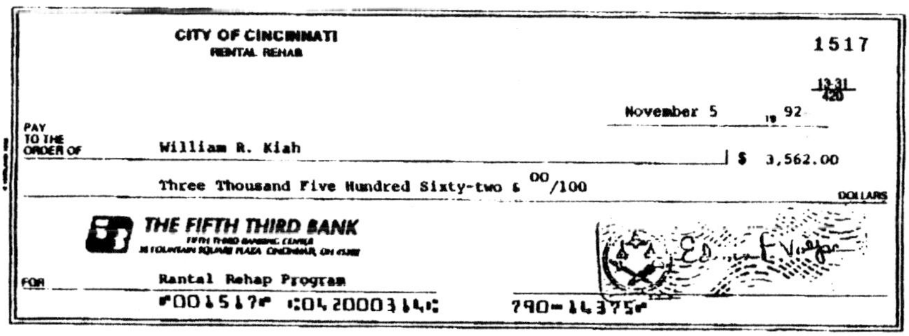

CITY OF CINCINNATI
RENTAL REHAB
1517
13-31/420
November 5 19 92
PAY TO THE ORDER OF William R. Kiah $ 3,562.00
Three Thousand Five Hundred Sixty-two & 00/100 DOLLARS
THE FIFTH THIRD BANK
FOR Rantal Rehap Program
⑈001517⑈ ⑆042000314⑆ 790-14375⑈

Contrary to what former United States President Bill Clinton's HUD reported to the U. S. Senate, these two checks totaling $25,062 consisted of the entire amount of federal HUD funds that William R. Kiah received. (See copy of letter from HUD on page 160.)

U. S. Department of Housing and Urban Development
Washington, D.C. 20410-8000

MAY 3 1994

OFFICE OF THE ASSISTANT SECRETARY FOR
CONGRESSIONAL AND INTERGOVERNMENTAL RELATIONS

Honorable Howard M. Metzenbaum
United States Senate
Washington, DC 20510-3502

Dear Senator Metzenbaum:

Thank you for your letter of March 24. 1994, on behalf of your constituent, Mr. William R. Kiah, of Cincinnati, Ohio. Mr. Kiah claims Federal funds have been misused and banking regulations violated, and requests a formal investigation of funds he received for the renovation of a building he owns in the central business district of Cincinnati.

The Department of Housing and Urban Development's (HUD) Office in Columbus was contacted regarding this matter because the City of Cincinnati is under the jurisdiction of that office. Based on information provided by the Columbus Office, the assistance Mr. Kiah received from the City was through the City's Rental Rehabilitation Program (RRP). The Housing and Urban-Rural Recovery Act of 1983 amended the United States Housing Act of 1937 by adding Section 17, which authorized the RRP. The National Affordable Housing Act, signed November 28, 1990, terminated the RRP as of October 1, 1991, but provided that grantees may use funds they received prior to that date.

The RRP provides funds on a formula basis to cities of 50,000 or more, as well as to urban counties, eligible consortia of local governments, and States. The program is intended to encourage the maximum use of private sector resources and the minimum public sector subsidy for rehabilitating rental properties. Consequently, the authorizing legislation included limits on the total amount of subsidy that each project can receive, i.e., there are limits on the amount of RRP funds that can be used per unit based on the number of bedrooms in the unit but the amount of RRP funds in a project cannot exceed 50 percent of the total eligible rehabilitation costs. The program operates with considerable decentralization in program administration, giving local officials broad discretion in determining the types of subsidy they make available to rental property owners.

Mr. Kiah received $45,000 in RRP funds from the City of Cincinnati in September 1992, and the rehabilitation of the property began in October 1992. Subsequently, due to cost overruns, Mr. Kiah sought additional funds from both the City and

This is page one of a three-page letter from the federal Department of HUD's William J. Gilmartin in the early stages of 124 West Ninth Street's U. S. Treasury theft cover-up. The bottom paragraph shows how former President Bill Clinton's HUD intentionally deceived a United States Senator (a felony) by not only misreporting the amount that William R. Kiah received from the City of Cincinnati, Ohio, but by also greatly under-emphasizing the significance of HUD's legal responsibility for the cost overruns of their making.

ALEXANDER / CAMABEAM & ASSOCIATES

Architecture • Planning • Development

AFFIDAVIT

I, Bertram Charles Alexander, attest and swear to the fact that I was under contract with the Department of Neighborhood, Housing & Conservation to provide architectural consultant services only, to various clients within the Rental Rehab Program. In this particular situation, Mr. Kiah was one of those clients.

Under my regular contractural duties, it was only my responsibility to:

1. Conduct an initial inspection of the complete building.
2. Prepare a preliminary Scope of Work.
3. Take photos of the building's elevations.
4. Develop a cost estimate for comparison purposes.
5. After acceptance of the above, NHC authorities direct me to prepare specifications.
6. Once bidding tasks are complete, I assist in the evaluation of the Owners' three competitive bids.
7. Make recommendation only, on Owner's selected contractor and bid pricing.
8. Attend the rehab loan closing and pre-construction conference (these usually happen simultaneously).

NOTE: Relative to items 1, 2, 4, 6 and 7, I was restricted from fulfillment of my regular duties by circumstances beyond my control.

I further attest that no where throughout this process did I nor do I have any legal authority to sign off on any rehab contracts, as may have been implied.

Furthermore, no contractural forms are required for me to sign, in order to officially approve or disapprove any rehab loan, throughout; this program process. The only place where a signature is required, occurs on the Certificate for Application for Payment, which essentially establishes the contractor's right to be paid an agreed upon amount. (Note that the loan had been approved by NHC before this process can even take place).

I further state that I was not allowed the opportunity to fulfill my standard duties, sequentially, to a logical and typically expected completeness level. Because of this, lack of proper procedures, I never felt comfortable with the rapid series of events that eventually lead to a "loan closing" on this case, and had verbally stated such more than once.

I, Bertram Charles Alexander to the best of file notes and memory attest that all the above statements are true and accurate.

Subscribed and sworn to before me this 11th day of July, 1994.

Kay L. Crise - My commission expires March 17, 1998

Notary Public State of Ohio

Member American Institute of Architects

2439 highland avenue • cincinnati, ohio 45219 • (513) 421-8345

Federally-suppressed United States Sixth Circuit Court evidence showing that the Queen illegally misused (a felony) HUD Treasury funding at 124 West Ninth Street.

EXHIBIT "B"

John R. Wirthlin (#0031526)
Attorney for The Provident Bank

IN THE UNITED STATES DISTRICT COURT
FOR THE SOUTHERN DISTRICT OF OHIO
WESTERN DIVISION

WILLIAM R. KIAH, ET. AL.,	:	CASE NO. C-1-94-150 J. Spiegel
Plaintiffs	:	
-v-	:	
THE PROVIDENT BANK, ET AL.	:	
Defendants	:	SUPPLEMENTAL AFFIDAVIT OF GEORGE FULFORD
	:	

: : : : : : : : : : : : : : : :

Now comes George Fulford and, being first duly cautioned and sworn, states as follows:

1) I have personal knowledge of the matters stated herein and am competent to testify hereto.

2) I am an Assistant Vice President with The Provident Bank Commercial Mortgage Loan Department.

3) The loan made by The Provident Bank to William R. Kiah and Sandra W. Kiah, which is the subject of their Complaint, was not part of, or approved by, any federally assisted or sponsored program.

4) Said loan was solely between The Provident Bank and William R. Kiah and Sandra W. Kiah and was not subject to any requirement by any federally assisted or sponsored program.

5) The Provident loan to Mr. and Mrs. Kiah was a commercial transaction, not a consumer transaction, and was not insured through the FHA.

Further affiant saith naught.

George Fulford

Federally-suppressed United States Attorney General Janet Reno Justice Department evidence that has been withheld in Cincinnati, Ohio's U. S. Sixth Circuit Court. It shows that billionaire Lincoln Bedroom guest Carl Lindner, Jr.'s bank, Provident, perjured itself (a felony) to conceal its direct involvement in the theft, misuse and cover-up of HUD Treasury tax dollars at the Queen's 124 West Ninth Streeet.

Chapter 7

Bananagate

"It is to law alone that men owe justice and liberty. It is this salutary organ of the will of all which establishes in civil rights the natural equality between men. It is this celestial voice which dictates to each citizen the precepts of public reason, and teaches him to act according to the rules of his own judgment and not to behave inconsistently with himself. It is with this voice alone that political leaders should speak when they command."

—Jean Jacques Rousseau

Like objects being pulled to the center of a celestial body by gravity, the weighty pieces of the 124 West Ninth Street cover-up puzzle started to come together in a collusively logical fit. At the middle of this criminal convergence, I could see that President Bill Clinton steadily dragged in a galaxy of 124 West Ninth Street cover-up conspirators. I knew that it was due largely to his success at hiding his federally indictable participation in the cover-up at my illegal HUD project that he was elected to his second term of office on November 5, 1996.

Although the White House was besieged with many other legal troubles, my resolute efforts continued to produce positive results by exposing a major ramification of Bill Clinton's subterranean compulsion to receive illegal federal campaign finance contributions. While the implications of my resistance went well beyond the potential damage of most other White House scandals that peppered his presidency, a more troubling scenario emerged for the American people as Bill Clinton increasingly used the full weight of his office to illegally hide 124 West Ninth Street's crimes. More significantly, it represented the highest level of America's loss of morality.

After growing up in a relatively secure period in America, it is the majority of my generation, the post-World War II " baby boomers" (born 1943-60), who has seen the dazzling optimism of our youth, with the strong promise of a better life, erode from underneath us. In coming up, we generally believed that you could achieve what you wanted if you went to school and worked hard. But a strange thing happened on the way to the 1990's. After President Kennedy was assassinated—a President that symbolized hope for America, seemingly, one event after another marred the country that Americans thought we were going to have.

I could see that a litany of problems had beset the nation: the concerns of job insecurity from corporate layoffs and downsizing; meteoric divorce rates; uneasiness about retirement; the working poor; unsafe streets; ubiquitous drug use; dead-end jobs; babies having babies; corporate welfare; increased taxes; a lower standard of living; the denigration of family values and the like could be seen on the faces of most Americans. While the moral leadership in the White House nose-dived, I irately watched as America was being ruled over by unscrupulous politicians who primarily had money on their minds. The moral strength of America showed real signs of collapse.

On January 20, 1997, Bill Clinton again put his hand on the Bible and swore an oath to God to "preserve, protect and defend the Constitution of the United States." But, this time, as I was America's number one believer that Clinton was nothing more than a tricky political opportunist whose hunger for money made his primary focus that of using his office to generate cash at any cost, I knew that defending the Constitution was the furthest thing away from what he was actually doing.

I occupied a rare position of being able to watch, unobstructed, a master of deception at work. With reasonable certainty, I also felt that the trail of federal incrimination had led to his doorstep, but the only evidence that I could produce was not as plausible as I wanted it to be. As I continued to plaster the Internet and telephone lines with gobs of faxes and email messages to U. S. Senators and Congressman, I sat back and patiently waited, hoping that a mistake would be made that I could capitalize on.

It was conventional wisdom that President Bill Clinton had been aggressively seeking financial contributions and, like most politicians, had put the influence of his office up for sale as his beleaguered presidency was strapped for cash. With more energy than a cyclotron, his administration pushed the donor envelope to near overload proportions. To the displeasure of many dyed-in-the-wool Americans who believed that the White House was sacrosanct, the Lincoln Bedroom, like a room at Motel 6, was used by Bill Clinton to make fast money, and lots of it.

According to a study for the Cable News Network (CNN) by a political investigation organization known as the Campaign Study Group, President Bill Clinton's guests in the Lincoln Bedroom gave a total of at least $5.4 million to the DNC during 1995 and 1996. The CNN study found 24 overnight White House guests who gave $100,000 or more to the DNC. CNN's $5.4 million figure did not include money given to the Democratic Congressional Campaign Committee, the Democratic Senatorial Campaign Committee, or any state party committees. *Mother Jones* magazine listed the Queen's Carl H. and Edyth Lindner of Chiquita Brands International and the American Financial Group, as being in the fourth position from the top of American campaign contributors.

On Tuesday, February 25, 1997, amidst a gathering political tempest that had embroiled the Democratic Party in controversy due to questionable fund-raising activities, the administration of President Bill Clinton released more than 500 pages of documents to a House committee investigating 1996 campaign contributions. Among the papers: a list of 938 who stayed overnight in the Lincoln Bedroom at the White House. Once I saw Carl Lindner's name on this list, the Bananagate scandal of 124 West Ninth Street was born and began to breathe life because of his nickname "Mr. Chiquita Bananas."

The Lincoln Bedroom sleepover list was the proof that I had been hoping for. It was the missing link that connected President Clinton to the receipt of 124 West Ninth Street's illegal quid pro quo campaign financing. It was the corroborating evidence needed to establish that President Clinton was ground zero for deeply illicit U. S. Treasury theft cover-up activity that had originated at my HUD project. Moreover, it was the Holy Grail of logical federal incrimination against the top two people that I could identify who were ultimately responsible for the cover-up of the U. S. Treasury theft crimes at 124 West Ninth Street.

Even though the White House did not provide the sleepover dates, I was still able to see to the end of the road where Bananagate was cast naked upon the earth, spilling the truth of the criminal relationship between the cash-starved Bill Clinton and the behind-the-scenes moneyman who had an ironfisted rule of the Queen, Carl H. Lindner, Jr. As the scrutinizing eyes of the nation began to focus in on his past campaign finance activities, public rancor began to build against President Bill Clinton's use of the Lincoln Bedroom for quid pro quo purposes.

The public question became not *if* President Clinton criminally misused this nation's highest office, but *how* he misused it. In the same vein, my private question became not *if* I could show that President Clinton misused the Lincoln Bedroom, but, with the power of the federal government being used against me, *how* I could show that he misused it.

While the Lincoln Bedroom sleepover list gave most in the American public an introductory inkling into a distasteful scenario that I had long recognized, I knew that it did not tell the full story of an unquestionably repugnant event that had happened in America's White House. I knew that there was a hidden agenda, an illicit federal ligature that connected two willing sleeping chamber participants to an illegal control of the U. S. Justice Department. As my federal case files provided a necessary—but sickening—window into the remorseless defiling of the nationally revered bedroom of President Abraham Lincoln, I witnessed the implementation of President Bill Clinton's crafty dodge.

From my insider's perspective, it was not hard for me to see that this list truly reflected a sin against the American taxpaying public. I could plainly see through Clinton's smooth and twisted public version of what he said his closed-door bedside performance had been with Lindner to what this unholy relationship had actually begotten. It was this list that allowed me to see the connection between the President's wanton lust for money and the existence of a sneaky, hanky-panky private relationship with the receptive Carl H. Lindner, Jr. From this list, and through the vileness of his desecration, I could see that President Bill Clinton was providing a loophole, a means of escape from hurtful U. S. Treasury theft prosecution for Lindner, all in return for having received cash—something for something.

On the next day, Wednesday, February 26, 1997, John Solomon of the Associated Press reported from Washington, D. C. that President Clinton sanctioned a top campaign fund-raiser's memo that identified "our top 10 supporters"—four of whom even eventually spent the night at the White House. Among the four was Carl H. Lindner, Jr. who was listed among, as *The Cincinnati Enquirer's* Washington Bureau reported, "friends and supporters" in the list of 938 persons who stayed overnight at the White House in the Clinton years.

On the same day, R. W. Apple, Jr. of *The New York Times* reported that "Contributions have always been made with the understanding that favors could be expected to follow. In the Clinton White House, the nature of those favors was made far more specific than before, and the linkage more explicit."

Similar to the effect of what Dorothy's dog, Toto, did in the movie *The Wizard of Oz*, my recognition of Bananagate was as if a curtain had been pulled back to reveal a calculated White House illusion. Like Dorothy, who had been denied going home after being led on many wild-goose chases, the Lincoln Bedroom list conclusively allowed me to see the concealed linkage as to why I had been stopped from returning to the home and business of my American dream.

Like the Wizard of Oz when he was first revealed, it was the sleep-over list that made it crystal clear to me—for the first time—that it had been the President all along that had been at the top of the 124 West Ninth Street decision-making pyramid. Unlike the Wizard who, at the end of the story, made good on the hurt that he had caused, Bill Clinton continued to damage and trick Americans by looking them in the eyes and telling them that they had not seen what they saw. It was this Lincoln Bedroom sleepover list that proved that President Bill Clinton was the shrouded evil ruler who had no clothes.

While I did my very best to spread the news about the true nature of the favors that the incriminating White House list exposed, a slick President continued to fool American taxpayers into believing that his pockets had not been padded with Carl Lindner, Jr.'s illegal Lincoln Bedroom money. As Provident Bank's criminal seal of approval from the top of the American government became dangerously close to being uncovered by me, circumstances revealed that there was a perfect marriage of convenience for the President. While Clinton had a vested interest in protecting HUD, Clinton also protected Provident Bank from 124 West Ninth Street federal incrimination in return for large campaign contributions that he received from Lindner.

It was not a crime for Clinton to have received money from Lindner per se. But, when money was given to Clinton from Lindner in a quid pro quo federal campaign contribution, infamous felonies were committed.

From my perspective, the 124 West Ninth Street HUD fraud cover-up scrap turned into a bare knuckled, no holds barred brawl at the birth of Bananagate. Forced into a solitary fight, the only weapon that I had to bare evil and help right what was wrong was the faxing and email capabilities of my computer. As my protracted witnessing revealed how politics had negatively affected the rulings of the Sixth Circuit District Court, it would not have made any sense for me to have gone to the Supreme Court: as far as I could determine, both courts were one and the same. As a result, my computer became the only arrow that I had left in my quiver.

As I exposed the criminal relationship between President Clinton and Carl Lindner without the fear of legal retaliation, they were in the awkward position of not dreaming of filing lawsuits against me for libel or slander, lest they would have brought unwanted attention to their federal crimes by making me a cause celebre. While they were not able to answer to the hard evidence that I kept placing on the public's front burner, they made sure that high-up efforts were continued to discredit me. Regardless, I made every attempt to show the influence that the Queen's billionaire wielded.

I broadcasted that Carl H. Lindner, Jr. is one of America's wealthiest men who has a reputation for being a veteran right-wing tycoon. As a rock-ribbed Republican, he has been a big giver to the Republican Party for years. As his friends defend his political giving as merely the generosity of a public-spirited citizen, his critics rightfully suspect that his money buys him political access and influence. With the help of Bill Clinton, I knew that only his raw power allowed him to evade the federal criminal laws prohibiting the type of U. S. Treasury theft that occurred at 124 West Ninth Street.

Born in Dayton, Ohio, he dropped out of high school to help run the family's ice-cream store when his father became ill. With a head for figures and a knack for financial deals, Lindner built the business into a chain of stores known as United Dairy Farmers. Today there are over 200 such stores run by his brother Robert. Dairy-store profits have fueled Lindner's investments in financial institutions. In addition to controlling Chiquita, he is a former part owner of the Queen's largest newspaper, *The Cincinnati Enquirer*, the newspaper that was used to disparage me. After initially acquiring savings and loan companies, and then diversifying into the insurance business, he went into running a corporate empire known as the American Financial Group.

As chairman and chief executive of American Financial Group, Lindner presides over business assets worth over $14 billion. As the Chairman and CEO of the powerful American Financial Corporation, Carl H. Lindner, Jr. is also on the Board of Directors and is the majority stockholder of Provident Bancorp, Incorporated, which has as a subsidiary Provident Bank. It was Provident Bank that was the federally-required private co-financier that participated with the public sector's Queen in the completely bogus and federally doomed HUD building renovation project at 124 W. Ninth Street. Provident Bancorp, a banking company with 71 Cincinnati area offices, is a government contractor because it holds federal funds and issues U. S. savings bonds.

Lindner has made a name for himself on Wall Street as an astute investor. He has a reputation for "bottom fishing"—that is, buying a financially troubled or undervalued company at a bargain price and transforming it into a profitable enterprise. He was an important customer of "junk" bond king Michael Milken, who worked for the now-defunct investment-banking firm of Drexel Burnham Lambert.

In his projected role as a philanthropist, Lindner has been generous. His estimated contributions to various charities over the past 10 years are at $60 million. As Lindner gives heavily to political campaigns, and while he is a staunchly conservative Republican, he hedges his bets in national races by giving generously to both of America's largest political parties.

Lindner, his family, and business associates also make donations directly to politicians. Among them: $106,000 to George Bush's presidential campaigns in 1988 and 1992; and $172,500 to former Senator Robert Dole since 1980. In a field of the "top ten career patrons" of Senator Dole, Lindner ranks seventh, reports the Center for Public Integrity, a nonpartisan Washington public interest research group. Dole has also made frequent use of private jets owned by the Lindner family—twelve flights in 1995 alone, according to the Federal Election Commission.

Lindner's money makes him so powerful that members of the Clinton Administration have moved to help Chiquita open European markets to its bananas. For years, Chiquita grew lots of bananas throughout Latin America and was the largest supplier to Europe. Then in 1993, the European Union announced changes to its trade regulations on banana import quotas. Colombia and Costa Rica agreed to this new

European "banana plan" and were key to making it work. Chiquita said because of this new policy, which it claims violated trade laws, sales and profits dropped. Bringing American trade power to bear by steering massive amounts of money into the Democratic maw through two dozen state parties—thereby avoiding the scrutiny given federal campaigns, Chiquita trounced the Europeans in trade by controlling President Bill Clinton through the DNC.

For example, on April 12, 1996, the day after U. S. Trade Representative Mickey Kantor, Bill Clinton's 1992 campaign manager, asked the World Trade Organization (WTO) to take up Chiquita's grievance to clear the way for it to make a bundle. Within 24 hours, notes *Time* magazine, Mr. Lindner and his men began shoveling heavy money into Democratic coffers in two dozen states. The WTO ruled favorably for Chiquita.

On May 6, 1996, when it gave the most recent listing the nation's leading Republican all-star political donors, the "CBS Evening News" reported that Carl H. Lindner, Jr. used his formidable financial clout by giving the Republican National Committee $1,128,220, as he sought American trade protection for his Chiquita Banana Corporation. In this news broadcast, one woman summed-up what was happening to not only my immediate family, but America as well, when she commented, "They (Lindner) buy access. It gives the wealthy the power to participate and leaves the others behind."

But as a small American, I had a personal witnessing of Lindner's power to corrupt and destroy. Like a Polaroid picture, the true image of Carl H. Lindner, Jr. began to develop with the public showing of the Lincoln Bedroom guest list. Even though Lindner went to great lengths to portray the image of a mild-mannered philanthropic gentleman, deep down, I knew that he was a conniving, exceedingly dishonest and grumpy old Cincinnati, Ohio billionaire. As I laid severely injured in his wake, he threw copious amounts of money around, fistfuls at a time, like trinkets being tossed from a New Orleans, Louisiana Mardi Gras float.

In the face of damaging U. S. Court evidence which could have severely penalized his growing financial empire, I could see from my vantage point that the Queen's billionaire was continuing to flex his far-reaching political and financial muscle in order to avoid detection of extensive government fraud involvement by Provident Bank. Under

Lindner's control and knowledge, a full charge was ordered to wipe out my legal threat against exposing Provident Bank's white-collar federal criminal activity. The more that I stood in his way, the more Lindner kept throwing money at the 124 West Ninth Street cover-up.

Similarly, the more I learned about Carl H. Lindner, Jr., the more I realized the danger that I was involving myself in by fighting one of the richest men in America. Nothing may be more aware of this fact than when I found out about the reverberative legacy of Chiquita's involvement in Honduras' "banana war of 1990." I discovered that, in its attempt not to allow its monopoly of banana suppliers to be broken, Chiquita Brands International was so intertwined in the historic, economic and political power circles of Honduras that it was once named "the Octopus."

There were death threats; a train was derailed; and there were accusations of bribery and government coercion. Chiquita's main competition, the Irish Fruit Company (Fyffes Plc), had three boatloads of bananas that were barred from leaving Honduras, three others departed successfully. Once, two hundred armed men boarded the Casablanca and, under gunpoint, unloaded and destroyed 100,000 boxes of Fyffes' bananas that were valued at $3.6 million.

The conflict culminated one hot Saturday in April 1990, when three armed men and an attorney working for Chiquita tried to arrest Fyffes' business agent, Otto Stalinski, in his hotel. Stalinski escaped out a rear exit, and later came back with a vengeance, charging in Honduran civil and criminal courts that the world's largest banana producer masterminded an attempt to kidnap and murder him.

I came to find out that the Council on Hemispheric Affairs (CHA), a nonprofit research group, published a scathing report on the Stalinski episode. The CHA's report noted the disappearance of the first judge on the Stalinski case, missing documents and problems with the U. S. Embassy in Honduras, and it questioned Chiquita's role in the "ongoing scandal."

Likewise, it was my knowledge of the ongoing scandal in the Queen—and Carl Lindner's concomitant association to it—that made me cautiously aware of his determination to win at all costs. Even though I requested, and was denied, federal protection by the United States Court and the FBI, I moved forward in my opposition to Carl Lindner, as I had been too beat up to fear his power. Knowing that

America could not continue to survive as a country as long as this type of aristocratic thing went on, I continued to act on my beliefs, remaining steadfast in standing up for my family and nation.

In the frantic pace of White House cover-up efforts, it was just as much who was not on the Lincoln Bedroom sleepover list as it was who was on the list. Prior to the release of this list by the White House, it was widely rumored that the Queen's Stan Chesley had slept at the Lincoln Bedroom in the Clinton White House. His sleepover was confirmed on Wednesday, February 26, 1997, when *The Cincinnati Enquirer* published "Clinton's List" of locals who stayed at the White House and reported, "Not on the list: local lawyer Stan Chesley." It was this blunder, this omission, this lie (another felony) to a House committee investigating 1996 campaign contributions that caused a further collapse of the President's legally weak house of cards.

Rather than distancing Chesley from the 124 West Ninth Street campaign finance illegalities of the President, Bill Clinton's feint backfired. In attempting to avoid detection of Carl Lindner's disgraceful back room sweetheart deal in the Lincoln Bedroom, Clinton foolishly blinked at Chesley's sleepover nondisclosure.

I realized what had happened and kicked my efforts into overdrive, further exposing a presidential faux pas that firmly linked Bill Clinton, Carl Lindner, Jr. and Stan Chesley to high government criminal activity that had emanated in the Queen. A dubious omission became a bigger Holy Grail of federal incrimination against the top three people who were ultimately responsible for the U. S. Treasury theft crimes against my family, my nation and me.

Chesley's unwise expurgation from the Lincoln Bedroom sleepover list only drew unwanted attention to a government investigation that posed a threat to President Bill Clinton's use of his office to sweet talk and sidestep. As a strategic criminal cover-up blunder, the conspicuous absence of Stan Chesley's name from this telling list only brought attention to his being there. Moreover, instead of hiding Stan Chesley's involvement in White House criminal activity, it revealed the magnum opus of all of President Bill Clinton's Machiavellian ruses. Capitalizing on this cover-up mistake by the President, I continued to set my telephone line on fire by calling widespread attention to this White House gambit that illegally called into play the infinite resources of the federal government's court system, HUD, FBI and IRS.

The 124 West Ninth Street cover-up was reminiscent of the political spying and dirty tricks of President Richard M. Nixon's handling of the Watergate scandal. In exposing Watergate, the American media—led by *The Washington Post*—created a sea change for United States journalism, an irreversible change for the better, by reporting information that helped oust a crooked president. As President Nixon changed forever the belief that Americans had in the presidency, I found it easy to draw many parallels between what had happened in the Watergate scandal and what was happening in President Bill Clinton's hidden Bananagate scandal.

By June 17, 1973, Nixon's waterloo had begun, as five burglars, loaded with electronic surveillance gear and employed by his reelection campaign, were arrested and charged with breaking into Democratic Party headquarters at the Watergate office complex in Washington. At that point, the Watergate break-in scandal was in full swing.

At first, President Nixon insisted that Watergate was the work of his enemies and stated, "I am not a crook." Then Nixon's press secretary dismissed the incident as "a third-rate burglary attempt." But the whole cover-up mushroomed into the biggest political scandal in American history, forcing a disgraced Nixon to become the first American president to resign. After he had tried many end-runs and power plays, it took two years and two months, from break-in to resignation, for Nixon's house of lies to collapse.

One of the charges against President Nixon was that he abused his power to cover-up what happened. President Clinton abused his power to cover-up what happened at 124 West Ninth Street. In Nixon's Watergate, the IRS was used against his enemies. In Clinton's Bananagate, the IRS was used to keep U. S. Treasury theft crimes hidden.

As President Nixon also tried to impede the due administration of justice, another charge against him was obstruction of justice. Clinton did the same. Just as a Senate investigation was conducted against Nixon, a House investigation was conducted against Clinton. As Donald Segretti performed for Nixon and there were resignations of top White House aides, Chesley performed for Clinton under similar conditions.

I was another Deep Throat that provided information that would have, otherwise, not been revealed. As hidden and dirty tricks were used to break into the Watergate office complex, my downtown office was also broken into. Just as surely as the Watergate cover-up was set into motion to hide high government crimes for political reasons, Bananagate was also instituted for the same reasons. As the Watergate cover-up happened at a time when the prestige of Nixon's presidency was waning, the Bananagate cover-up happened at a time when the prestige of Bill Clinton's presidency was waning. Most significantly, as Bananagate was one of the largest—if not the largest—threats to his presidency, my name had to be on a list of Clinton's enemies, like Nixon's enemies were during Watergate.

I saw how the cumulative effect of Clinton's past behavior was also impairing his presidency. On the heels of his "I did not inhale" scandal, his Jennifer Flowers scandal and the feeble justifications that he gave regarding the letters that were written allowing him to avoid the Vietnam War draft, the cumulative effects of President Bill Clinton's behavior generated a cloud of doubt that followed his every move. As a field of political land mines had already been set that made it treacherous for his administration to move forward, the 124 West Ninth Street scandal was added to a list of political conundrums that President Clinton struggled to put behind him.

In the Travelgate scandal, the political pressure that Bill Clinton faced put him into such a position that he could ill afford the incremental weight of Bananagate. Besides, on top of First Lady Hillary Rodham Clinton's role in these White House travel office firings, she faced obstruction of justice. Seeing how it took the U. S. Senate six months to get information from the White House regarding her Travelgate involvement, it was easy to understand why it was virtually impossible for a small American like myself to get requested 124 West Ninth Street information from the government.

In the Whitewater real estate scandal, just as it was in Bananagate, the obtaining of false financing was the main focus of controversy. As the Rose Law firm's Webb Hubbel was sent to prison, and as U. S. Treasury Department officials resigned because they lied to the federal government's Whitewater Committee, the Clinton administration avoided Bananagate like the plague.

As *The New York Times* had covered the Paula Jones story more than 39 times in 1994, the Clinton eschewal of Bananagate took on epic proportions. While independent counsel David Barrett had also investigated HUD Secretary Henry G. Cisneros to determine whether some of the 40 hours of taped conversations between Mr. Cisneros and his former mistress, Linda Medlar, were altered, President Clinton was in no mood for dealing with anything close to Bananagate.

Watergate did, however, have a favorable impact on campaign finance contributions. Watergate was the spur for what was actually a pretty good law that was passed in 1974 that limited contributions by individuals and political action committees. The end result was that the Federal Election Commission essentially created a new category of campaign funding called soft money, allowing political parties to accept unregulated and large donations if the money was not used for a specific candidate.

As soft money's impact started in 1988 and was huge in '92, by '96, both parties had raised and spent three times as much soft money as they did in 1992. As it exploded and destroyed the law that was passed in 1974, it made a mockery of it. As Bananagate attested to, I saw that both parties used it for purposes that are illegal.

The same type of questionable political contribution phenomenon existed in the politics of the Queen. From 1983 to 1994, Cincinnati City Council election spending went from where hardly no one spent more than $100,000 to where it was common to spend up to $500,000 for a single election campaign in pursuance of a two-year stint that paid between $40-45,000 per year; the math just did not add up. Essentially, as the Queen's Councilpeople increasingly depended on the deep pockets of Carl Lindner, Jr., his political control of them was a foregone conclusion. For all intents and purposes, Lindner was the Queen.

As the national campaign financing issue opened a fast-growing fissure in the Clinton dam of vulnerability, my faxing and emailing connections to the outside world reached a fever pitch. I would often times stay up all night getting the word out, hoping beyond hope that I could reach someone who had the will and the power to censure Clinton's criminal use of the White House. As the campaign finance issue ran neck and neck with the other scandals, more and more resources were erected against me to keep 124 West Ninth Street out of public view. In the meantime, President Bill Clinton increasingly came under attack from all sides.

As part of an ever-widening crescendo of citizen outrage against Clinton administration campaign financing activities, a nationally syndicated columnist for *The Fort Worth Star-Telegram*, Molly Ivins, wrote in *The Cincinnati Enquirer* on Sunday, March 2, 1997, "The problem is not who spent the night in the Lincoln Bedroom. That's the most innocuous OPO (obvious payoff) in recent history...Don't blow it [the Lincoln Bedroom investigation] by focusing on who got invited to coffee parties."

Ms. Ivins went on further to say, "Focus on who got what in terms of public money: subsidies, tax advantages, loopholes, special regulatory favors. That's where the rot is, and that's where the public interest is. The entire corrupt system costs the people of this country billions of dollars and is destroying our faith in democracy..."

In this editorial, Ms. Ivins not only thanked James Ring Adams, writing in *The American Spectator*, for an "interesting connection between Bob Dole and Carl Lindner of Cincinnati", but she also mentioned that Adams reported "that Mr. Lindner's interests have bumped up against federal regulation, including a complaint from the SEC in 1979, featuring Mr. Lindner's protégé Charles Keating as a co-defendant." Charles Keating, a Cincinnati, Ohio native, was sentenced in 1992 to 10 years in prison for defrauding depositors at (of all places) the Lincoln Savings and Loan Association. It is interesting to note that, for years, Carl Lindner's American Financial employed Charles Keating, as corporate counsel and executive vice president.

On Sunday, March 2, 1997, *The Cincinnati Enquirer* published yet another withering denunciation by nationally syndicated columnist William Raspberry of The Washington Post Writers Group. Speaking of President Clinton's use of the Lincoln Bedroom by political donors who stayed overnight at the White House, Raspberry said, "...the implications stink...The assumption has to be that they thought they were buying something besides bed and breakfast...this one comes too close to a straight-up deal: You want an audience with the President? A sleep-over? Show me the money."

Raspberry continued by writing, "What big givers—whether the Lincoln Room occupants or the foreign businessmen whose contributions fueled the scandal that barely preceded the present one—want is access. They think access is worth big bucks, and Mr. Clinton seems to share the opinion...But when it comes to this latest affair, enough is too much."

On the same day, *The Cincinnati Enquirer* lambasted President Clinton's statement that "The Lincoln Bedroom was never sold." by responding, "Of course not. It was rented with more turnover than a room in a skid-row flophouse. It was used for 'one nighters' by hundreds of donors who discovered that it takes an open wallet to open doors at the White House. This is just the most smelly sink-hole in a fund-raising swamp that needs to be drained by a special prosecutor, to find out if foreign policy and other favors were auctioned for donations."

Speculating about what President Abraham Lincoln might have said about renting his former office so fat cats and Hollywood hustlers could spend a night in the bed where his son Wille died, *The Cincinnati Enquirer* further stated, "To President Clinton: If you once forfeit the confidence of your fellow citizens, you can never regain their respect and esteem. It is true that you may fool some of the people some of the time; you can even fool some of the people all the time; but you can't fool all of the people all the time.'" This large newspaper concluded by saying, "Yes, it's crude to talk about who is in bed with the President, even figuratively speaking. But not as crude as prostituting our White House."

On March 6, 1997, United States Attorney General Janet Reno said on a CNN broadcast that she would only call for an independent council to investigate illegal campaign contributions "based on evidence, not politics." By this time, as I understood her role in the illegal protection that she was providing for her boss, I applied pressure on her by plastering the world's Internet with information that revealed her latest stratagem. I knew that she was secretly aware that her U. S. Justice Department case files had all of the evidence needed to remove President Bill Clinton from office due to flagrant federal campaign fund-raising violations that tied him to U. S. Treasury theft at 124 West Ninth Street. There was no doubt in my mind about the high stakes that were involved in her attempts to conceal Bananagate.

While Janet Reno was deeply involved in a federally indictable criminal conspiracy against me, there was another aspect of her cover-up efforts that revealed a more serious ramification of her hidden offenses against the American nation. She knew that I knew that my federal case files contained facts and evidence showing that U. S. government incrimination policy was illegally changed solely because of the secretive quid pro quo Lincoln Bedroom pillow talk between President Bill Clinton and the billionaire Carl H. Lindner, Jr. Contrary to what she had previously said, it was quite apparent to me that the real reason why no criminal investigation was conducted was due exclusively to the playing of politics by a corrupted Madame Attorney General.

Working hard to maintain his "Teflon Kid" image, even as his words rang more hollow with each passing day, President Clinton continued with his Lincoln Bedroom cover-up by saying in his March 7, 1997 news conference, "I don't believe that you can find any evidence of the fact that I have changed government policy solely because of contributions," and "They bought access—not influence."

By March 10, 1997, Attorney General Janet Reno had appointed four independent counsels to investigate Whitewater and other White House scandals. As she had become the Clinton administration's point man in hiding Bananagate, Reno continued to stand in the way by saying that the threshold for naming a special counsel—suspicions that a high-level official committed an illegal act—had not been reached.

In the meantime, while the evidence of Carl Lindner's illegal 124 West Ninth Street Bananagate campaign contributions were craftily excluded as a consideration by Reno, the White House strongly defended its aggressive money-raising activities. Regarding illegal campaign contributions, the White House insisted that President Clinton and other senior officials had only done what was necessary, and legal, to meet the Republican challenge in the 1996 elections.

Former White House chief of staff Leon Panetta acknowledged that the Democratic National Committee spent about $35 million in unlimited and unregulated soft money donations on television advertising to undergird the Clinton reelection campaign. But, even after I had contacted his office, he denied that campaign laws intended to keep party operations at arms length from the White House were violated.

The screws were tightened on Attorney General Janet Reno's Bananagate cover-up on March 13, 1997 when Republicans on the House and Senate judiciary committees urged her to take action that could lead to the appointment of an independent counsel to investigate President Clinton's 1996 campaign fund- raising abuses. Senate Judiciary Committee Chairman Orrin Hatch released a letter sent to Reno signed by all 10 Republicans who controlled the committee seeking an independent counsel. A similar letter was sent by Republicans on the House Judiciary Committee urging an outside prosecutor to delve into the growing allegations of improper campaign funds to Democrats to help President Clinton in the 1996 campaign.

Hatch, a Utah Republican, noted that the committee previously had not joined other calls in Congress for an independent counsel but added "recent developments over the past few weeks, however, have persuaded us that such an appointment is now necessary." His letter argued that an independent counsel appointed from outside of the administration was needed since a Justice Department probe alone could present a real or apparent conflict of interest. As Hatch had received many faxes and emails from me concerning Bananagate, just the consideration alone that I could have been included in his recent developments did my heart good.

At this time, a stooge task force from Reno's Justice Department that included 31 FBI agents was investigating the fund-raising matter including allegations the Chinese may have funneled money illegally into U. S. campaigns. "If the FBI truly is investigating these allegations, as is reported, and this investigation extends to high level Executive Branch officials, it raises an inherent conflict of interest," said the Hatch letter to Reno. Hatch suggested several areas of inquiry into the White House, including campaign fund-raising activities.

Earlier, Republicans on their own—and several Democrats as well—asked Reno to appoint a special prosecutor to investigate widespread reports of irregularities, nearly all of them involving improper, illegal or questionable donations to Democrats for the 1996 campaign. Seeing how it was her role to be out in the front of the Clinton administration to take Bananagate flack, I was reminded how the front line of my fight had taken a quantum leap from NHC's Wayne Chapman in the Queen to the President's Reno. As she continued to obstinately turn down investigative requests by continuing to say that there was no "specific, credible evidence" of a crime that would specifically trigger an independent probe, like clockwork, I began to flood cyberspace again with credible evidence of her participation in Bananagate's cover-up.

Under the independent counsel law, a majority of either Republican or Democratic members of the House or Senate judiciary committees could ask the attorney general to start the process toward naming an independent counsel. Once Reno would have gotten the request, she had to submit a report within 30 days on whether a preliminary investigation would begin and give her reasons.

The way that this whole process worked was that, if she decided to start a preliminary investigation, Reno would have another 90 days to decide if there were "reasonable grounds" to believe there should be a further investigation by an independent counsel. If she concluded there were reasonable grounds, she could apply to a special three-judge federal panel that could appoint an outside counsel. In this regard, I continued to use my limited power to disseminate torrents of federally indictable Bananagate information to practically any person, place or thing that I could get and email address or fax number for. By taking a shotgun approach with the hope of making someone, anyone, in the federal government aware of Bananagate, I regularly hit scattered federal agencies, departments and bureaucracies with information from my juiced up computer showing that there were reasonable grounds for an independent counsel.

Putting many Republicans who were also receiving illegal campaign contributions in a precarious position, Judiciary committee Democrats fired back. In their own letter to Reno, they said that if it was determined an independent counsel was warranted, the probe should include the "full scope of fund-raising irregularities" involving Republicans as well as Democrats.

On March 14, 1997, U. S. Congressman Bob Barr, R-Ga., asked the House Judiciary Committee to hold a meeting to discuss whether campaign fundraising activities by Clinton and Vice President Al Gore warranted impeachment proceedings. Feeling that I was no longer fighting Clinton by myself, I was encouraged, as it appeared that powerful people were joining in with me on warranted attacks against a crooked President.

The next day, I was encouraged even more when House Government Reform and Oversight Committee Chairman Dan Burton, the head of a House panel investigating allegation of illegal fund raising by the White House, vowed to get to the bottom of the mounting controversy and said he would soon issue more subpoenas. Burton told CNN's "Evans & Novak" television program he hoped that his investigations would not point to an impeachable offense by President Clinton.

The Indiana Republican told CNN "I quite frankly would hope that it would not come to that. I think it would be tragic for the country to have another problem like we had with Watergate. I would hope the president is not guilty of anything like that," Burton said. "If we get to the point where we find information like that, of course we'll have to take the proper actions. But I hope it never comes to that."

"We're going to be very diligent. We're going to be very fair but very thorough in getting to the bottom of this," Burton continued to say.

"I think it's important for the country. I think it's important for the presidency and I think it's important to show that the Congress is doing its job." He said further subpoenas would be issued "in the not too distant future", probably over the next three or four weeks.

It was as if the tide began turning in my favor when Clinton came increasingly under attack. On March 17, 1997, House Judiciary Committee Chairman, Henry Hyde, R-Ill., said he was having staffers look into impeachment laws. By this time, Rep. Bob Barr, R-Ga., had written to Hyde asking him to consider an inquiry into impeachment charges against Clinton because of "an alarming abuse of the political process." Senate Judiciary Committee Chairman Orrin Hatch's committee demanded that Attorney General Janet Reno seek appointment of an independent counsel to investigate Democratic fund raising activities. Sen. Arlen Specter, R-Pa., said Reno, as the ultimate head of the FBI which is investigating possible China connections to illegal fund-raising, may know more than she is telling the public and, as such, may have a conflict of interest. "I think at some point there is a dereliction of duty," he said on ABC's "This Week."

By March 19, 1997, according to *The Washington Post*, a former lobbyist for Pakistan accused Indiana Republican Representative Dan Burton, chair of the House committee investigating possible White House fund-raising abuses, the House Government Reform and Oversight Committee, of shaking him down for donations. In the Senate, a non-binding resolution was passed by a 55-44 vote, asking Attorney General Janet Reno to petition a federal court for a counsel to investigate possible illegalities during the 1996 presidential campaign.

As U. S. Attorney General Janet Reno continued to hide her recalcitrance to not let Bananagate come to the surface, like Watergate's Donald Segretti, she performed for President Clinton by supposedly initiating a Justice Department investigation. In so doing, she pledged to petition for a counsel if legal requirements were met: specific and credible evidence of a felony by high U. S. officials covered under law; or specific and credible evidence in cases involving conflict of interest. Even though I had both of these bases of legal requirements covered, Reno intentionally continued to ignore my federally incriminating evidence because it could have landed both her and her boss in jail.

It was on this same date that Bert Brandenburg, the attorney general's spokesman, executed an almost imperceptible shift in word play that was fast becoming a trademark in the Bananagate cover-up methodology. Correcting a glaring error that his boss had made on a March 6, 1997 CNN broadcast, Brandenburg said "The decision to ask for an independent counsel is based on the *law*, not politics." The American public was not aware of the way that he changed Janet Reno's words as she had recently said that she would call for an independent council to investigate illegal campaign contributions "based on *evidence*, not politics."

As I had provided a plethora of Bananagate evidence to the world via my computer, I knew that my little electronic box was working—smoking but working. I could see that, in a small but very real way, I was playing a part in forcing the Clinton administration's Justice Department to fall back on its legal ability to illegally control the American laws that it capriciously interpreted and ruled upon.

In response to Congressman Henry Hyde's ordering of a study of U. S. impeachment procedures in case a "smoking gun" emerged in the White House fund-raising affair, on Monday, March 24, 1997, I wrote a letter to the Senate Judiciary Committee Chairman, Senator Orrin Hatch. In this letter I wrote "Based upon the federally incriminating 'smoking gun' information against President Bill Clinton that I faxed to your office on January 31, February 10, February 20, and March 14, 1997, impeachment proceedings against the President are justified and should be initiated immediately."

I went on further to say, "I fervently desire to be subpoenaed to testify in front of Congress!....Contrary to what Congressman Henry Waxman, D-Calif., said on the CBS television show "Face The Nation," this is not about getting even for Watergate... this is about a basis in fact, evidence, and in law for Bill Clinton's impeachment. Moreover, this is about a smoking gun."

By April 6, 1997, the great national showdown between the Democrats and the Republicans practically brought the government to a standstill. Outside of the budget, congressional bipartisan pledges of action were forgotten amid campaign finance investigations. Votes by majority Republicans to exempt themselves from a burgeoning investigation of campaign-finance violations further strained congressional relationships and cast a shadow over attempts to reach bipartisan agreements on other important national issues. I, like most people in the United States, watched the political games that were going on at the expense of the American people.

A hands-off policy seemed to prevail, as campaign reforms could not gain enough backers. For all the flaws in the system, the unregulated gifts to political parties from individuals, corporations and unions, most of the people in the Senate and Congress saw the same redeeming virtue in leaving the laws alone: it was, after all, the system that got them elected. It became all too apparent that national politicians were not going to change a system that benefited them unless they felt they had no choice. In the middle of this rumpus sat my publicly unacknowledged Bananagate information that had been sent all over Congress.

As the leadership of both President Bill Clinton and House Speaker Newt Gingrich, R-Ga., was under intense fire, it was difficult for them to deal with tough issues. Mr. Gingrich, in the wake of his admitted ethics violations, had faltered in his bid to re-exert strong leadership. There were growing rumblings by Republicans about replacing him as speaker.

A little over one week later, while attempting to mount a defense against the Bananagate evidence that I had spread both far and wide, U. S. Attorney General Janet Reno faced a high-pressure deadline for a decision in the campaign funding controversy, as she was ready to defy a visible Republican clamor for an independent counsel. Saying she had yet to see the sort of specific, credible evidence of wrongdoing the independent counsel law requires, Reno hid Bananagate and continued to resist calls to seek a Watergate-style investigator to probe the fund-raising practices of President Clinton's Democratic Party and White House.

I remembered how the independent counsel law derived from the Watergate scandal of 1972-74 in which then-President Richard Nixon fired Archibald Cox, the first official appointed to investigate the abuse-of-power allegations that eventually drove Nixon from office. Just as Congress later established a system for appointing investigators independent of such influence and beyond retaliation, I knew that Janet Reno had risen from the sludge and was illegally blocking America's exercise of its rule of law by illegally protecting her boss, the President.

The evidentiary pressure that I placed on Janet Reno further exposed her role in the Bananagate cover-up, thereby, necessitating the urgent need of my elimination as a threat in her special domain, the U. S. Justice Department. On April 23, 1997, my federal case was politically thrown out of Clinton and Reno's U. S. Sixth Circuit Appeals Court when it affirmed the lower district court's ruling. In a total disregard of the rights of Americans to not have their Treasury robbed, the Appeals Court said, "Accordingly, plaintiffs' complaint was properly dismissed. For the foregoing reasons, plaintiffs' requests for counsel and for other relief are denied, and the judgment of the district court is affirmed."

As the U.S. Sixth Circuit Appeals Court's ruling was not consistent with existing U. S. laws and the Constitution, it was obvious that anti-constitutional powers were continuing to negatively dictate my legal destiny. It had not mattered that federal laws were on my side, nor did it matter that I had provided to the Sixth Circuit Appeals Court a preponderance of federally incriminating evidence proving a U. S. Treasury theft conspiracy. What did matter was the importance that I placed in making the American public aware of the fact that Bananagate had become a major problem for their interests, and that a top priority had been placed on me by the Bill Clinton Justice Department to not let my voice be heard.

In the face of the bad news, the good news was that, had I not mounted a strong opposition for such a long period of time prior to this latest higher-level ruling against me, undoubtedly, I would have been summarily ruled against long before then. As I had become proficient in the use of a graphical software package for my computer that allowed me to construct and publish a professionally formatted newsletter, I only intensified my emailing and faxing to continue my Bananagate exposure efforts.

By the Week of April 28, 1997, the national press was applying pressure to the Clinton White House by asking embarrassing questions about all of his scandals and comparing Whitewater to Watergate. President Clinton's old business partner, James McDougal, said he was tired of lying for the Chief Executive and the First Lay, Hillary Clinton. Mark Middleton was ready to tell all he knew about the money trail from the Lippo Group, an international financial conglomerate based in Indonesia. Kenneth Starr had just gotten a six-month extension on his Whitewater investigation to get Susan McDougal to sing. Starr was also positioned to call Hillary Clinton to testify again. Vice President Al Gore was losing his public credibility.

A 27-page report from Empower America had been released detailing hush money to the former Associate U. S. Attorney General Webster Hubbell. Hubbell, an early focus of special prosecutor Kenneth Starr's

Whitewater investigation, resigned his Justice Department post in early 1994 and pleaded guilty later that year to embezzling $400,000 from his former law partners in Arkansas and their clients.

The Empower America report also detailed how Clinton knew that illegal payments were made to Hubbell; the Chinese connection, including John Huang, the Commerce Department, and Lippo; Asian-related policy reversals tied to campaign contributions; money laundering; the role of Johnny Chung and his Chinese connections resulting in campaign contributions; ignoring warnings from the National Security Council when they called Chung a "hustler"; $450,000 in contributions to Clinton's Legal Defense Fund from Little Rock, Arkansas restaurateur Charles Yah Lin Trie; the Democratic National Committee's use of the CIA for Roger Tamraz, an international fugitive and major donor to the Democrats; Chinese arms merchants, Russian Mafia members, drug dealers having their pictures taken with Bill and Hillary Clinton; mishandling of the FBI files; House Democrats Jim McDermott and David Bonior's possible indictment for getting caught leaking Republican Rep. Newt Gingrich's tape to *The New York Times*; and, most importantly for me, illegal fund-raising at the White House.

In May of 1997, the Supreme Court ruled that the Paula Jones lawsuit could go ahead while Clinton held office. On May 6, 1997, I filed a "Petition for Rehearing En Banc" in the U. S. Sixth Circuit Court of Appeals. In this brief, I clearly laid out in specific detail the names, facts, motives, dates, places, events and circumstances that proved that the City of Cincinnati misappropriated public tax dollars in a bogus operation that involved deception and trick of the U. S. government.

By June 16, 1997, I filed in the U. S. Sixth Circuit Appeals Court a "Motion to Set Aside Judgment and Memorandum To All Active Judges Who Serve In The Sixth Circuit." This court document was a scathing criticism of broad-based bipartisan political corruption and cover-up activities by higher-ups, including malfeasance and the suppression of admissible evidence by judges in the lower U. S. District Court who incorrectly dismissed my case by turning their heads the other way. Moreover, it gave a rare, firsthand and factual insight into the reciprocal relationships that existed between a scandal-weary Bill Clinton White House that was strapped for cash and named individuals who used their financial power and political connections to gain access to the White House.

In moving the Justice Department's U. S. Sixth Circuit Court of Appeals to set aside its judgment against my case, I sent memorandums to the Chief Judge, all Senior Judges and all active Judges who served in the Sixth Circuit for purposes of accuracy and history. I wanted to make sure that I established a federal record of their participation in the 124 West Ninth Street HUD Treasury theft crimes against America.

These memoranda were addressed to the following judges at their locations in the Sixth Circuit Court of Appeals:

Chief Judge Gilbert S. Merritt, Nashville, Tennessee
Circuit Judge Alice M. Batchelder, Medina, Ohio
Circuit Judge Danny J. Boggs, Louisville, Kentucky
Circuit Judge R. Guy Cole, Jr., Columbus, Ohio
Circuit Judge Martha Craig Daughtrey, Nashville, Tennessee
Circuit Judge Cornelia G. Kennedy, Detroit, Michigan
Circuit Judge Boyce F. Martin, Louisville, Kentucky
Circuit Judge Karen Nelson Moore, Cleveland, Ohio
Circuit Judge David A. Nelson, Cincinnati, Ohio
Circuit Judge Alan E. Norris, Columbus, Ohio
Circuit Judge James L. Ryan, Detroit, Michigan
Circuit Judge Eugene E. Siler, Jr., London, Kentucky
Circuit Judge Richard F. Suhrheinrich, Lansing, Michigan
Senior Judge Bailey Brown, Memphis, Tennessee
Senior Judge Leroy J. Contie, Jr., Akron, Ohio
Senior Judge Albert J. Engel, Grand Rapids, Michigan
Senior Judge Ralph B. Guy, Jr., Ann Arbor, Michigan
Senior Judge Nathaniel R. Jones, Cincinnati, Ohio
Senior Judge Damon J. Keith, Detroit, Michigan
Senior Judge Robert B. Krupansky, Cleveland, Ohio
Senior Judge Pierce Lively, Danville, Kentucky and
Senior Judge Harry W. Wellford, Memphis, Tennessee

I filed federal court papers to all of these Appeals Court judges saying, "...all of you have been fully apprised about the true merits of this case in reaching your decisions not to get involved... As we [Sandy and I] have been effectively hamstrung by the U. S. District and Appeals courts, and as it is a foregone conclusion that the original panel [which decided against us] has implicated all of you in participating in federally indictable U. S. Treasury theft cover-up activities, now is the time to distance yourselves from these treasonous crimes by seeing to it that these erroneous judgments are reversed... it is important that you clear your names. Cover-ups—especially of this magnitude—do not work."

My constellation of emotions continued. On July 8, 1997, the Senate began long-awaited hearings on the campaign finance improprieties of 1996 with politically disingenuous pledges of fairness and cooperation. However, with the perfect vision that I had from inside of the Bananagate scandal, I witnessed a repugnant political shift that agonized me. Instead of U. S. Senators and Congressman pursuing the sure-fire federal indictments that Bananagate campaign finance prosecutions could bring, the campaign investigation, instead, focused on accusations that the Chinese government was trying to buy influence with American politicians.

In the most direct and aggressive statement to that point about alleged foreign interference in the U. S. political process, Sen. Fred D. Thompson, R-Tenn., said that investigators from the Governmental Affairs Committee that he was presiding over had found evidence of a Chinese plan "designed to pour illegal money into American political campaigns." He said its aim was to "subvert our election process" and that it touched the 1996 presidential campaign and state elections that year.

Following Sen. Thompson, the President's senatorial Bananagate cover-up pointman, Sen. John Glenn, D-Ohio, the committee's ranking Democrat, also sought a dramatic beginning, disclosing that John Huang, a central figure in the morass of questionable Democratic fund-raising practices during the last election cycle, had agreed to testify before the committee if given a limited grant of immunity from prosecution. After months of partisan bickering, this session was largely cordial and restrained. But beneath their vows of mutual cooperation, both sides made clear that they had vastly different visions of what the hearings should be about and where they should lead.

From the sideline of my television screen, my spirits rebounded when GOP members of the panel refocused their attention on allegations of widespread campaign finance abuses during the last election cycle by the DNC, the White House and President Clinton's reelection campaign. "There apparently was a systematic influx of illegal money in our presidential race last year," Thompson said. "We will be wanting to know: Who knew about it? Who should have known about it? And was there an attempt to cover it up?"

Other Republicans echoed these sentiments. Asserting that "we are here today largely because of an ethical indifference which some in the Democratic National Committee and the White House displayed toward fund-raising in the 1996 presidential campaign," Sen. Susan Collins, R-Maine, urged Democrats on the panel to "go where the evidence leads."

"The White House and others under scrutiny must be more forthcoming," she added. "The president cannot credibly preach the gospel of campaign finance reform unless his aides and supporters are prepared to let the light of day shine on their activities." In light of the fact that I had sent Sen. Collins volumes of evidence that implicated the DNC, the White House and President Clinton, I was hoping that my email messages and faxes to her had been working in favor of American taxpayers.

With its massive size and resources, Provident Bank was able to absorb the punishment that I meted out to it. This was not the case with Suburban Federal Savings Bank. As it buckled, in part, under the pressures of possible federal prosecution for what it did to me, Suburban Federal Savings Bank went out of business on July 30, 1997. Regardless, as this occurrence was of little consequence to my immediate situation, I drifted in legal limbo and waited for another opportunity that would avail itself to me.

In a strange twist that started a downhill slide for him, it was President Clinton's sex drive that breathed new life into the Bananagate scandal. As October of 1997 was when Independent Counsel Ken Starr ruled that former White House lawyer Vince Foster committed suicide on July 20, 1993, that was pretty good news for President Bill Clinton. As November of 1997 was when Ken Starr sought videotapes from the White House into allegations that payments made to Webb Hubbell were hush money, that was bad news for President Bill Clinton. But, when December of 1997 arrived, life changing news events began to occur that made life appreciably worse for the President.

It was in December of 1997 that a woman by the name of Linda Tripp began secretly taping extensive conversations of a friend who worked with her in the Pentagon, former White House intern Monica Lewinsky. The tapes revealed that Monica had a sexual affair with the President of the United States, Bill Clinton, and that he tried to cover it up. On top of all of these developments, things degraded further when the White House learned that lawyers for Paula Jones had Ms. Lewinsky on a list of potential witnesses. From that point on, a lengthy succession of rapid-fire dates, critically punishing to the President, began to wear away at Bill Clinton's image of invulnerability.

The image-killing opening salvo against the President began by December 23, 1997, when Bill Clinton was forced into providing sworn, written answers in the sexual harassment lawsuit filed by Paula Jones. By January 7, 1998, Monica Lewinsky, subpoenaed to help prove a pattern of Clinton philandering, said in a sworn affidavit given in the Paula Jones sexual harassment suit against Clinton that the two had no sexual relationship. Consequently, this made her a target of Ken Starr's investigation.

On January 17, 1998, Paula Jones' lawyers deposed President Clinton, via videotape, for six hours concerning the sexual harassment lawsuit filed by Ms. Jones. In this videotaped testimony, he denied a sexual relationship with Ms. Lewinsky. Exhibiting the conduct of someone who had not testified truthfully, shortly afterwards, Mr. Clinton, called his secretary, Betty Currie, to get their stories straight about Ms. Lewinsky.

The detached sexual motif of the Monica Lewinsky scandal gave me comfort in knowing that something was forcibly wiping the smugness off of Bill Clinton's hugger-muggering face. As the President had made his bed and was lying in it, the two-fisted events of January 21 and 22, 1998 revealed a level of wincing that had never before been seen coming from the Oval Office.

Reversing what she had said two weeks earlier, the first body blow was delivered to the President when Monica Lewinsky said on tape she had an affair with him. Clinton soon thereafter put his best face forward in further denying the affair when he responded to a National Public Radio correspondent, Mara Liasson.

On the next day, January 22, 1998, Clinton had two broadcast interviews about the alleged Monica Lewinsky affair. During one of them, a noticeable change was evident on his face when he used the present tense to say there "is" no relationship between him and the twenty-four year old Lewinsky. My observations were confirmed when the President came under criticism for what some commentators described as "a faltering denial." At a photo opportunity in the White House, Clinton flinched further when he again denied the affair to reporters after being asked about his sexual affair with the White House intern.

On January 26, 1998, Bill Clinton's public persona became uncharacteristically discombobulated when he jumped out of the frying pan and into the fire. In a noticeable attempt to crawl into his shell during a White House announcement on child-care initiatives, the Chief Executive, in more determined tones, repeated his denial of a sex relationship with Monica Lewinsky, rebutting the charges that many of his detractors said threatened his presidency.

In a forceful denial of the charges that had swirled around him for five days, the President uttered these infamous words, "I want you to listen to me; I'm going to say this again: I did not have sexual relations with that woman, Miss Lewinsky," as he wagged his finger and spoke with the only defense that he could muster, a scowl on his face. He went on further to say, "I never told anybody to lie, not a single time, never. These allegations are false."

The evasion continued when the President did not go into detail and declined to answer questions after the brief statement. When he publicly said, "I need to go back to work for the American people", it was as if his inner thoughts were saying, "Damage control is now officially in order and it is imperative that I see that a lot more money is thrown into my cover-up's—Bananagate included." The irony of this White House announcement was that, even though the president's remarks came at the end of the kind of routine White House event that usually gets little notice, given the heat of the building controversy that had surrounded him, this particular one was broadcast live by the major television networks.

While hellfire and brimstone rained down upon the President of the United States of America, on Capitol Hill, Democrats and the Republicans alike were using grave terms to discuss the mounting Lewinsky scandal. Even though Democrats across the country were privately begging Clinton to quickly provide a full accounting of his relationship with Lewinsky, the President continued to suffer unimaginable political losses.

His closest allies, even some senior administration officials, expressed doubts about whether Clinton was telling the truth and could survive. Though he tried to avoid a growing erosion of support while his favorable rating dropped in the polls, the president telephoned elected officials and donors, reiterating his denial but providing no details. Sen. Daniel Patrick Moynihan, D-N.Y., called this a "crisis of the Regime" and warned that the presidency will crumble if Clinton had sex with Lewinsky. "If it's so, it represents a disorder," Moynihan said.

On January 27, 1998, with his not mentioning the Monica Lewinsky scandal, President Clinton gave a State of the Union address that was awkward. As Linda Tripp gave Ken Starr tapes of Ms. Lewinsky's description of Clinton affair and Ken Starr opened a federal grand jury probe of Lewinsky matter, January of 1998 was a very bad month for Bill Clinton.

February was not much better either. Whenever the reptilian Bill Clinton was forced into crawling out of his shell, he came across as being smarmy—and rightfully so, as was the case on February 5, 1998 before he met with British Prime Minister Tony Blair. Like swarming flies over summer roadkill, the national press was all over President Bill Clinton when he, again, denied the allegations of sexual misconduct by Monica Lewinsky. To the growing embarrassment of the American nation, the eyes of the world became fixated on the hollowness of America's moral leader, as Bill Clinton was commonly viewed as lying through his teeth.

Even though I could not see what U.S. Senators and Congressmen were doing behind the scenes, I was determined not to rest on my laurels in anticipation of what they would or would not do. All I knew was that there had to be a better way for me to get the appropriate people to act.

I continued to move forward as a lone wilderness fighter whose mission was that of exposing the 124 West Ninth Street fraudulent activities to indictment. As a result, I steadfastly focused on ways of improving the electronic information base that I was using to combat the hidden Bananagate scandal and determined that it was of uttermost importance for me to upgrade my computer capabilities. Because my massive email and fax address base was growing by leaps and bounds, like the Internet itself, it was absolutely necessary for me to enhance my delivery system of Bananagate information. Also, in order to help level the playing field against those who were illegally abusing the power of the federal government to hide Bananagate, I needed the 24 hour a day presence on the Internet that only a web page could provide.

As the limited memory, processing speed and hard disk space of my 486-computer system could not cut the mustard for my needs, I made two synchronized tactical moves to arm myself much better. On February 16, 1998, I made my first move by buying a state-of-the-art digital color scanner that allowed me to place suppressed federal Bananagate evidence—both photographic and text—onto an Internet web page. After teaching myself how to put up a Web page in cyberspace, my computer processing capabilities took a quantum leap forward when, on March 2, 1998, I upgraded from a slow 486 MHz computer with 8 MB of memory, a 540 MB hard drive and a 14.4 KB modem to a blazing 233 MHz Pentium processor with 64 MB of memory, a 3.5 GB hard drive and a 56 KB internal voice/fax modem.

Even though I was at the starting line, ready to launch my presence into cyberspace, a very interesting current event occurred, causing me to delay my move. As the local press announced that President Bill Clinton was coming to Cincinnati on March 10, 1998 to visit Stan Chesley again, I said to myself, "Hmmmm." With all of the intense political pummeling that the President was taking at the time, and with all of the large legal problems that rained down upon him like grapefruit-sized hail on a Midwestern wheat field, I questioned the timing of the President's return to the solace of a trusted confidant—and Bananagate co-conspirator. Immediately, a red flag went up.

At the same time, in remembering that I had learned from the national press that there was a move afoot in the federal court system requiring the U. S. Secret Service to testify against the man that they protected, Bill Clinton, I realized that I had not contacted them. I contacted them prior to the President's March 10, 1998 visit to Stan Chesley's house and took a calculated risk that was fraught with all of the possible negative ramifications of exposing Bill Clinton's private army to the knowledge of Bananagate.

I immediately received a return telephone call from a U. S. Secret Service voice that reminded me of the Cigarette Man's voice from the Fox Television Network's science-fiction television drama, "X-Files." High intrigue was carried on when, in an attempt to intimidate me, a pair of U. S. Secret Service agents showed up at my residence on March 8, 1998. Behind the closed doors of the place that their boss forced me to live in, I stared into the steely-cold eyes of people who let me know through their actions that they could—and would—kill or physically hurt me at the drop of a hat.

While my wife and kids were in the house, the two federal Secret Service agents made it a point to get their message over to me loud and clear: don't mess with the President. In driving home their point by brandishing their weapons in a matter-of-factly way, it was at that point that I understood their role in insulating Bill Clinton from Bananagate.

As the U.S. Secret Service was the most powerful armed force that is available to the President (outside of the CIA, FBI or U. S. armed forces), I stood in my doorway as they pulled away from my residence and realized that they had just pulled off a gestapo-type of mob intimidation move on me. The deep involvement by those who were so close to the President, his personal army, signaled the extent to which Bill Clinton had gone in the nefarious use of his power. It was not surprising that federal protection by the United States Justice Department, in particular, the FBI, had been denied to me. As before, I continued to move forward in my opposition to the President and the Queen, as I was prepared to die, if need be, to defend my family and nation from having their future taken away by organized white-collar criminal activity.

Two days after President Bill Clinton came to a $10,000-a-couple fund-raising dinner at Attorney Stan Chesley's Cincinnati home, the inside view that I had of his Bananagate cover-up reunion was significant enough of an inducement to cause me to launch my web page with impassioned enthusiasm and interest. After many fits and starts, and in the wee hours of the morning, I was amazed beyond compare when I saw my uploaded computer server files come together to form a hyperlinked presence in cyberspace on the worldwide web.

In the absolute astonishment and elation that I went through in seeing my web page for the first time, I woke up several members of my family from the uncontrollable rebel yells that I let out in the middle of the night. I knew that I had carefully arranged an assemblage of pixels that had established a brand-new 24-hour a day information source that was the worst drawback to the President and the Queen's Bananagate cover-up.

While using his whip hand to maintain the solid wall of opposition that blocked Bananagate's painful repercussions against him, Bill Clinton slid further in the polls while being bombarded with other negative developments to his presidency. Five days from the launching of my web site, Kathleen Willey, a personal friend of President Clinton, appeared on television accusing the President of committing a sexual assault against her just outside the Oval Office. Seventeen days from that, a federal judge threw out Paula Jones' sexual harassment lawsuit against President Clinton. Mrs. Jones appealed.

Like the modus operandi of a serial rapist, a characteristic method employed by President Bill Clinton in performance of repeated Bananagate criminal cover-up acts recurred upon his return to the Cincinnati area on April 9, 1998. Framed exclusively as a fund-raising event, I knew that many of the people who were responsible for the financial success of this latest presidential foray into the land of the Queen were prominent Bananagate cover-up conspirators. The only difference between a serial rapist and President Bill Clinton was that, instead of his violating the personal rights of a handful of unsuspecting and unwilling individuals, he violated the public rights of all American taxpayers. By maintaining the Bananagate charade, he satiated his lust for all-important cash.

By the week of April 13, 1998, the Republican congressman heading the probe of President Clinton's election fund raising, Rep. Dan Burton of Indiana, chairman of the House Government Reform and Oversight Committee, told the editorial board of *The Indianapolis Star*, "If I could prove 10 percent of what I believe happened, he'd [Clinton] be gone. This guy's a scumbag. That's why I'm after him." The following week, he backed away from his comment and said that he felt the president was not a "man of integrity."

When Independent Counsel Ken Starr's office communicated with me in writing on April 27, 1998, acknowledging the "receipt of my recent communication", I knew that I had reached a threshold of federal power that could censure the President. Moreover, the Independent Counsel's communication to me signaled the federal government's awareness of Bill Clinton's federally indictable criminal involvement. Besides, with the receipt of this correspondence, I had proof that the Independent Counsel's office saw the evidence of Clinton's Bananagate crimes on my web site.

I was further lifted when Monica Lewinsky replaced her family lawyer, William Ginsburg, with Washington insiders, Attorneys Jacob Stein and Plato Cacheris in June of 1998. Because of her move, I knew that the former White House intern's camp was getting serious about the federal prosecution of a man who deserved it.

July of 1998 was another particularly bad month for U. S. President Bill Clinton. Linda Tripp testified to a grand jury; Monica Lewinsky was offered broad immunity from prosecution and agreed to testify before the grand jury in the Clinton sex and perjury scandal; Ken Starr subpoenaed the President and Bill Clinton volunteered testimony that was to be televised from the White House; the U. S. Court of Appeals said that the

Secret Service must testify; Monica Lewinsky turned over the dress that she wore in the Oval Office with the President; and the dress was tested for DNA by the FBI.

In the same month that Monica Lewinsky testified before a federal grand jury, August of 1998, President Clinton underwent videotaped questioning as he testified in Ken Starr's federal grand jury. In his grand jury testimony on August 17, 1998, President Clinton gave his now-famous response to the question of whether or not there "is" a relationship between him and Lewinsky, he responded, "It depends upon what the meaning of the word *is* is." Stuck in slick mode, President Clinton later told the nation that he had a relationship with Monica Lewinsky that was "not appropriate" and was "wrong."

With the perfect vision that I had from my Bananagate watchtower, I continued to look in on the similarities of how U. S. President Bill Clinton played on words to avoid federal prosecution by Ken Starr, and how the U.S. Sixth Circuit Court played on words to avoid federal prosecution of the President. The same type of deceptive wordplay that Clinton was responsible for using against the nation was the same type of deceptive wordplay that was being used by the U. S. Sixth Circuit Court against me.

On September 11, 1998, Independent Counsel Kenneth Starr delivered a report to Congress. The House later made public the report from Ken Starr alleging "The president has pursued a strategy of deceiving the American people and Congress, " and Mr. Starr named 11 grounds for impeachment. Within one week, like a recurring cancer that is resistant to cure, President Clinton was back in Cincinnati for another suspicious Stan Chesley-arranged fund-raiser.

For only the third time in history, a House panel voted on October 7, 1998 to begin a formal impeachment inquiry. However, by the time November of 1998 arrived, Independent Counsel Kenneth Starr advised the committee in a daylong appearance he had found no evidence of impeachable offenses in controversies involving FBI files at the White House, the firing of White House travel office officials and Whitewater, the failed Arkansas land deal he was originally appointed to investigate. I began to get worried.

The good news was that Ken Starr, at least, did not specifically mention the dropping of campaign finance. As far as I could deduce, the issue was still alive. Knowing that there was a window that was rapidly closing on my attempts to reveal Clinton's illegal campaign involvement at 124 West Ninth Street, I could not help but to wonder if my Lincoln Bedroom evidence was being considered. It was so quiet that I could hear a feather drop.

In the midst of the din, the November 3, 1998 off year elections produced a surprising result. Republicans, overconfident against a scandal-weakened president, lost five House seats to the Democrats in national elections. The State of Minnesota elected former professional wrestler Jesse Ventura governor. Not long after that, it was somewhat refreshing for me to hear the flamboyant professional wrestler Hulk Hogan strike an American nerve by announcing his run for the U. S. presidency "because no one appears to be representing ordinary Americans."

With the ability to generate mind-boggling amounts of cash for the defense of his battered administration, the to-and-fro political tide began to move in favor of the President. November 7, 1998 was a day that House Speaker Newt Gingrich, once brash, self-confident and tough, saw the revolt that was going on in his Republican Party and resigned. By November 13, 1998, using his propensity as a political opportunist, President Clinton agreed to pay Paula Jones $850,000 to withdraw her case, and with no apology.

Emboldened from the recent occurrence of events that he deemed were positive, I noticed how on a slow Saturday, November 28, 1998, President Bill Clinton hurriedly made a shadow radio announcement that HUD was making a move to implement the spending of $700 million in grants for the nation's housing needs. With respect to all of the things that I had personally witnessed pertaining to HUD financing for housing needs, I knew that if President Clinton continued to have unregulated access to the nation's Treasury via HUD, the nation was in trouble. The real issue that needed to be in front of the American people—beyond the significance of sexual lying—was that President Bill Clinton was illegally using HUD as a vehicle to rob the Treasury of the United States.

As President Clinton had a very real problem in disconnecting with his obsessive criminal behavior, he was no fool. He knew that his administration had suffered serious damage. Like a crazed pirate who was desperately preoccupied with only salvaging the booty from his sinking ship, I knew that Bananagate's federal evidence showed that

President Bill Clinton remained at America's helm to be in a position to plunder the Treasury of the United States.

Another pivotal time came when I did not know if my incriminating Bananagate evidence was being considered by the national legislature. On December 2, 1998, the House Judiciary Committee gained access to unedited, internal Justice Department memoranda relating to the agency's inquiry into alleged irregularities in Mr. Clinton's 1996 re-election campaign. As Bananagate had all of the elements that tied Bill Clinton to glaring federal campaign finance violations, I knew that this particular juncture was the golden opportunity that the American taxpaying public was deserving of to nail an extremely dishonest President who had just undergone a long-term lapse from grace. Within hours, two committee lawyers journeyed to the Justice Department to read the memos that had been shielded from public view.

My worst fears were realized on the following day. As the GOP suffered unexpected setbacks in the preceding month's elections, polls indicated that the public wanted the curtain to come down on the long-running national drama involving the president and the former White House intern. Chastened by these disappointing off-year election results, 1996 presidential election campaign financing was cut from the majority Republican-led House inquiry, clearing the way for the historic House Judiciary Committee vote during the following week over President Clinton's relationship with Monica Lewinsky and his effort to cover it up.

Since the issue of campaign finance violations was removed as a congressional deliberation, it was as if the wind had been taken out of my sails. I had just witnessed how a slick President had illegally slipped through the legal fingers of America's laws. As America's highest politicians had him solidly cornered in his 124 West Ninth Street Lincoln Bedroom U. S. Treasury theft involvement, and then let him escape, there was no doubt that tricky Bill Clinton had again abused his power to evade the waiting hook of public damnation.

On this same day, Rep. Henry Hyde relayed the results of reading the December 2, 1998 Justice Department memos to GOP members of the panel in a morning conference call. There was "no clear evidence of impeachable acts by Clinton requiring further inquiry" Hyde said. "The committee will not address allegations involving abuse of campaign finance laws in its deliberation currently scheduled for next week," he later said in a written statement.

As I had made the U. S. Congress and Senate aware of the 124 West Ninth Street federal crimes for many years, I saw that Rep. Hyde allowed the President to avoid federal prosecution by turning his head away from unquestionable and subterraneanly suppressed federal evidence of Bananagate crimes. The decision to abandon the campaign finance aspect of the impeachment inquiry came a few days after Republicans similarly decided not to look in depth at allegations by Kathleen Willey, a former White House volunteer.

I knew that there was a hidden political dynamic at work. It was the only explanation as to why Bill Clinton was allowed clear passage through the legal mine fields of American laws that were set out to stop the type of corrosively illegal campaign finance contributions that were given by Carl Lindner, Jr. in the Lincoln Bedroom. As the former head of the Justice Department's campaign finance inquiry, Charles LaBella, received the news of Mr. Hyde's decision, he later said of the Republicans, "I think they're running for the hills."

But they were not running for the hills for nothing; a formidable Bananagate-influenced subculture was causing the stampede. Increasingly, as I dug deeper and deeper as to why this all was happening, time would show that LaBella was right.

Coinciding with the impeachment vote, it was like stink in the nostrils to me to watch the commencement of President Clinton's Operation Desert Fox on December 16, 1998. As the United States attacked Iraq, I did not draw any questions about its timing and its motive: it was nothing more than another Clinton diversion.

I continued to sit back and watch the political circus unfold as the start of the full House impeachment debate against President Bill Clinton began on December 19, 1998, the first in 130 years. As the House Judiciary Committee approved two of four impeachment articles—one for perjury and the other article alleging that he tampered with witnesses and helped hide evidence—but rejected two other articles on perjury and abuse of power, President Clinton was charged with "high crimes and misdemeanors" for lying under oath and obstructing justice to cover up his affair with Monica Lewinsky. I found it to be incredulous that the nation's highest politicians were going after the President for his carnality instead of his criminality.

Rep. Henry Hyde, chairman of the House Judiciary Committee, picked a U. S. Congressman from the Queen, Steve Chabot, to be one of the 13 managers of the presidential impeachment case when it reached the Senate floor. While House speaker-designate Bob Livingston dumbfounded Congress by announcing his intention to resign from the House after his admissions of past sexual indiscretions, and challenged President Clinton to follow his example, I was astounded at Carl Lindner, Jr.'s ability to control not only the Queen, but America as well.

Watching history unfold from a distance, I knew that if 124 West Ninth Street had been an active congressional consideration, I would have been part of the historical record. As everything that was needed for Clinton's removal from office was included in Bananagate, from its outset, I could see that the whole Monica Lewinsky national mesmerism was a waste of America's money and time.

By January 14, 1999, opening presentations started in the U. S. Senate trial of President Bill Clinton. The team of 13 House prosecutors not only began laying out the case against Mr. Clinton, but also made a strong pitch for presenting witnesses later. As Representatives challenged the 100 senators to recognize that the high crimes Mr. Clinton was accused of by saying that the President's crimes went to the very core of American principles of law and government, I knew that they were acting hypocritically because they chose to drop Bananagate from their own deliberations.

By the next day, House prosecutors asserted that "a merger of the law and the facts" proved that President Clinton committed perjury and obstruction of justice in attempting to conceal his affair with Monica Lewinsky. On January 16, 1999, facing an uphill struggle in convincing 67 senators out of 100 to vote for conviction, the House wrapped up three days of arguments in the Senate to weakly demand that President Clinton be found guilty of high crimes and misdemeanors and removed from office for violating laws to conceal an extramarital relationship.

I stared into my boob tube and watched the frail congressional effort against Clinton fizzle away. Clinton had slicked his way out of the Bananagate conspiracy charges while being able to shift the political focus over to a slap-on-the-wrist private sexual affair because the nation's most powerful politicians wanted to protect their access to large sums of unquestioned money: campaign finance contributions.

In the height of duplicity, chief prosecutor Rep. Henry Hyde said "The office of president of the United States has been debased and the justice system jeopardized...He has broken his covenant of trust with the American people." "This is not a question of who we hate," Hyde said. "It's a question of what we love. And among the things we love are the rule of law, equal justice before the law and honor in our public life." As Mr. Hyde had been made aware of Bananagate, I knew that he was talking one way and acting another.

Former United States Congresswoman Barbara Jordan is best known for her argument to impeach President Richard M. Nixon during the Watergate hearings. She long ago quoted my beliefs by saying, "A President is impeachable if he tries to subvert the Constitution...I feel right now, my faith in the Constitution is whole, it is complete, it is total. I am not going to sit here and be an idle spectator to the diminution, the subversion, the destruction of the Constitution." The then Congresswoman went on to make the case for Nixon's impeachment, arguing that the evidence against him was so compelling that if the committee did not act, "then perhaps the eighteenth-century Constitution should be abandoned to a twentieth-century paper shredder."

By January 21, 1999, the one-year anniversary of the disclosure of President Clinton's relationship with Monica Lewinsky, the first phase of the impeachment trial ended as the president's defense closed. Almost immediately after the White House team finished presenting its side of the case, Republican senators appointed by Senate Majority Leader Trent Lott went behind closed doors to prepare for the Senate's two-day question and answer period on the following day. Senators Fred Thompson of Tennessee, Orrin Hatch of Utah and Mike DeWine of Ohio met to get rid of duplicative questions and help to figure out exactly how the questioning should proceed.

By the next day, convinced that the necessary two-thirds for conviction were not there and that they were not likely to develop after they watched their first chance to question lawyers for both sides turn into a free-wheeling debate on constitutional theory and evidence, Senators sought a fast exit strategy to dismiss the two articles of impeachment.

In throwing together words to go through the motions of appearing to be doing what was legitimate and just, Senator Phil Gramm, R-Texas, said "Justice is not just a conviction or an acquittal, justice is a process," and it is important that the process be fair. As I would find out that he was part of a large group of national legislators that had financial connections to the Bananagate cover-up scandal, it was they who criminally stopped the American public from seeing that the process was not fair.

Even as President Bill Clinton was again scheduled to be at Attorney Stan Chesley's residence in the Queen for another fund-raiser on March 25, 1999—but was canceled due to the crisis in Kosovo and Serbia, I was determined not to give up my fight against a true threat to America. However, as I knew that the threshold of legal government activity had been lowered to new depths upon the president's return to Stan Chesley's house on July 23, 1999, I could sense that a Bananagate archetype of high government White House corruption had been set, further endangering America.

Chesley's relative importance to the Bananagate cover-up was indicated by the placement of this latest fund-raiser in the schedule of the President of the United States. Two days before this presidential visit to Chesley's, Clinton was at John F. Kennedy, Jr.'s New York City memorial service. One day after this latest visit by the President to Chesley's house, Air Force One arrived in Rabat, Morocco with Bill Clinton for King Hassan's funeral.

I delved deeper and determined that U. S. Senate and House politicians had been paid for their participation in the Bananagate cover-up with the Queen's money. Consequently, I uncovered a federal track record that revealed an out of control political lust for money that threatened the stability of America. Even though Bananagate conspirators wanted to assign the whole cover-up to oblivion as quickly as possible, I went forward undaunted, remaining the lone soldier in defense of my country's fight against the buried 124 West Ninth Street Treasury theft scandal. In the process, I uncovered convincing proof that my beloved country's financial lifeblood was being imperiled by a growing outbreak of documented political graft and malfeasance.

Chapter 8

Politicians Playing Politics

"The creation of constitutional government is a most significant mark of the distrust of human beings in human nature. It signalizes a profound conviction, born of experience, that human beings vested with authority must be restrained by something more potent than their own discretion."

—Raymond Moley

I knew that the Bananagate cover-up could not have happened without the help of national politicians who were in position to block any and all federal investigations and prosecutions of 124 West Ninth Street HUD Treasury theft crimes. My fight had reached a point in determining not if Carl Lindner, Jr. was paying politicians to hide these federal crimes, but whom he was paying to hide them. I decided to look at available public records of national campaign contributions that were listed at the Federal Election Commission (FEC).

The FEC has exclusive jurisdiction in the administration and civil enforcement of laws regulating the acquisition and expenditure of campaign funds to ensure compliance by participants in the federal election campaign process. It's chief mission is to provide public disclosure of campaign finance activities and effect voluntary compliance by providing the public with information on the laws and regulations concerning campaign finance.

In searching through FEC records on the Internet, like the visual bombardment of light one gets when coming out of a dark tunnel on a sunshiny day, I was suffused with an abundance of campaign contribution information that linked the receipt of Carl Lindner, Jr. machine money to prominent national politicians. This FEC window showed me for the first time how Carl Lindner, Jr.'s money corrupted politicians and, as a result, I saw how a Bananagate cover-up payroll allowed America's Treasury to be robbed with a wink and a nod.

It became even more obvious to me that Carl Lindner, Jr.'s power was but one aspect of a multifaceted American political campaign fundraising dynamic that was plaguing America, and was getting worse. I saw that he was contributing to a runaway national political process that was causing U. S. Treasury theft losses for all American citizens while politicians gained personal cash.

I thought of how far things had gone awry when comparing the relevant words of Abraham Lincoln to the current campaign finance environment that allowed President Bill Clinton to defile the Lincoln Bedroom. President Lincoln once referred to political leadership as "The wise employment of individual meanness for the public good." He had no idea that one day, conversely, a symbol dedicated to his honor, integrity and sacrifice would be collectively used by many of America's national political leaders in an unwise way to harm the public.

In the damaging wake of political campaign fundraising practices that had been redefined by seven years of Bill Clinton policies run amok, I saw how politicians became more audacious in their capricious following of the dollar. Standing on the inside of a hidden presidential scandal looking out, I was able to see that the nature of politics was sullenly teetering on the edge of acceptability, as most national politicians, in their obsessive hunt for political money, conspicuously said what they did not believe and believed what they did not say.

With the Clinton-led defeat of campaign financing investigations in the House inquiry on December 3, 1998, the moral fiber of America continued to degrade and be undermined, becoming open season for national politicians to fatten their political pockets. To the distinct disadvantage of the vast majority of taxpaying Americans, Bananagate's apropos frame of reference made it a certitude that, at least, national politicians were using the cover of their offices to curry favor while hiding secret deals to represent the interests of the rich and the powerful.

Helpless, I could only sit back and watch the ruthless greed and the obligatory activities of national politicians, as they snorted-up all of the money that they could, while they could, like pigs to gruel in a trough. To me, Bananagate's salient example, if anything, was that there was little honor in politics; politicians were selling out the interests of the public, as they converted into cash the political influence of their offices. Since they, too, were subverting the Constitution, like Nixon, they were impeachable. After all, U. S. Senators and Congressman, like public treasurers, are duly elected officers who have been entrusted with the receipt, care and disbursement of federal funds.

In many ways, when thinking of the national politicians that were involved in the Bananagate cover-up, I was also reminded of stories in the Bible of Judas Iscariot, the Treasurer. As one of the twelve apostles in the Gospel accounts who betrayed Jesus, over the millennia, the name of Judas has become synonymous with being a traitor and being one who betrays under the guise of friendship.

To be Judas-like is to be a person treacherous enough to betray a friend. Like this disciple who betrayed Jesus, I knew that the national politicians who were made aware of what happened at 124 West Ninth Street were traitors and false prophets to American taxpayers. Also like Judas, the FEC campaign contribution listings let me see how bipartisan national politicians had their hand in the bag while illegally raising non-issues to defend the President, Carl Lindner, Jr. and Stan Chesley from justified Bananagate prosecution.

In a Bill Clinton political shell game designed to use diversions to shield big donors, FEC records revealed to me that the Democratic National Committee (DNC) and the Republican National Committee (RNC) channeled millions of dollars in campaign donations to state Democratic parties, therein, effectively hiding big contributions from Carl Lindner, Jr. Because the money was not deposited in the accounts of the national party, Lindner's name did not appear on the DNC's federal disclosure reports. Instead, his donations were reported on the state level, where they are far more difficult to track. To protect Lindner, it was like the DNC was keeping a second set of books to evade the FEC's disclosure requirements. My jaw dropped when I saw the millions that had been directed to state parties by the Democrats.

But there was another way that the FEC records revealed to me how Carl Lindner, Jr. and his firms gained added political influence by skirting FEC limits on the additional millions that they gave to the DNC, the RNC and political action committees (PAC's). In a practice referred to as bundling, Lindner, his family, his executives and their family members contributed heavily to many of the same candidates. As a result, there was no FEC requirement to report the millions that were funneled directly to political parties in the name of one of the Lindner firms rather than by an individual.

FEC records revealed that wherever organized bundling took place, the person who delivered the checks to the candidate gained considerable political leverage. I witnessed how this process created a new influential political class with Carl Lindner, Jr.-types at its head. As I felt the sting of the influence that he created, Carl Lindner, Jr. was able to actively participate in stealing from the U. S. Treasury through HUD, and then walk all over me and other American taxpayers in the process by giving money to Bill Clinton in the Lincoln Bedroom. In seeing the company that Carl Lindner, Jr. was in, I was also made aware how former savings and loan executive Charles Keating was a prominent bundler.

Notwithstanding the hidden Lindner political payoffs, page after page of FEC records disclosed a well-coordinated Lindner political machine consisting of dozens of Lindners who switched at the delivery of cash to hungry politicians whenever and wherever the political whims of Carl Lindner, Jr. dictated. With irresistible cash bait hung out in front of them like a carrot in front of a donkey, the federal record was clear that hungry politicians walked or ran towards the Lindner money. Before accepting the money, though, scores of them knew that there was a price to be paid: allegiance to Carl H. Lindner, Jr.—even if it involved the self-serving swindling of the American taxpayer by covering-up Bananagate's U. S. Treasury theft.

For documented, irrefutable and unquestionable U. S. Treasury theft to be completely wiped away from the slate of federal prosecution, Lindner had to control both the U. S. House of Representatives and the Senate. The FEC list of prominent U. S. Congressmen and Senators who received soul-selling cash payments from the Carl Lindner, Jr. political machine is far too long and extensive to list, but the strategic placement of its controlling campaign contributions speaks volumes.

Even though the House Appropriations Committee and the Senate Appropriations Committee share oversight of all federal spending, the House committee typically addresses spending bills first before its Senate counterpart. Together they allocate money and outline new spending power for each new fiscal year. On the Lindner payroll in this House Committee was the prominent New Hampshire Republican John E. Sununu. With Sununu in place, I did not stand a chance of making sure that this segment of the federal legislature would enforce the federal laws that prohibited the misappropriation of the public's money at 124 West Ninth Street. Lindner was in control.

International and domestic financial matters including money, credit, banking and monetary policy fall under the jurisdiction of the U. S. Government's House Banking and Financial Services Committee. Its members also oversee HUD. In the Senate, the Committee on Banking, Housing and Urban Affairs deals with the same issues. On the Lindner payroll in this House Committee was the prominent Georgia Republican Bob Barr. With Barr in place, any efforts that I made to get this Committee to act were nipped in the bud. Lindner's financial power ruled here also.

The House Government Reform and Oversight Committee has wide-ranging oversight duties, including the national archives; public information and records; population and demographics including the Census and federal paperwork reduction. However, its most visible role is as the House's investigative body. The Senate's Governmental Affairs Committee oversees many of the same issues. On the Lindner payroll in this House Committee was also the prominent Georgia Republican Bob Barr. Again, with Barr in place, my efforts to get this Committee to act in accordance to the federal laws that required it to conduct a meaningful investigation of the U. S. Treasury theft that occurred at 124 West Ninth Street were summarily put to an end.

In the House Judiciary Committee, Criminal and civil judicial proceedings fall under its jurisdiction, as well as civil liberties; the federal judiciary; constitutional amendments; bankruptcy and counterfeiting. The panel also deals with presidential succession; interstate contracts; trade protection; patents; penitentiaries and immigration and naturalization. The Senate Judiciary Committee has similar jurisdiction.

It was this Committee which assessed Ken Starr's Independent Counsel report and decided if grounds existed to impeach President Bill Clinton. Carl Lindner, Jr.'s hometown boy, Cincinnati Rep. Steve Chabot, and, again, Bob Barr ensured that I would go nowhere in this Committee. Primarily, it was because of the strategic positioning of these two Lindner large cash recipients that 1996 presidential election campaign financing was cut from the House inquiry on December 3, 1998. Additionally, it was because of these two nationally televised and crooked politicians that America's time and money was wasted in the House Judiciary Committee's investigation of President Bill Clinton's sperm-depositing relationship with Monica Lewinsky and his effort to cover it up.

The House Ways and Means Committee oversees revenue programs and issues such as Social Security; deposit of public money; customs; reciprocal trade agreements; tax-exempt foundations and charitable trusts. Cincinnati area U. S. Congressman Rob Portman was positioned in this Committee to nix any moves that I made to have America enforce its laws. He was also additionally positioned in this Committee's Subcommittee on Oversight. Every time I went to this Committee's Internet home page, I guffawed when I read the welcome of Chairman Bill Archer when he said, "...I am glad that you have taken an interest in how your Federal Government works and how it spends your money."

The powerful Senate Appropriations Committee oversees all federal spending, along with the House Appropriations Committee. Its panels help define spending powers for each new fiscal year and allocate money to agencies, departments and programs throughout the government. On the Lindner payroll in this Senate Committee were the prominent Lindner grafted plants from Pennsylvania, Sen. Arlen Specter; from Missouri, Sen. Christopher S. Bond; and from Kentucky, Sen. Mitch McConnell.

My initial grin at the blatant hypocrisy that is displayed on their home page turned into a serious stare when my thoughts turned to the nationwide damage that their playing of political games was causing. With my eyes glued to the computer screen, I read an Internet device that was allowing the robbery of the American Treasury.

At the very top of the front page of this Committee's web site, I personally knew, beyond a shadow of a doubt, that they were lying to the world by quoting the U. S. Constitution, Article One, Section Nine which said, "No money shall be drawn from the treasury, but in consequence of appropriations made by law; and a regular statement and account of receipts and expenditures of all public money shall be published from time to time." Seeing that they were charlatans only made my resistance to them stronger.

In the Senate Banking, Housing, and Urban Affairs Committee, finance and monetary policy are a large part of this committee's jurisdiction, including the Federal Reserve System and all other financial institutions; price controls; economic growth and stabilization and industrial and commercial financial aid. More importantly to Bananagate, this Senate committee also oversees HUD.

Throughout most of Bananagate's time span, New York Sen. Alfonse M. D'Amato was this Committee's Chairman. He was on the Lindner political payroll. With Texas Senator Phil Gramm, Florida Senator Connie Mack and Colorado Senator Wayne Allard being bought and paid for by the Lindner political machine on this Committee, 124 West Ninth Street's HUD federal criminal activity was, and had been, covered-up, due to their receipt of profuse Lindner campaign contributions.

The Senate Select Committee on Ethics, like its House counterpart, investigates alleged misconduct of Senate members and employees, and also keeps senators and staff abreast of new rules and regulations of conduct. On the Lindner cover-up payroll in this Committee were its Chairman, New Hampshire Republican Sen. Bob Smith and former Ohio governor, Republican Sen. George Voinovich. As Ohio's governor, not only was his run for the Senate largely financed by Lindner, but Sen. Voinovich led a state-wide cover-up of misappropriated 124 West Ninth Street HUD financing that Ohio was federally responsible for.

The powerful Senate Finance Committee oversees financial issues including the federal debt limit; taxes; customs; trade agreements; revenue measures and tariffs. Social Security, Medicare and Medicaid also fall under the panel's jurisdiction. Prominent Lindner-paid Republicans on this Committee were Senators Chuck Grassley from Iowa; Phil Gramm from Texas; Trent Lott from Mississippi; Connie Mack from Florida; and Fred Thompson from Tennessee. With them there, I stood no hope of success in getting the federal government to act against Carl Lindner, Jr. Orrin Hatch from Utah is also a member of this Committee but, instead of being paid to keep Bananagate quiet by Lindner, I was able to see that he was paid handsomely by Stan Chesley.

The panel of the Senate Governmental Affairs Committee oversees budget and accounting measures, intergovernmental relations, nuclear export policy, statistics and the Census. Agencies under the Governmental Affairs Committee's jurisdiction include the federal civil service, the U.S. Postal Service, the District of Columbia, the National Archives and the organization of both Congress and the executive branch.

On the Lindner cover-up payroll in this Committee was, again, Chairman Sen. Fred Thompson from Tennessee; Sen. Susan Collins from Maine; Sen. Arlen Specter from Pennsylvania; and Sen. George

Voinovich from Ohio. Additionally, Republican Sen. Sam Brownback from Kansas had been a longtime Lindner cash recipient and Democratic Senator Joseph I. Lieberman from Connecticut had received cash from Stan Chesley.

Similar to the House Judiciary Committee, perhaps the most visible duty of the powerful Senate Judiciary Committee is confirming or rejecting nominations for the Supreme Court and other openings on the federal bench. The committee's job is more far-reaching, however. As a Stan Chesley campaign finance recipient, Senator Orrin G. Hatch, the Chairman of the Senate Judiciary Committee, oversees the Justice Department and all of its agencies. The FEC records that I saw gave new clarity as to why Stan Chesley was appointed to be my lawyer by the U. S. Sixth Circuit Court and why the FBI did not intervene into the white-collar criminal activity that occurred at 124 West Ninth Street: indisputable Lindner political payoffs.

Other Senate Judiciary Committee members who received Lindner political machine money are Senators Storm Thurman from South Carolina; Chuck Grassley from Iowa; Arlen Specter from Pennsylvania; Fred Thompson from Tennessee; Mike DeWine from Ohio; and John Ashcroft from Missouri.

The past and present Democratic U. S. Senators who knew about the U. S. Treasury theft crimes that occurred at 124 West Ninth Street and did nothing are John Glenn, Howard Metzenbaum and Edward Kennedy. In view of the fact that HUD Secretary Andrew Cuomo married into the Kennedy family, I gained new insight as to why the disfavored brother of the beloved American President John F. Kennedy, U. S. Senator Edward Kennedy, did nothing about the 124 West Ninth Street HUD Treasury theft that he was informed of.

As the true picture of what was going on focused and sharpened, other national politicians who received Carl Lindner, Jr.'s "keep quiet and look the other way" political campaign finance money came into sight. On the Senate side, John McCain, Tom Daschle and Gordon Smith were involved in intentionally not exposing Bananagate and, on the House side, David McIntosh, Mark Foley, Jim Moran and Charles Stenholm were likewise involved.

Politically, it is a sad day in America as Bananagate-type political games are being played. As America's national politicians are charged with enacting the nation's laws and making sure that the laws are upheld, it is shameful that the overwhelming majority of them have placed a higher value on pursuing money-making political objectives rather than holding the nation's constitutional core values as being sacrosanct.

Chapter 9

The View From The Pinnacle

"We have forgotten in America that a democracy is the most difficult kind of government to maintain. It is the hardest kind of government under which to live. It is hardest to maintain because of the widespread political corruption to which it so easily lends itself. Our drift today toward complete totalitarian bureaucracy is one that threatens immediately the very freedoms for which our own boys are dying."

—Ernest R. Palen, D.D.

In addition to the U. S. Senate and House being kept under the thumbs of the President and the Queen, other insightful reflections at my path of pain and agony revealed a much clearer picture of raw Bananagate cover-up mastership. It was this introspective look backward in time that allowed me to see how 124 West Ninth Street's criminal concealment had been methodically carried out from its inception to its latest point.

It was as if I had reached the pinnacle of a steep and high elevation of land that was providing me with an unobstructed view into the scandalous federal cover-up machinations that had befallen my homeland. Like greatly magnified binocular images of a nearby valley from a lofty mountaintop observation post on a bright sunshiny day, I reexamined the people, places and things that had been involved in the 124 West Ninth Street conspiracy.

From this perspective, I could see how all of the unknown pieces that caused me to eke out a years-long battered existence came together in a revealing anti-Bananagate tapestry. I saw how a timely assemblage of unknown parts were woven together that produced a picture revealing the totality of how long, difficult and dangerous of an experience I had travailed through. All I had to do to get answers to the questions of "How did or could Bananagate happen?", or "Who or what were the supports for such a far-reaching cover-up?", or "What was the continued cover-up agenda?" was to look back from this pinnacle of my mind's eye.

From my mind-packed view that stretched over a series of years and events, I could see a presidential artifice that was designed to be slipped past the public's eye. As this standpoint provided a sight into the sum total of what the President and the Queen had done, for the very first time, I garnered a far different perspective on the great breadth of the cover-up that had overwhelmed me.

I knew that the view went well beyond what was required to convict the President and the Queen, as a flush of incriminating motives and methods teemed over my visional senses. It did not matter which direction I looked towards; 124 West Ninth Street's criminal activity led back to the President of the United States, thereby clinching Bill Clinton's role in the Bananagate cover-up. While surrendering to the daunt of the Bananagate anarchists was not an option, I could see how Sandy and I had dug in our heels opposing evil politicians while the moral decay in America continued.

As the view was like a story of personal and national tragedy without words, it provided a sad image that left a lot of negative, but true, things to be said about the people that were involved in the whole Bananagate mess. Although I was comforted in knowing that I was able to substantiate what I was seeing, the picture that I saw was like a mental snapshot, a transfixing intermediate somewhat between a thought and a thing.

In all actuality, I had an exclusive perspective of being able to peer into a presidential scandal that had sidestepped the national news media. Yet, beyond Monica Lewinsky, I knew that my facts and evidence were irrefutable and convicting that tied the President of the United States to his most successful hidden lie on the American public.

Foremost, while my undistorted view reconfirmed the intricacy of the President and the Queen's ruse, I could see that they had to go to great lengths not to expose their stratagem. As a grand jury never was convened, an indictment was never handed up, a subpoena was never issued, or that anyone was ever legitimately investigated pertaining to 124 West Ninth Street's federal crimes, ocular images reaffirmed that the U. S. government all along the way had hoodwinked Sandy and me.

We could see that, as there was a preponderance of evidence that left many malefactors extremely vulnerable to front, rear and flank attacks, cover-up plotters neutralized our damaging thrusts by painstakingly ignoring our convicting, admissible and probative evidence. It became clearer that we had been systematically stonewalled whenever and wherever we brought up pertinent issues, or referenced specific federal laws that applied to the Treasury theft at 124 West Ninth Street.

It became evident that Sandy and I had been routinely blocked in the U. S. Justice Department, from the top down, as it vagariously controlled the flow of incriminating documents and factual information while glossing over crucial evidence. With total indifference to the U. S. laws that prohibited U. S. Treasury theft, I could see that the U. S. Justice Department was disregarding the American public's demand that our laws should serve the masses from the bottom up, and not the other way around.

As optic images gave me an eyeful when I glanced back over my path, I could see what should have happened. While justice should have been fair, equitable and clear, the strict line of legality that the U. S. Sixth Circuit Court was federally required to follow became illegally blurred, drifting between rulings that were blatantly wrong and those that were even more specious. While laws are only good if they are rigorously adhered to, instead of being selectively enforced, I had an increased sense of the maxim that *justice delayed is justice denied.*

More and more, the revealing panorama that I beheld shed light on the truths of what the HUD conspirators had tried to do. As 124 West Ninth Street's cover-up by the President and the Queen was intended to be a master stroke of superior power to defeat Sandy and I, its overarching stratagem was to cut off our legal head by not allowing us court representation. In turn, they figured that our legal body would die and that we would go away.

In attempting to make people believe that their legally contorted version of truth was legitimate, they tried to cast the illusion of fairness and justice. Knowing that exposure of their federal cover-up could sink them quicker than the *Titanic*, they devised a gigantic wall of silence strategy that would circumvent the law. Although the Bananagate conspirators had legal success against me, I could see that they would not have stood a snowball's chance in hell in a fair court of law.

Looking down into my protracted struggle from afar, it was also as if I could see the dust rising that had been kicked up from the hustle and bustle of the battlefield arbitrament of my constitutional sword. From this field of view, it was uncannily real when I could hear the clinks and the clangs of the gives and takes from my resistive exertions against the President and the Queen. In this mindset, I was inspired to the nth degree when I finally realized that the shimmering that I was seeing through the dust was the glistening sun, as it kissed off of the blade of the trusty sword of patriotism that I continued to defiantly wield.

As the President and the Queen faced stiff evidentiary and factual opposition from me, I could also see that they resorted to ever-increasing levels of subterfuge to save face. With their control of the all-important clock, I checked out how they had played a backyard waiting game of postponing their moves on the many legal matters where I held them at bay in the courts that they controlled. After finding my cases impossible to dismiss for lack of evidence, and to no avail, they desperately tried to get them dismissed for lack of prosecution by intentionally making my cases creep along.

I could see what the President and the Queen had done to me. As the majority of civil cases get settled and very few go to trial, my civil case was deliberately not settled and there was no trial. Settling for them would have been a leaning, whether perceived or not, towards guilt. The maintainers of the Bananagate cover-up, in their pompous way, would not have any of that.

Instead, they passed Sandy and I off to one another like a hot potato while conveniently sweeping their wrongdoings underneath the rug. In tampering with justice, they violated my constitutional rights along with the letter and the spirit of the law.

I saw clearly how the federal and the state courts in Cincinnati made sure that I did not succeed in exposing the U. S. Treasury theft that I was trying to reveal. The tragic experiences that Sandy and I encountered in fighting the President and the Queen's U. S. Treasury theft involvement set off a chain of events that gave us an up-close and personal view of what most Americans do not see: massive federal judicial corruption, fraudulent activity and rampant malfeasance.

Like on a movie screen, I could see, in their low-minded pursuit of legal correctness, how they obstructed, burdened and frustrated the search for truth while showing no compunction whatsoever to the illegal activities that involved much of their attention. In ignoring federal law, they struck at the very undergirding of American democracy, demonstrating that there was no independence in the judiciary. In using their influence and power to weaken my case, the integrity of the judicial process in the U. S. court system was damaged for all Americans.

If but for nothing else, it was the President and the Queen's aberrant behavior that signaled their mask. They wrongly used pomposity and pretense instead of dignity and decorum in their reckless willingness to break the laws of the United States. I reviewed their activities to see how they used high political corruption to defeat my damaging federal actions against them in order to stage a federal Treasury heist cover up.

Quietly studying every nuance of a vista that was smeared with my blood, sweat and tears, I was able to see to the bottom of federal measures that should have been performed in an entirely different way. As we had an overabundance of incriminating facts and evidence to prove hidden U. S. Treasury theft by many, Sandy and I initially believed that the American legal process would protect us.

The word *fact* is commonly described in law dictionaries as "an event that has occurred, circumstances that exist, or events whose actual occurrence or existence is to be determined by the evidence." In deciding a case, a court is supposed to find facts on the basis of the evidence presented to it, and then apply the law to those facts.

Based upon codified procedures in American courts of law, facts must be established by competent evidence, such as the testimony of witnesses or the presentation of real evidence to the court. With respect to the fountainhead of facts and competent evidence that sprang from the 124 West Ninth Street crime scene, I could clearly see that the U. S. Sixth Circuit Court shirked its responsibilities, as it should have been bound to prosecute 124 West Ninth Street's infamous crimes.

The pinnacle's outlook also allowed me to pierce the President and the Queen's shaky defenses to see what they did not do. I could openly see that they talked law, but their actions did not follow what was legal. As the constitutional requirements of the U. S. were subordinate to their private agendas, there were massive discrepancies between their words and deeds. It was obvious that they did not come clean.

From my unrestricted observatory, I could see the many things that the President and the Queen were. They were wolves in lambs clothing who had a clandestine and an esoteric purpose. They were ground zero for the detonation of a virulent scheme that had been designed for release on the American public's right to protect its Treasury. They were treason incarnate. They were self-righteous and shamelessly manipulative. They were the linchpins that held together the criminal cover-up of 124 West Ninth Street's federal crimes. They were machinators for the devil.

Peering remotely into the depths of a full-blown presidential scandal when the light of day removed their obscurity, I could see what they were not, what they should have been and how they appeared. They were not creatures of conscience; they should have been bastions of fairness; and there was a palpable sense of dread on their part.

The ideational frame of reference that was imparted to me altered the way that I looked at the effects of the President and the Queen's acts. I could see that they appointed themselves as police, judge and jury and remained unrepentant in their participation in the 124 West Ninth Street crimes against America. I also saw that, as the word spread in legal circles about what was actually going on in the Queen, lawyers stayed away from me in deference to, and fear of, the powers that be.

As I looked down upon much of what I had already known, I could see that Sandy and I had been criminally mugged in the state and federal courts. Seeing what I saw, it was of little surprise that I had lost practically all of my faith and objectivity in the American judicial system.

From my high footing, it was quite easy for me to zero in on a pattern of the President and the Queen's conduct that belied the seriousness of their stations. All that I had to do was to look at how their callous disregard for federal laws prohibiting the U. S. Treasury theft at 124 West Ninth Street was part of America's undermining. As the effects of their actions further eroded the sense of security that Americans entrusted to politicians who were confident in their abilities to hide their snide self-aggrandizement, I watched them bask in the afterglow of their corrosive influence.

The unconfined panoramic sweep of my view gave me a perfect line of sight into the President and the Queen's past and present HUD fraud behavior. However, even though the perspicuity of what was to come was not as certain, I, nevertheless, had astute observations and grounded beliefs.

With the precious treasure of my eyesight not lost, I could see that the President and the Queen's artful defense still went unpunished. Concurrently, at the bottom of my heart, I believed that, ultimately, 124 West Ninth Street's case would be settled in the court of public opinion, and that concerned Americans would eventually come over to my side. I knew that they should all face indictment for obstruction of justice and should be charged with conspiracy to commit fraud on the U. S. government.

But of all of the views that the pinnacle provided, Sandy and I were most proud when we looked back upon things past and saw what we had done in opposition to the President and the Queen. Awash in strong beliefs in our nation and ourselves, without hesitation, we could see how we had intrepidly stood up to challenge observable sins against America. In the dearth of opposition to the form of HUD U. S. Treasury theft that occurred at 124 West Ninth Street, we realized that someone had to serve the larger national interests regardless of the costs. Despite all of the efforts to debunk us, threaten us and make us a non-issue, we could see that we proudly stood alone.

Had it not been for the wholesale participation in the 124 West Ninth Street HUD Treasury theft cover-up by the highest levels of the U. S. Justice Department on down to the Hamilton County, Ohio state court, the Bananagate cover-up would not have had the success that it had. A focusing squint was not required to plainly see the connective bonds that linked President Bill Clinton, Carl H. Lindner, Jr. and Stan Chesley to a criminal cover-up in corrupt federal and state court systems. Applying William Shakespeare's words to what could be seen from the pinnacle, there were "warnings, and portents and evils imminent."

As Sandy and I had appropriately gathered federally incriminating evidence that was backed up with straight talk and hard facts, we submitted the evidence of our case to the proper federal officials and waited for a ruling based upon the evidence. That is how America's rule of law should work; that was what we did. But, as we could see from a solid perch, that was not what happened. Our eagle eyes did not allow the President and the Queen's ploys to escape detection.

America's courts were designed to uphold the laws of the United States by resolving legal questions. In the Preamble of the U. S. Constitution, the introductory clause that states its intent and purpose, the sixteenth and seventeenth words from its beginning are to

"...establish Justice..." That is the obligatory purpose of the American court system. This function is indispensable for the good of United States society.

Before we roosted on our pinnacle, Sandy and I had already known that the justice system was only as good as the people that worked within it. But it was only after we had gained a position of unobstructed vision that we got the perspective to see the immovable barriers that had been erected by the President and the Queen. We had also already known that America had been established wherein the rule of law was constituted as its foundation. Yet, while we knew that the concept of the rule of law meant deciding matters in court rather than through an aristocracy or through corruption, we also had gained a firsthand appreciation for the fact that corrupt lawyers were bad enough, but corrupt judges were worse.

I could see that the judges that Sandy and I came into contact with were atrocious. As their gratuitous insolence had no legitimate place in American law, their actions were arbitrary and contrary to law. But, as they sat in judgment, usurped their legal powers and were derelict in their duties, they had the legal dexterity to run their trick on us.

My eyes had long ago read Article III, Section One of the U. S. Constitution that says that judges shall hold their jobs as long as they have good behavior. With the evidence that exists of widespread judicial bad behavior regarding 124 West Ninth Street, the pompous jobs of the judges that handled Bananagate's legal questions should no longer be sacrosanct, as they have demonstrated that they have outlived their usefulness to society.

Bananagate's judges were most interested in the protection that they provided to—and the reciprocal recognition and/or compensation that they would get from—the President and the Queen. They were more interested in image than justice, and more interested in a public relations ploy than in an honest effort to abide by the law.

By seeing hideous crimes being shielded by the pernicious rulings of those who pass judgment, it was rather strange—and paradoxical at the same time—to see United States judges who saw little incongruity in their participation in 124 West Ninth Street criminal activity. It was stranger still to see them pronounce the virtues of truth, fairness, freedom, liberty, impartiality and equality while they were legal entities acting illegally in courts of law.

The criminal legal environment created by the President and the Queen was not about the fair, equal and impartial administration of justice. From my crow's nest, I saw that what happened was a mockery of justice—federal laws and righteousness be damned. In their own particular brand of justice, they rigged court proceedings to avoid the requirements of the federal laws that they were facing.

By ensuring that we were not allowed the opportunity to make any discovery or give any depositions, the Bananagate influenced judges who handled my court proceedings gave the defendants in my lawsuit an illegal advantage over my wife and I. Criminally, they marched in lockstep to a politically oriented drumbeat in order to cover federally indictable crimes.

Like a fly on the wall, I could see the story of how a labyrinth of kangaroo courtrooms had been stealthily assigned to deny me due process of law. Since the judges could not dismantle my case, they resorted to the use of tricky court maneuvers to make sure that Sandy and I never got to tell our story in open court. Under the color of authority, federal and state judges used chicanery to violate their oaths in a conspiracy of silence to hide federally indictable white-collar criminal activity.

From the pinnacle, there never was a time that my view was clouded; I always had twenty-twenty vision. As I stared deeper, and deeper yet, into a highly esoteric place where villainous courtroom officials dwelled, my penetrating eyes allowed me to see past the President and the Queen's curtain of fog and iron. I telescoped into a place where mass underworld attempts were made to withhold crucial federal information to change a factual history that could not be changed.

Every time the 124 West Ninth Street facts came to light, the credibility of the U. S. court system took an unwanted hit. As judges illegally erected firewalls of protection to shield themselves and higher-ups, still, their attempted use of smoke and mirrors could not hide the federal crimes of 124 West Ninth Street. The sad irony was that it was not so much that these federal crimes were committed, as much as it was the federal court's active involvement in covering-up these crimes.

I knew from what I saw that the very idea of the existence of an inner circle, a secretive and illegal mode of operation from within the U. S. court system, goes against everything that democracy stands for. From my stakeout, I could see how the cast of the Queen's shadow owed its darkness to the ability of America's courts to be guided and influenced by dirty money. I had no doubt what I saw: the federal criminal events that occurred at 124 West Ninth Street demonstrated that the politically oriented American court system is for sale.

With the bird's-eye view that I had during President Bill Clinton's Monica Lewinsky sex scandal, I knew that U. S. Attorney General Janet Reno was not going to appoint an independent counsel to investigate the president's illegal campaign contributions. With the knowledge that she and her boss had in the 124 West Ninth Street HUD criminal cover-up, there was no way that she was going to provide the boots to kick herself and her boss in the butt.

My sharp eye could also detect the signature pattern of the U. S. Justice Department's use as a conduit and a shield to deflect incrimination away from Attorney General Janet Reno. When the U. S. Justice Department wrote to me regarding the blatant crimes at 124 West Ninth Street and said "there was no basis for action by them," like Nixon's Watergate, I knew that I was seeing a deep cover operation.

I riveted my eyes upon how, under Federal Rules of Civil Procedure 52(a), the Sixth Circuit Appeals Court should have set aside the lower District Court's finding of fact made by Judge Weber because his decision against us was clearly erroneous, in that it involved a mistake. As his decision was a deviation from the requirements of the law, I checked out how the District Court's judgment was clearly based upon an erroneous application of legal principles.

The pinnacle's fresh view only reconfirmed what I had seen for a long time. Instead of the District Court trying to reinvent the wheel of legal application science, it should have applied the federal legal regulations and guidelines of 24 CFR Part 511 that had already been invented to deal with the HUD RRP U. S. Treasury theft infractions that occurred at 124 West Ninth Street.

In staid revulsion, I took a long, hard look at the legal abomination that was of Judge Weber's frantic making. As my unassailable facts and evidence gave him fits, and in an attempt to establish a basis for the dismissal of my case, he had to resort to making almost imperceptible changes to the wording of my court filings, thereby transforming and misconstruing the sense and meaning of my assertions. What District Judge Weber attempted to do to my wording was like deducing that Mary gave birth to a baby sheep by reading "Mary had a little lamb."

In the recesses of my mind, the visional images just kept on coming from the pinnacle, bathing my mind's eye in a whirlpool of retrospective simulacra. I saw how my knowledge-starved eyes had been opened in the legal library of the Sixth Circuit Court after a passing and intellectually intensive chance meeting with an unheard-of jailhouse lawyer godsend.

I saw how his cherished input gave me the ammunition that I so desperately needed to put unyielding pressure on the federal court's obligation to appoint a government attorney to me. From that instant in time, my legal fighting batteries were charged sufficiently. From that moment of enlightenment, my perceptions had been altered forever from gaining an effective grasp of legal research techniques. Yet, with all of the exposure that I had to him, I could not determine whether he was my attendant spirit, my guardian angel or not. All I know is that he mysteriously came into my life, uplifted my soul through understanding and encouragement and then he vanished without a trace.

With an unaided eye, the focus upon 124 West Ninth Street's dark past became clearer to me. As my legal savoir faire sharpened, I could see how the President and the Queen's exposure and vulnerability to detection grew. As if I was viewing a theatrical scene, I directed my eyes at how cover-up efforts repressed crucial facts while evading punishing federal laws. In another tragic act, the U. S. Justice Department's strategy took yet another flawed turn.

Like the slow motion playback of videotape, I was able to review and analyze in detail U. S Attorney Janet Reno's involvement in protecting her boss from criminal indictment and/or removal from office. Undoubtedly, she felt the oppressive legal pressure from a successive barrage of motions that two common citizens like Sandy and I filed in her Sixth Circuit Court. Reno then quarterbacked a public attempt to give the appearance that she was doing what federal law mandated by seeing to it that Attorney Stan Chesley was appointed to represent me. In hindsight, I could see that it was the October 24, 1994 Trojan horse appointment of Chesley under her auspices that was secretly done to do me harm.

As the stakes were high and Attorney Stan Chesley was extremely close to Bill Clinton, the overriding fact of the matter was that I had come too dangerously close to exposing President to 124 West Ninth Street Treasury theft crimes. Just as surely as the cover-up effort was in dire straights, Stan Chesley was chosen to be the President and the Queen's ace-in-the-hole.

I could see what the U. S. Justice Department's rationale for Chesley's appointment to me was. First of all, the Clinton White House had sanctioned it. Secondly, he was sent to stop my lawsuit. Thirdly, he was chosen to step into a hornet's nest of White House incrimination, due to the seemingly impeccable nature of his legal community standing.

As ostensible political payoffs of 124 West Ninth Street's whitewash were settled, I gaped at the waxing emergence of greater sins against America. It was horrific enough to see that Chesley had illegally shielded a member of his law firm, former Cincinnati City Mayor and Councilman Dwight Tillery, from federal prosecution. It was worst yet to see what President Bill Clinton did for Chesley's wife, Attorney Susan J. Dlott, after my first federal court appointed attorney saved face for the Clinton administration by getting my case thrown out of lower court.

The public reward for Chesley's faithful West Ninth Street felonious cover-up service was sickening to me. I goggled in seeing how Attorney Dlott breezed through a brief September 28, 1995 U. S. Senate Judiciary Committee confirmation hearing as a federal judge nominee to fill a vacancy caused by U. S. District Judge S. Arthur Spiegel's decision to take semi-retirement. As the Clinton/Lindner/Chesley alliance continued to do a number on the American public, I painfully observed two Bananagate senatorial mainstays stepping forth to earn their crooked spoils: U. S. Senator Mike DeWine, R-Ohio, chaired the hearings while U. S. Senator John Glenn's, D-Ohio, picture appeared in a national newspaper article congratulating Dlott.

I felt sad for my nation to see Stan Chesley making jokes on one of the White House videos that were released during the week of October, 14, 1997, two months before Linda Tripp began secretly taping extensive conversations that revealed Monica Lewinsky's sexual affair with the President.

In steady view of Chesley's appointment to me, I relived the President and the Queen's government cover-up spectacle that snowballed in front of my commanding perspective. After I had filed an overwhelmingly convincing negligence and legal malpractice lawsuit against Stan Chesley that undeniably linked him to White House HUD Treasury theft incriminations, it was quite astonishing to behold how U. S.

District Judge Carl B. Rubin took his Bananagate hanky-panky to his grave.

Appointed to the federal bench in 1971 by President Richard M. Nixon, United States District Judge Carl B. Rubin served in the Southern District of Ohio for more than twenty years. Most notably, Judge Rubin presided over the handling of the huge lawsuits that followed one hundred and sixty-five deaths in Chesley's Beverly Hills (Kentucky) Supper Club fire case. He also presided over the handling of the large federal actions that followed hundreds of birth defects among women who used the anti-nausea drug Bendectin, which was made by Merrell Dow Pharmaceuticals of Cincinnati.

Some attorneys dreaded having their cases assigned to Judge Rubin, assuming his conservative social, political and judicial views would work against them. After I presented clear-cut evidence to Judge Rubin's attention that Chesley's attorney, Terrence L. Goodman had perjured himself to the Court (a felony) and Judge Rubin did nothing, I saw how he worked against me in the mishandling of Chesley's federal negligence and legal malpractice lawsuit (Case No. C-1-95-219).

Continuing my gaze from the pinnacle, I could see that criminal cover-up activity did not matter in the world of political patronage that lived and thrived in the U. S. Justice Department. As evidenced by Attorney Stanley M. Chesley's presidential clout in the Sixth Circuit District Court, he operated with impunity. There was no price to pay by those who broke federal laws in illegally protecting the corrupt command structure of President Bill Clinton.

While the President was in control of America's supreme legal body that abetted the hiding of his Bananagate crimes, Reno, Chesley and Rubin were untouchable, as their backs were ultimately watched through the stratagem of a chronically immoral and lying president. Like the cyclicality of a rolling echo in a high-walled canyon, I saw how the Judge Rubin's District Court was the latest part of a federal cover-up, that was on top of another cover-up, that was on top of another cover-up, ad infinitum.

Based upon what I observed, I could not help but to keep thinking about the intricacies of how the cover-up was craftily constructed. I saw how, on March 15, 1995, just four and one half months prior to Judge Rubin's ruling dismissing Chesley, U. S. Magistrate Judge Steinberg had said at my injunction hearing that "Judge Rubin is ill (with terminal cancer) and is not available" for that court hearing.

It was precisely for that reason that serious questions were raised when, in such a short time before his death, Judge Rubin was able to prepare and file an eight page, logically bereft court order to dismiss Chesley from criminal prosecution. With no legal scrutiny that could be applied to Judge Rubin beyond the grave, the President and the Queen's court even attempted to use the death of one of its accomplices as a means to deliver an unapproachable coup de grace to Sandy and I.

I saw again how the Trojan horse that Chesley rode in on had backfired on the President and the Queen. As Judge Rubin's death was opportunely used as an additional cover-up mechanism, the Bananagate scheme was forced into shifting back to an unending line of Sixth Circuit court judges who were willing to participate in the cover-up and win at any cost.

Implicit to the U. S. Treasury theft strategy from within the Sixth Circuit court was the following rationale that they posed to the American public: "If there was a mistake made, it was Judge Rubin's mistake, not ours. If you have a question about or a problem with what he decided, ask him about it." The Queen's 124 West Ninth Street Treasury theft conspirators figured that the truth had been buried.

Most of all, Judge Carl Rubin's ruling to dismiss did not square with the glaring negligence and legal malpractice charges against Chesley. I could easily view how the only answer to the legal conundrum that the Queen's court had worked itself into was to use the ruling of a dying judge to attempt to bail them out. Ironically, it was no surprise that the same frightening concept of abuse of power that was used by the imperial presidency of Rubin's mentor, President Richard M. Nixon, was the same type of corrupt decision that came from the imperial judgeship of Carl B. Rubin.

Pulling another trick out of their hat, the District Court parlayed Judge Rubin's death in such a way that I could not contend with it. As a result, my evidentiary court advantage and my winning momentum shifted away from me and back into other politically corrupt Sixth Circuit courtrooms. Stretched extremely thin by not having the resources to successfully appeal Judge Rubin's court decision, by cover-up design, Sandy and I were forced to continue to legally fight in propria persona (without the assistance of an attorney).

Upon his death, Robert Rubin, Judge Rubin's son said, "What many people don't realize about him was that while he was a very conservative person in his political views, I don't think I met anybody who felt more strongly about the importance of individual liberty and his responsibility to protect that liberty. He viewed that as the most important thing he did as a judge." Just as the deathbed of President Lincoln's son was secretly used by Chesley for rest, public eulogies did not accurately reflect the fact that Judge Rubin's deathbed was actually the federal focal point where Chesley's link to presidential incrimination was secretly put to rest.

Speaking from firsthand experience, nothing was further from the truth to me. To Chesley, his personal friend on the other end of the spectrum, the most important thing that Judge Rubin did as a judge was to keep him from the public embarrassment of being heavily fined and/or jailed for jutting crimes against America. Judge Rubin had seen to it that the charges of negligence, legal malpractice and complicity in a presidential HUD Treasury theft cover-up scheme were conveniently dropped against him.

From the loftiness of a topless tower, my eyes continued to be opened by the sight of the federal government's power being used against me. From my reading in the U. S. Sixth Circuit Library, I was able to determine that the U. S. attorney's office had the federal responsibility to intervene and to prosecute when federal laws were broken. As Edmund A. Sargus, Jr. was head of the U. S. attorney's office for the Southern District of Ohio, an area encompassing 124 West Ninth Street, I made note of how the dirty hand of President Bill Clinton reached down to influentially touch Sargus' Queen City base of corruption.

Admittedly, I was rather encouraged when I originally called his office on September 9, 1994 informing his secretary, Nonnie, about the Queen's federal infractions. From my highland gander, I could see precisely how my early optimism abounded. The problem for me thereafter was that nothing happened; I had run smack-dab into the wall of silence again. It was from this fated moment that things became more open-and-shut in clinching his role in the Bananagate cover-up.

On November 28, 1994, I received a letter from Sargus that stated, "Our office is the prosecutive arm of the Department of Justice. Our office is not authorized to investigate alleged criminal conduct." He went on further to say, "I have forwarded the information you sent to me to the FBI, Cincinnati division. That office will then determine if an investigation is warranted. In the event such an investigation is conducted the matter may be re-referred to this office for prosecution."

But that was where the hoax ended. From that time forward, instead of abiding by the laws of this nation that he swore to uphold, Sargus followed the dictates of America's latest political fund-raising dogma to allow Bill Clinton-influenced federal government Treasury theft fraud to go on unabated. As Sargus was completely aware that my two active federal lawsuits contained case files that were rife with clear-cut evidence of federal misconduct, he remained conspicuously mum with respect to his selective prosecution of America's laws. An elaborate system of criminal cover-up against the American public remained hidden under Sargus' watch.

Just as Attorney Stan Chesley's Bananagate cover-up efforts were rewarded, Sargus was rewarded for his. On September 29, 1995, thirty-nine days after U. S. Judge Rubin died, it was announced that Sargus was going to take his place. From aerial heights, I could see how political cogs interconnected, serving as mechanisms that were performing a specific function in a complete cover-up machine.

Towering above a view of my past, the incriminating linkage between indictable presidential criminal activity and Sargus' participation in it became increasingly palpable as the political payoff became unmistakable. First, I was able to make out that Sargus had been the unanimous choice of a five-member, bipartisan commission appointed to screen federal judicial candidates by U. S. Senator John Glenn. Next, I was able to comprehend that Senator Glenn sent his recommendation to President Clinton for a decision. But, it was after Clinton's nomination of Sargus to be a Sixth Circuit Judge that I knew that I had a greater chance of changing the leopard's spots, fetching water in a sieve or catching the wind in a net than beating debauched feds in their own back yard.

Like seeing dust arising from a bovine stampede, my upland slope position allowed me to see signs of a large herd of people that were moving against me. The perspicuity of this situation caused me to see my being up against an army of Bananagate cover-up soldiers in a special light. They were a massive array of institutional American government and private forces that were evading U. S. Treasury theft laws, consumer protection banking laws, civil rights laws and federal perjury and obstruction of justice laws.

Even though this army had different types, ranks and levels of soldiers, each of them figured that they could hide behind their collective efforts to deny Sandy and I our constitutional rights, while keeping Bananagate hidden. As I witnessed the marching of the President and the Queen's soldiers, it was ever more apparent how much was at stake.

I saw that they were a body of persons organized to advance a cause. In the true definition of esprit de corps, the 124 West Ninth Street cover-up conspirators also had a common spirit existing within their ranks that inspired enthusiasm, devotion and strong regard for the honor of the group. Seeing how they were in cahoots with one another, I was able to distinguish how they had cocooned themselves, and had gone to exceeding depths to win against Sandy and I.

As we faced the wrath of the Queen's soldiers, they conjoined to aim their barbs at us, to spurn us, and to loathe and deride us. To aid their trick, they resorted to fancy footwork to keep their secret. Thinking that Sandy and I were in awe of them, they expected us to be compliant, accommodating and submissive while they did their evil deeds.

Overhead, I could see how the President and the Queen's soldiers had amassed, giving me the final, irrefutable piece of evidence that something was terribly wrong in America. Helpless, I espied their gaining of an impressive foothold that was undermining the American system of judicial checks and balances.

Like stink in the nostrils, I reacted with a sick feeling in my stomach, abhorred from seeing how their behavior was leeching over to infect the rest of society. After the dust settled, I could see that the general of the cover-up army was U. S. President Bill Clinton. It was not as if the Commander in Chief's office was not aware of what happened at 124 West Ninth Street: I wrote to him, faxed him and emailed him constantly.

It was also not as if the Bill Clinton White House did not know of the rampant problems that existed at HUD. From my view, I did not have to crane my neck to see that the President gave the Queen a gift in the Lincoln Bedroom, and that it was the fear of the White House that scared people away.

I did not have to tiptoe to see that Carl H. Lindner, Jr. was like a five-star general of the Bananagate cover-up army who had considerable influence in the White House. As his extensive corporate financial empire was inextricably involved in defrauding the U. S. government at 124 West Ninth Street, I could see that the whole Bananagate cover-up was nothing more than a mere ad hoc measure that was used as a demarche for unrestrained political power.

My earthward view made it as clear as day that Carl H. Lindner, Jr.'s Provident Bank used its untrammeled political clout to sway politicians and judges deep from within the government of the United States. I could see how cover-up efforts took on an additional dimension when Sandy and I resisted and Lindner shoveled out tons of money against us to avoid federal incrimination.

Neither did I have faulty eyesight when I visually revisited the hidden absurdity and lunacy of the federal government's HUD from the time that Sandy and I signed a binding contract with it in 1992. It was this cathectic look back in time from my toploftical field of vision, however, that allowed me to see the conditions under which Clinton, Lindner and Chesley criminally advantaged HUD's last two leaders, Secretaries Henry Cisneros and Andrew Cuomo.

Looking back into time with my heavenly eye, and into places that were beyond my initial line of sight, I could see how at the beginning of the Clinton and Cisneros administration, the national press reported troubling news about HUD. In the March 11, 1993 edition of *The New York Times,* it was reported that, "A series of internal reports on operations within HUD warned about further scandals; reports say problems in staffing, data systems and accounting controls are leading to misuse of hundreds of millions of dollars, leaving the Department with an uncertain grasp of more than $1 trillion in financial commitments."

I could also see that, two days before I led a picket of Cincinnati's City Hall, the October 27, 1993 edition of *The New York Times* reported that Deborah Gore Dean, Executive Assistant to former HUD Secretary Samuel R. Pierce, Jr., who found herself at the center of an influence-peddling scandal during the Reagan Administration, was convicted of 12 felony counts of defrauding the Government and lying to Congress. With a slight cutting of my eyes, it was not hard for me to see that she was sentenced in 1994 to twenty-one months in prison and fined $5,000.

I saw much, much more with respect to the HUD theft of government tax dollars at 124 West Ninth Street. Four days before I determinedly infiltrated HUD's headquarters in Washington, D. C., the June 18, 1994 *New York Times* reported that, due to a legal technicality, the Federal appeals court overturned the conviction of the onetime top aid to former HUD Secretary Samuel R. Pierce, Jr., Lance Henry Wilson. Even though this article revealingly reported that Wilson had been tried, convicted and sentenced to six months in prison after an investigation of bribery and kickbacks at HUD, I could see that the stigma on the Department remained.

Above all, my eyes feasted on how President Bill Clinton's Bananagate role tied into Cisneros' demise. I saw how, regardless of the political baggage that he carried by keeping him in his Cabinet, President Clinton said publicly that he would stand behind Secretary Cisneros. As a besieged and scandal-ladened White House and HUD had become extremely reticent of any additional flack that they could have received, they covered-up what happened at 124 West Ninth Street, lest the nation would have had yet another reason for their removal from office.

I could see how the President required that the underling Queen handle the Bananagate scandal by the same old tired songs of playing dumb, and by digging into an old bucket of bones by pulling out anemic assertions of "no comment." But, regardless, I knew that their impotent strategy did not matter. I had already seen that, under federal conspiracy law, the people in the Queen who participated in the Bananagate conspiracy were just as guilty of felonies as the feds who participated in the 124 West Ninth Street HUD criminal activity.

I could see how Carl H. Lindner, Jr.'s Lincoln Bedroom sleepover also occurred subsequent to the filing of my lawsuit that would have incriminated him and his bank, Provident. Based upon the way in which events evolved, it was as clear as the nose on one's face that only the financial power and the corrupt political connections of this billionaire kept the federally indictable facts and evidence of my lawsuit from being revealed.

Looking down from the pinnacle, I could clearly see the Brobdingnagian systematization of a cover-up scheme that I could not have seen from below. My broad view allowed me to see how a mountain of people, who had authority over many others, misused their high ranks, positions and powers to illegally participate in the Bananagate HUD U. S. Treasury theft conspiracy.

More important than anything else, my view from the pinnacle allowed me to get a historical perspective of what had happened to my family. I could see that the Bananagate cover-up was the type institutional discrimination that spawned the passage of the Civil Rights Act of 1964, passed to amend statutes passed after the Civil War to provide stronger protection for rights guaranteed by the Constitution. At bottom, based upon the President and the Queen's actions, Sandy and I had fallen victim to a historically recalcitrant pattern of biased and discriminatory conduct that was a legacy of America's past.

Chapter 10

The Quasi-slave System

"There can be no freedom of the individual, no democracy, without the capital system, the profit system, the private enterprise system. These are, in the end, inseparable. Those who would destroy freedom have only first to destroy the hope of gain, the profit of enterprise and risk-taking, the hope of accumulating capital, the hope to save something for one's old age and for one's children. For a community of men without property, and without the hope of getting it by honest effort, is a community of slaves of a despotic State."

—Russell C. Leffingwell

Something was terribly wrong with the prolonged picture that I was seeing. The glaring shutdown of help to Sandy and I from America's government remained in place, violating the Constitution of the United States of America. My perspective of the 124 West Ninth Street federal cover-up reminded me of the adage made popular by the French author Jean Baptiste Alphonse Karr (1808-1890) which read, "The more things change, the more they remain the same."

I read the handwriting on the wall and developed a precise and vivid understanding of how the existing state of national racial relations, buttressed by a historic ideology of white supremacy, had been a driving factor in my institutional demise. With America's racial legacy as a backdrop, it was quite easy for me to draw unmistakable parallels between observable social phenomena and the subterranean existence of a constitutionally outlawed slave-like condition that affects most African-Americans: a quasi-slave system. I saw it for what it was: a cultural way of thinking that grips the consciousness of America's status quo.

Although it was not nearly as severe as the once constitutionally-sanctioned chattel slave system that existed during America's past, in many striking ways, I saw how the current-day and incognito quasi-slave system was twinned to its forbidden societal predecessor. Though it is far more pervasive and damaging than the corrosive and potentially calamitous pattern of racist U. S. Treasury theft that is the distinguishing characteristic of the Queen syndrome, I knew firsthand that the Queen syndrome was only a pointer to a much larger quasi-slave system. It is the quasi-slave system that implements an institutional standard of separate laws and separate understandings of what America should be.

In the immediacy of the trouncing that Sandy and I had received in the microcosm of the Queen, there was no doubt in my mind that the quasi-slave system's reach continued to be of historic significance. It became even more apparent to me that America's history of recalcitrant enslavement was defining its current national policy and what we, as a nation, believed.

My test of the U. S. Constitution that had begun more than twenty years prior made it absolutely clear to me that the enduring and most significant legacy of America's chattel slavery system was the continued acceptance of African-American discrimination by large numbers of the U. S. citizenry. I saw that it was a way of American governance that was reinforced and supported by most politicians and their constituents who believed that they had the right and option to permit racial intolerance, no matter how unconstitutional it was, or whom it hurt.

Sadly, with respect to America's inherent constitutional contradictions regarding race, I knew that many white Americans regularly flew Old Glory because they felt that it was their duty to honor their right to enjoy life in the way that they know it. Conversely, I could also see that it was sad that most African-Americans did not proudly fly the American flag because they knew that their constitutional rights were regularly infringed upon.

Regardless of the overall success of the American experiment since it was begun, I knew that the American political character had brought through time the burdensome baggage of a racial predicament that, from its outset, has been negatively influenced by money. It was, after all, the influence of money that brought African slavery to the Western Hemisphere in the first place.

I was cognizant of the fact that the American Revolution provided us an opportunity to reconsider our choices, but the American Constitution chose slavery, as the plantation system had taken hold and

America had become too dependent on slave labor to give it up easily. Likewise, the Civil War was fought over slavery, but, by that time, the whole concept of African slavery had become the foundation on which America's social order rested.

Despite the fact that there was considerable Southern sentiment against slavery during the colonial and early national periods, the institution always had its defenders. From its beginning in America until today, no attack on slavery has gone unanswered.

When there was some doubt regarding the future of chattel slavery under young America's new national government following America's Revolution, most of the Southern delegates made it clear that they would tolerate no interference with the institution. From the time that Jefferson's Notes on Virginia, circa 1782, were made public, Southern leaders did not hesitate to use his work to strengthen their contention that Negroes were by nature an inferior race and therefore should be enslaved. Some Southerners conceded that slavery was a political evil; but almost none agreed with anti-slavery proponents that it was also a great moral evil.

There was no doubt in my mind that, even though the Thirteenth Amendment to the Constitution of the United States effectively abolished chattel slavery in America in 1865, the carry-over effects of this institution of racial servitude stubbornly persisted, in a very real sense, all around me. In many ways, I could see how, in today's America, those same race-based conditions were still guiding the conscious governance of the United States of America.

Just as early America's numerous slave codes protected slave owners in their domination over Negroes, I saw how the federal government was still fostering a prevailing attitude that was largely responsible for suppressing its African-American population. From the beginning, just as America's politicians practiced racial hypocrisy as an art form, similarly, I knew that it was the typical evasion, denial and deception of President Bill Clinton's White House modus operandi that was to blame for the slave-like racial madness that was tormenting my family. Events in Washington demonstrated to me that there was a fully operational quasi-slave system in place and that America's political ruling class had not much changed.

As an undeniable drain on the U. S. society, I realized that the pernicious effects of institutional racism were flourishing in America; that it was insidious; and that it was suicidally shaking the bedrock foundation of America's constitutional form of government. Furthermore, as I eked out a very strained existence from the trenches, I saw that the quasi-slave system was real, underground, not hard to prove and inconsistent with the American constitution. Most of all, I saw how its conservative ideology was institutionally marginalizing most African-Americans by forcing them to live beyond the pale of the law.

Conservatives, by definition, are people who have something to conserve. With society's fast paced technological advances and lifestyle changes drastically changing the way that we do things these days, I, personally, do not know of anyone who does not have some sort of sentimental attachment to the past.

By definition, I knew that *conservatism* was not necessarily a bad thing. In many ways, there is nothing wrong with being disposed to keeping established ways; many positive conservative things occur all of the time that are transparent to race. With respect to holding on to those types of things that are universally valued, such as cherished neighborhood institutions, the family structure, respect for elders, and the like, African-Americans are just as conservative as white Americans. However, I could not help but to see how America's controlling right wing conservatives were doggedly trying to hold on to racial beliefs of the slaveholding past.

As they are in many positions of power throughout the American body politic, I had an inside view on how they have many tools that are available to them which are used to undercut established law in order to carry out their stratagem. Unable to legally carry out their true agenda of outlawed racial privilege in the open, they try to cloak their real intentions and feelings in a functioning underworld of hidden codes and actions.

Without coming out directly and saying what they mean from their prejudicial points of view, they use code words that have racist overtones to communicate their real intentions. They sometimes imbed and weave racially discriminatory themes into normal jargon. For example, when they mention *family values*, they, more ofttimes than not, are referring to protecting and upholding the conservative pro-white racial beliefs that were instilled in white families of yesteryear which gave American whites distinct advantages over African-Americans. When the conservatives speak of *law and order*, typically, that means that they want to keep the enforcement of historic laws that keep blacks in the order of the slave, replete with many of the built-in inducements from the throwback days of chattel slavery.

To most of America's right wing conservatives, being *tough on crime* is synonymous with being tough on African-Americans. Look at how Willie Horton's picture was used by President George Bush during his 1988 presidential campaign against George Dukakis. As much as most African-Americans loathe what welfare has done and is doing to the black community, conservatives use the term *welfare reform* as another code word for working institutionally against African-Americans who have been inordinately disadvantaged by the quasi-slave system. The paradox, though, is that most of the people on welfare are white.

By no stretch of the imagination do white folks have a lock on being clannish: blacks like being amongst their own kind just as much as whites, Mexican-Americans, Asians, native Americans, or any other racial group—whether in this country or not. Fundamentally, there is absolutely nothing wrong with this human characteristic, as it is natural. If various individuals want to be together with others in their own racial groups, providing that laws are not broken, then, that is their American right. However, if laws are broken in pursuance thereof, in a nation of laws, that is illegal.

Having visited other nations of the world, in my opinion, the American political experiment, on balance, is the best on earth. However, for those Americans who attempt to defend the United States legal, political and economic system from much warranted reproach by saying that "it's the only thing that we have," that response is way off target. Instead, circumstances dictate that efficacious approaches are required for the corrections that are needed in America's handling of its African-American racial dilemma.

In seeing how America's conservatives attempted to justify the quasi-slave system, I listened to what they were saying. Many conservatives argue that, because American blacks have the privilege of living in the world's best society, they should not complain. As beliefs like that are, at their core, inherently racist, the lack of responding to such a nonsensical utterance only denotes my not dignifying the statement.

Conservatives also feel that if they allow blacks into the mainstream of America, they will lose their heritage of racial superiority, which is the fabric of their perception of what this nation should be. If left up to many conservatives, African-Americans will either remain locked positionally in the status quo; we will be denied full American rights even more than now; or we will be shipped to Africa.

As they are relatively comfortable basking in the sunshine of the quasi-slave system's present-day clampdowns, conservatives do not need the Ku Klux Klan. They reason that as long as planned economic deterioration endemically besets the black community, the Klan can hang up their robes and take a breather. As their societal strategies and expectations for America's Negro population only mirrors the high levels of addictive and mind-stealing drugs that make their way into African-American neighborhoods, quasi-slave system proponents do not need to lynch Negroes from trees: by design, Negroes will lynch themselves.

Conservatives also know about the collateral damage that guns have in the areas where blacks are concentrated. As a result, they have no reason to instill fear in blacks because, with their seeing to it that handguns are disproportionately out of control in African-American communities, blacks will instill fear in themselves.

Conservatives say, "I'm not responsible for what my ancestors did." Nobody is saying that they are. However, when they have an unfair racial advantage in American society over millions of African-Americans, based upon the discriminatory groundwork that was institutionally laid by their ancestors, there is a troubling constitutional problem. When they say and do nothing to eliminate this embedded racial advantage, they are, in effect (whether they want to admit it or not), beneficiaries of a perpetually unequal system that their forebears created. Their arguments of convenience do not begin to adequately address, let alone solve, America's vexing race problem.

As the *L* word (for liberal) has become a curse word for conservatives since before the Reagan administration, I have heard conservatives saying things like, "Affirmative action is race discrimination in reverse and it is just as wrong as the discrimination that blacks experienced." I knew that the truth of the matter was that these complaints were only acknowledgments of conservative unwillingness to deal with the painful process that America has to go through in order to remedy the far more destructive quasi-slave system.

Other contemporary factors forced the conservative pendulum to swing further to the right, adding to already increased levels of negrophobia. With the existence of the *angry white men phenomenon*, the misconception that white jobs were going to African-Americans (when they were being eliminated or were going overseas) kept giving life to right wing conservatism. Even as black images uncontrollably entered into their residences via the television, the Internet and the news media, quasi-slave system negrophobes could alter many things in their lives, but time and change were two things that they could not.

It was easy for me to recognize that American chattel slavery still lived; it just existed in another form. My firsthand 124 West Ninth Street experience gave me an insightful perspective that allowed me to see that there were quasi-slave system *masters* in place who had disinterested socio-economic control over African-Americans.

As my 124 West Ninth Street experiences had proven, the governments of the United States and the State of Ohio were masters in this regard. My treatment was proof of how they quarterback institutional racism and work in conjunction with powerful anti-black sentimentalities in the status quo that maintain racially discriminatory barriers, standards and norms.

For example, two prominent national politicians, U. S. Senate Majority Leader, Trent Lott, R-Miss. and former U. S. Attorney in Atlanta, Georgia, Representative Bob Barr, R-Ga., openly spoke to the Council of Conservative Citizens (CCC), which has links to white supremacists. Among other things, the CCC's race-based warnings assert interbreeding between whites and racial minorities will destroy the white race and lead to the decay of civilization. As the CCC has been the most successful far-right organization in establishing ties to elected officials, it has been somewhat successful in cloaking itself in the mantle of conservatism to underlie its racist agenda. Their real agenda, however, is opposition to the American ideal of equality for all people.

The CCC was formed in 1989 from the now-defunct Citizen's Council of America, also known as "the white-collar Klan," active in the 1950s and '60s opposing the integration of public schools in the South. Based upon the CCC's web page, its goal is "to conserve the traditional heritage, culture and way of life that Euro-Americans have practiced since the inception of this country." With Sen. Lott's and Rep. Barr's public leanings being the way that they are, it is easy to see how they were actively involved in the Bananagate cover-up against me.

Based exclusively upon race, there are also quasi-slave system *overseers* in place who overlook, aid, abet, inspect, supervise and give feedback to the masters within the quasi-slave system. In this regard, and from firsthand experience, I saw how America's courts and banks did the overseeing work for the quasi-slave system.

Just as *chains* were once used to fetter Negroes in the chattel slave system of the United States, the funneling of drugs into black neighborhoods, high unemployment, massive underemployment and the fostering of economic disfranchisement are classic examples of the chains that are being used against African-Americans today. In a nationally televised interview that was conducted by the ABC's Barbara Walters on the Honorable Minister Louis Farrakhan, head of the Nation of Islam and organizer of the Million Man March on Washington, D. C., one thing, in particular, was said by the black Muslim leader that most American blacks are in accordance with.

Farrakhan said, "If the United States government is not responsible for the drugs in the African-American community, then why don't they stop them from coming in?" Farrakhan, like many others understands the connection between the slavery of the past and the deliberate injection and national condoning of drugs into American black communities. Even though cocaine is cocaine, African-Americans are disproportionately penalized for using the cheaper variety of crack cocaine that floods our neighborhoods.

Another jutting indicator of chains that exist within today's quasi-slave system is the second-class citizenship condition that exists within most of America's black communities. As many African-Americans feel anger from being left out of sharing all of the freedoms that white Americans have, millions of America's blacks are institutionally trapped in a large section of the national economy that institutionally drains their neighborhoods of cash. Consequently, large numbers of us know that we must survive via a fringe, underground, drug or ignoble economy in order to survive.

On the streets of a significant percentage of America's black neighborhoods, it is commonplace to hear the coined term *deal a meal* when one sells drugs in order to eat. On the welfare recipient side, the limits of African-American pocketbooks are controlled, keeping them dependent upon the handouts of the quasi-slave system. There are those who call this the American "chitterling strategy."

As *whips* were used in the chattel slave system of yesterday, the police, jails and prisons serve a similar function in today's quasi-slave system. Even though law enforcement is absolutely necessary for American society, the specific use of law enforcement officers for implementing the discriminatory racial practices of those who control them is readily apparent. Cops and cans (jails) should not be used as extensions of quasi-slave system masters and overseers.

The signs of the negative impact that the quasi-slave system's whips are having on America are all around us. Of the three fastest growth industries in America today, temporary employment, gambling and prison construction, the latter is most indicative of the emphasis that is placed on this quasi-slave system whip. By looking at America's prison population numbers, one can easily see that there is a systemic warehousing of a disproportionate number of the African-American population.

As public works are being neglected for prison construction, only the temporary employment industry, which pays no benefits, and the gambling industry, which bets on the future instead of building it, dubiously lead the pack. If predictions hold true, for example, California alone will build only one new state college to twenty new prisons beginning around the year 2000. As building new jails is not the answer, California—like America at large—should be providing for the common good, not just for race-based prisons.

In America's quasi-slave system, *slave codes* still exist as the taking away of African-American rights continues to be codified. Just as the historic purpose of this nation's slave codes was to serve as a system of principles and rules excluding its Negroes from entering into the mainstream of society, nationally sanctioned constructs continue to remain in place for the same purpose. I was a perfect example of this fact.

By code, slaves were not supposed to own anything of significance: my valuable real estate was systematically taken away from me. By code, slaves were forced to live in a caste system of institutional inequality: the highest levels of the America's federal government made sure that the nation's institutions would not serve me equally. In order to institutionally destroy their dignity and sense of personal worth, slaves had no constitutional rights: by code, mine were taken away. As codified muzzles were placed on African-American slaves to prohibit them from communicating through the beating of their drums, in effect, my story of bona fide HUD U. S. Treasury theft was muzzled and silenced by the White House and the Sixth Circuit Court.

During the chattel slavery days of America's past, *house Negroes* and *Uncle Toms* used to roam the American landscape as designees, serving the function of assisting their oppressors. Today, house Negroes and Uncle Toms still roam the land and serve the same function.

Generally speaking, house Negroes of yesterday and today are almost always chosen by masters or overseers, and are strategically placed in positions of influence. If they do not deliver, and while house Negroes fully understand the job that they have to do, what is expected of them and the price that they will have to pay, they run the self-serving risk of being kicked out of their sporadically propped up positions of influence and back into institutional positions of disadvantage within the masses of the rest of America's *field Negroes*. While personally benefiting from their subterfuge, they are used as the eyes and ears of the principals of the quasi-slave system, serving a mainly threefold purpose, as they sell their souls and act counter to equal and full African-American economic participation in America.

Similar to their chattel slave system counterparts who operated from positions of privilege, first, today's house Negroes are used as window dressing to give the appearance that African-Americans are being treated well. Secondly, they serve as inside informants against other African-Americans who fight for their constitutional rights of equality, as they give insightful and immediate feedback to the *big house* to quell quasi-slave system rebellions and unrest. Thirdly, they serve as shields to deflect attention away from the masters or overseers who violate the constitutional rights of America's Negro population. Tragically, when an American black face speaks on behalf of the quasi-slave system, the problem does not seem to exist nearly as much.

Typically, wherever African-American self-hatreds breed, one will find fertile ground for house Negroes. With blinders firmly affixed, house Negroes are both victims and beneficiaries of a self-defeating system of residual chattel slave system indoctrination. Implicit to their belief system is the goal of self-aggrandizement at the expense of other African-Americans.

They fall basically into two categories: either they don't fully understand the big picture that they see or they don't care about the big picture that they understand. If they don't fully understand the magnitude and the ramifications of the socio-economic plight of themselves and the other African-Americans that they see, it is because they have been living in a vacuum. On the other hand, as they don't care about inflicting pain, misery and self-deprecation—even upon the ones who are closest to them in their own immediate families, the effects of their own self-hatreds perniciously spread into the American black population at large.

It is precisely for these reasons that African-Americans with these types of personalities are sought after by the controlling authorities of the quasi-slave system, as they assist in illegally controlling the African-American population from within. Classic and notable house Negroes that I know of who are directly involved in the U. S. Treasury theft cover-up at 124 West Ninth Street are U. S. Appeals Court Judge Nathaniel Jones and former Cincinnati City Councilman Tyrone Yates.

It should be noted, however, that there are many different levels of House Negroes. This is important to know because of the subtle distinctions that exist between them. Although house Negroes are typically appointed to the big house by those who are non-black, the establishment of house Negro status is not just exclusive to extraracial appointment: there is also an intraracial phenomenon that results in their appointing themselves. Most of the times when this happens, but not always, house Negro types are usually known as Uncle Toms.

By definition, Uncle Toms are commonly known as American blacks that are overeager to win the approval of whites. But from the dregs of humanity that they snake from, they are easily recognized for being unique hybrids, a subset group operating from within the overall house Negro milieu. Make no mistake about it, *Toms* (plural for how they are oftentimes addressed from within the American black neighborhoods) can be just as vile and destructive to the best interests of the African-American community, if not more so, as house Negroes.

Classic and notable Toms that I know of who are directly involved in the U. S. Treasury theft cover-up at 124 West Ninth Street are former Cincinnati Mayor and City Councilman Dwight Tillery and former

Cincinnati City Councilman Charlie Winburn who, paradoxically, is one of the five State Commissioners for the Ohio Civil Rights Commission.

It is the consensus of large numbers of African-Americans that the most prominent Uncle Tom in America is United States Supreme Court Justice Clarence Thomas. From his controversially conservative political appointment to the federal bench to his notable anti-American Negro decisions, all of the signs point squarely to his *Uncle Tomism.* As he has willingly accepted and executed his designated position, overwhelming numbers of African-American's would say that, unlike his predecessor, the Honorable Thurgood Marshall, Justice Thomas has *Tommed,* is a Tom, and will be *Tomming.* California's Ward Connelly is running in a close second place to the top Tom Thomas.

House Negroes and Toms are not stupid. They know that they have very slim chances of equally and effectively entering into the mainstream of American society to take advantage of all American freedoms, such as operating a business and other opportunities that are afforded to American whites and most other immigrants.

Under the unconstitutional conditions of quasi-slave system slim pickings that daunt them into panic, they, instead, go into the business of defeating other African-American's as sycophants to masters and overseers. Both House Negroes and Uncle Toms emphatically know about the extensive racial barriers that have been erected against African-Americans and take the path of least resistance by selling themselves out to a never-ending surplus of willing quasi-slave system financiers.

In the vacuum of effective black leadership in the United States, quasi-slave system masters and overseers scramble to maintain the void by placing favorite house Negroes and Toms at the forefront of visible puppet assignments as spokespeople for the black community. The effectiveness of most of the large national African-American civil rights organizations has been tragically jeopardized, influenced and compromised by financial contributions that have been made to house Negroes and Toms in leadership positions.

Usually, through their secretive and poisonous support of the quasi-slave system, they gain significant community prestige and political power as they are positioned to pose as representatives of African-Americans at large. In January of 1996, for example, the leader of the National Urban League implied that African-Americans should cut out "wedge tactics and divisive techniques" in order to be good Americans.

As they are usually under considerable pressure to simultaneously juggle between two conflicting roles, many house Negroes are hard-pressed to smoothly change hats while they shuffle back and forth from one side of the fence to the other. Appearing in many guises, they run with the hare and hunt with the hounds.

Many times, in order to be accepted as a so-called brother or sister in the African-American community, they are quick to camouflage themselves with all sorts of afrocentric dress and expressions that gives the false impression of their afrocentricity. Like wolves in lambs clothing, they ofttimes opportunistically wear, among other things, African Kinte cloth that has been made into all kinds of garments and accessories, African jewelry, lapel pins, etc.

Although many of these charlatans will try to stay as far away as they possibly can from anything that remotely resembles African accouterments, most house Negroes and Uncle Toms will use any device that they can to escape detection. They deceivingly talk the talk, but they don't walk the walk.

Sometimes called *Oreos*, like the cookie that is black on the outside and has white filling on the inside, they generate a key spark to a destructive internal combustion that occurs in the African-American community just as they did during America's chattel slavery days. Instead of shouldering the burden of removing themselves from the choking yoke of a quasi-slave system that uses them, they are like camp followers who join movements solely for personal gain.

They remind me of the stories of Moses' people in Exodus from the Bible wherein, after their departure from Egypt, they were drunk on their freedoms and did the wrong things. Like crabs in a basket, house Negroes and Uncle Toms see to it that African-Americans keep pulling one another down. As a reward, they are given distinct advantages by masters and overseers for seeing to it that no blacks get past them.

In today's quasi-slave system, *slave quarters* still exist. These places of African-American habitation are highly recognizable areas with fixed territorial divisions and distinguishing characteristics. Their delineation is marked by unequal and underclass communities where a state of perpetual economic deprivation and deterioration thrives. They are places where most African-American dreams of upward mobility are permanently interrupted by the socio-economic nightmare of the quasi-slave system.

Obtrusively, they are often littered places where substandard housing, high crime rates, alcoholic beverage billboards, old cigarette advertisements and graffiti typically plaster the neighborhood—and where minimum subsistence levels are maintained. As places where many African-Americans have been marginalized and locked into the periphery of the United States economy, they are peopled by consuming non-producers who are kept away from financial opportunities that allow them to go into business for themselves.

Worse yet, it is a purposely designed place where non-black businesses feed off of African-Americans, as blacks are systematically used as stepping stones by new and old immigrant groups who use us to enter into the mainstream of the American economy. It is a place where African-Americans are forced into buying even their toilet paper from those who do not have a vested interest in reinvesting profits back into their communities.

As a quasi-slave system population, African-Americans have been forced into being an indigenous consumer-based population. By design, relative to our numbers, we do not own commensurate factories, production facilities, distribution centers, retail outlets, grocery stores, gas stations, etc. Due to government-sanctioned economic policies, we are being blocked by stratagem from establishing our own self-sustaining businesses.

As these embedded societal limitations severely restrict the ability of African-American's to financially pull ourselves up by the bootstraps, our ability to play on a level playing field is dampened by the continual and hushed politics of the quasi-slave system. As a result, normal and otherwise healthy economic activity in America's black communities is curtailed, stagnated or, as in most cases, completely eliminated. Therein, by design, the slave quarters are maintained.

The 124 West Ninth Street scenario fits perfectly into this paradigm. Sandy and I were denied our constitutional rights by being forced to exist in this netherworld of depravity. Due to illegal racial impositions, we were denied our American right to be able to own a business. Individually, as we had created a lucrative business opportunity for ourselves from our successful challenge of quasi-slave quarter doctrine, we were severely retaliated against and forcibly steered into slave quarter confinement.

Collectively, in trying to climb the slippery slopes of the American banking and finance industry in order to obtain much needed access to business capital (like most successful businesses require), the existence of quasi-slave quarters verifies that African-American business development is methodically thwarted. As many different tactics, schemes and tricks are employed to keep qualified blacks away from financing opportunities, those African-Americans who get through the initial gauntlet are still typically faced with increased and unequal levels of difficulty in acquiring additional financing. If they do get through, they typically get smaller loan amounts, more difficult lending terms and higher interest rates.

Based upon my personal experience, banks have proven and tested ways to clandestinely stretch, pull, twist, turn and manipulate banking figures to make it appear that they use propriety and fairness in their business dealings with African-Americans. They ofttimes use house Negroes in attempts to smooth over criminal activity to make everything look okay.

On a regular basis, as we are faced with being cut off from mainstream bank financing, many blacks are forced into getting their money from untraditional sources. The illegally imposed race-based difficulties that make money scarcer in the black community increase the demand for it. Consequently, when alternate sources of financing are sought and acquired by African-Americans in the quasi-slave system slave quarters, the interest rates are much higher. The ubiquitous loan sharks in the pawnshops stand in testimony to the financial and economic shackles that exist there, as ridiculously expensive money is lent to literally get away with stealing pawned items.

In the upside-down world of American economic opportunity that exists in today's slave quarters, if all else fails in getting money from the banks and the pawn shops, many African-Americans go to an alternate source of getting much needed financing: they go to the respected and feared moneymen. As no questions are asked in their use of radically unorthodox lending practices, these people should absolutely be one's last resort under the sun for obtaining much needed financing.

Their cost of money is so high that one can almost get a nosebleed by getting a loan from them. As they typically lend money at fifty cents on the dollar (to the people that they like), payback on the dollar can easily be over one hundred percent. While they are often unsavory characters, several of the moneymen that I know of in the Queen look like their first names could be "Kneecap" or "Ankles" or "Fingers". Thanks, but no thanks.

As *slave justice* still exists for African-Americans, the wheels of justice did not roll evenly for Sandy and I. American slaves used to be denied the right to testify in the courts; the same thing applied to us. American slaves used to not be allowed to accumulate or acquire property; again, the same thing applied to us. Just as American slaves were not allowed to engage in trade like freemen, Sandy and I were not either.

What happened to Sandy and I was only the tip of the iceberg of what I saw happening to African-Americans collectively. Practically all of us were institutionally being illegally treated with scorn and contempt in a de facto national government that operates like a speakeasy. Like the chattel slave system, a mob and lynch mentality continued to prevail, as slave justice was selectively meted out in persecution of America's Negro population. Implicit in America's quasi-slave system was the notion that African-American rights are okay just as long as they did not conflict with the rights of white conservative ideologues. I knew that practically nothing could have been more dangerous to American society.

Just as trains of slaves were fastened together in *coffles* and forced to walk together while obeying the commands of their captors, most African-Americans of today know of this type of entrapment that exists inside of the quasi-slave system. Like the slave coffle experience, the truth of the matter is that most African-Americans have to watch what they say or do, lest they be severely disciplined or retaliated against by masters or overseers. Just like the experience that American slaves went through in being forced to walk in a coffle, the behavior restrictions that quasi-slave masters and overseers institutionally saddle African-Americans with today—both subtlety and overtly—denies us our constitutional rights while requiring us to pay taxes.

Unlike European-Americans, much of the economic base and many of the financial opportunities of African-Americans is being unfairly and illegally tampered with, thereby eliminating the meaningful capitalistic participation that is essential for parity. It is not that way purely by happenstance, but by design—historic design.

The salient truth of the matter is that African-Americans are blamed for not being able to climb up and out of greased slopes that have been institutionally designed to keep us down. What makes it worse is that the current government of the United States of America categorically disavows and repudiates the existence of, its involvement in, and its constitutional obligation to remedy the quasi-slave system. All one has to do is to look at what happened at 124 West Ninth Street to see that, by virtue of its actions, the American government has remained desensitized to the plight of the historic unfair treatment of its blacks.

Like an easily recognizable mental disorder, the quasi-slave system's outward manifestations are just as psychological as they are physical, in that a great deal of nervousness surfaces from its status quo. Just as anxiety is defined as a state of apprehension and psychic tension found in most forms of mental disorder, it is also marked by an unsettled and an uneasy state of mind. Consequently, as America's status quo scrambles helter-skelter in resolving the race problem that confronts it, troubling societal ills are revealed.

In this regard, the status quo's anxiety manifests itself in many ways: through distress that is caused by the perception of danger or misfortune from African-Americans; by painful uneasiness of mind, usually over anticipated ills due to the African-American presence; from abnormal apprehension and fear, often accompanied by physiological signs (as sweating and increased pulse); by doubt about the nature and reality of African-Americans themselves; and by self-doubt.

While the collective racial behavior of America's past and present status quo shows classic signs of mental disorders and psychiatric disease, many of the standard medical classifications that are used by psychiatrists and psychologists are easily transferable to the discussions of America's race conundrum. Because of their applicability, these terms lend themselves very well in describing many thought processes of the race experience that many in the United States majority are undergoing with great difficulty.

For example, it is quite evident that the American body politic has long suffered from something that can realistically be characterized as a racially generated emotional disorder that dominates its personality, like psychoneurosis, where it regularly experiences feelings of anxiety, obsessional thoughts, compulsive acts, and physical complaints.

In providing a salient example of the extent to which anxiety has deep roots in the America's racial personality, I hasten to offer President Thomas Jefferson as an example. Acknowledged to have been one of the most brilliant ornaments of the Enlightenment, an age that produced in America a group of men whose political genius astounded the world, President Thomas Jefferson recognized the difficulties that race would play in America's constitutional future.

Known as the "Scribe of the Revolution" and the "Father of the Declaration of Independence," he was instrumental in defining the racial character of the United States of America. However, due largely to his financial dependence upon American chattel slavery, Jefferson turned from a flaming advocate of slavery's abolition in his younger days to becoming less zealous in the cause during his later years. Even though he lived in an America of days gone by, his circumspection of American racial anxieties was timeless. Jefferson's ageless and angst-ridden words from over two hundred years ago defined the true neurosis of America's racial consciousness both then and now.

Concerning slavery, in his *Notes on Virginia*, Jefferson also wrote, "I tremble for my country when I reflect that God is just; that his justice cannot sleep forever." But he also declared much later in 1821, "Nothing is more certainly written in the book of fate than that these people [American Negroes] are to be free; nor is it less certain that the two races, equally free, cannot live in the same government."

These feelings of a troubled, uneasy state of mind that were caused by suspicion and fear of future evil accurately set the tone for what was to come in America. As the hand of time swept fundamental changes into America, Jefferson's accurate prognostication of the future came into fruition when the United States ended up fighting its Civil War. That same potentially destructive racial dynamic which was the cause of much national tumult during that time of our past is still in place today in the America that Thomas Jefferson foreordained.

The true colors of America's constitutional *mania* become visible as it takes on distinct appearances of being *unstable*. When viewed through an objective eye, it can readily be seen how America's *aberrant behavior* strays significantly away from the weighty implications of its precepts of constitutional fairness and equality.

There are many *manic-depressive*-like tendencies that are nationally exhibited, where alternate extremes of excitement and depression revolving around race is noticeable. When black sports figures, black entertainers, black military service people and other American blacks are cheered at one moment and capriciously castigated in the next, these are all signs of both a disordered and troubled mind and a split personality. This condition can also be indicative of *schizophrenia*.

Because of the status quo's controlling mental state, and the resultant national racial stance of the quasi-slave system, America's body convulses on a regular basis; another symptom of this underlying race-related mental disorder. The Watts, California race riot of 1965; the Martin Luther King assassination riots of 1968; the Rodney King riots of 1992; and the racially polarized reaction to the verdict of the 1995 O.J. Simpson trial are but some in a continuum of famous racial flash points that have erupted because this problematic phenomenon that has not been successfully addressed or treated. As American racial tremors continue to signal problems in all kinds of deeply embedded ways, constitutionally twisted thought patterns still come from the ugly and reared head of United States racist dogma.

America's obsessive and compulsive racial behavior of the past, as has ofttimes been recorded in photographs from mob scenes at African-American lynchings and burnings, also still bubbles beneath the surface today. The Union, South Carolina, Susan Smith incident ignited a national firestorm of African-American bogeyman hate mongering. Not that long ago, the public display of our national neurosis was tapped into as this nation's deep-seated racial fears came into view by the issuance of a fictitious composite drawing of an African-American male. The accompanying *delirium* triggered mass confusion, *hallucinations* (false sightings) and *frenzies* (paroxysms resulting from manias, which are forms of *insanity* characterized by great excitement).

As the personality of America's status quo displays disconcerting traits of being *withdrawn* and *isolated* from the objective world (as through indifference or disaffection), signs of *abject alienation* are visible too. In addition, America's racial attitude is *incoherent*, as its is without logical connection to its constitutional precepts, and it is *rambling*, as it wanders aimlessly on a stupefacient course that is constitutionally unsound.

As a nation, our *unbalanced behavior* indicates that we have taken leave of our senses by adopting a policy of national race relations insanity. Although our national credo espouses "freedom and justice for all", in reality, this is not true, as we, as a nation, try to cover-up this fact. With regard to full African-American inclusion in America's society, 124 West Ninth Street reflects the true state of U. S. racial relations. Our national preoccupation with racial fears and hates has clouded our view of the big picture, and has left us looking rather *deranged* and *bereft of reason.*

And so we continue to collectively go down our national trek into the unknown, apparently oblivious to the consequences of the bed that we are making for ourselves. In this unforgiving world's overall scheme of things, we, as a nation, will have to lie in that bed if we do not wake up. American laws, as set forth in the Constitution, must be stringently followed. For our own sake, we should want to get better. If left unchecked, God forbid, these treatable societal ills will lead to the most severe form of mental derangement: *suicide*.

Another analogy can be drawn that is indicative of the quasi-slave system. Just as it was designed to do in its chattel slave system days, America's dichotomous racial relationship with its Negro population continues to be responsible for our being treated like foreigners—not equal participants—in our own homeland. To a very real extent, African-Americans receive the type of treatment that mirrors U. S. foreign policy tactics used in dealing with many Third World countries. The similarities here are also striking.

We send our troops to foreign nations that have been decimated by tyrannical regimes, unfair political states and failed economic systems for selfish reasons. It is done in this manner to promote not only their economic and political development, but, moreover, to protect our vital interests. It is ironic that we do not use our national resources to effectively help this nation by making similar changes that affect the African-American community within our own borders that have been hurt by similar causal factors. We also send foreign-service officers and consuls abroad to promote trade, protect the rights of foreign citizens, issue visas to aliens, etc., yet we do not effectively use our national resources to sufficiently promote economic vitality to this nations' African-American community.

Instead, like the *Big Stick* foreign policy, America uses the threat of power from its police and military forces to intimidate African-Americans to capitulate and acquiesce to the quasi-slave system. As in *gunboat diplomacy*, where a sovereign exercises its domain of political control over a dependent state, America's Negroes are targeted by their government to be controlled. Similarly, America's foreign policies of *colonialism* and *neocolonialism*, where there is control by one power over a dependent people, applies to African-American treatment.

The list of United States foreign policy similarities that are institutionally used against America's Negroes goes on. In *containment*, the policy, process, or result of preventing the perceived expansion of a hostile power or ideology, we are kept in quasi-slavery and out of the American mainstream. As in *deterrence* and *militarism*, the maintaining of vast military power, weaponry and preparedness in order to discourage war, African-Americans have been prevented from acting in pursuit of constitutional freedoms.

Through *isolationism*, a policy of national separation by abstention from alliances and other political and economic relations, we have been shut out of full participation in American society. Through the use of *imperialism*, the policy, practice, or advocacy of extending the power and dominion of a nation, especially by direct territorial acquisitions or by gaining indirect control over the political or economic life of other areas, the ongoing quasi-slave system violations against African-Americans goes on unceasingly.

The reality that makes African-American treatment worse is that not only are we taxed without meaningful representation, but hundreds of thousands of our numbers in America's fighting forces serve as quasi-military conscripts for the defense of the quasi-slave system. As an unwritten—but technically in force—national racial policy is firmly in place that has quite visible and negative results, it is scandalous for the quasi-slave system to require tax paying African-Americans to be unequally confined to the economic periphery of the United States while we financially support and die for this land.

At the drop of a hat, the White House will apply sanctions and order embargoes against selected nations of the world for human rights violations etc. However, as a country that professes freedom, justice and equality for all of its citizens when it habitually violates the human rights of its own Negro citizens, the United States sanctimoniously acts like it does not violate these human and equal rights by looking the other way.

In many ways, the difficulty that I encountered in attempting to fight against the all-pervasive quasi-slave system reminded me of the many-headed Hydra, a marsh serpent monster in Greek mythology that Hercules encountered which, when each head was cut off, was replaced by two others. Similarly, as the quasi-slave system symbolized to me a persistent and many-faceted problem that presented new obstacles each time I solved one, it truly was a multifarious evil that could not be overcome by my single efforts.

There was one more way in which I perceived the chattel slave system's latest American form: the vortex of the quasi-slave system. Like the downward spinning suction of a giant whirlpool, I envisioned the quasi-slave system vortex as an entity where perpetual states of American status quo energies were devoted exclusively to the maintenance of white privilege and black bondage. As the sheer force of this vortex made life insufferable for far too many African-Americans, I could see how African-American lives were imperiled, minds were lost, hope was dashed and dreams of true equality were crushed into smithereens.

Yet, in the hellish vacuum-like vortex of the quasi-slave system, Uncle Toms suck up to the masters, overseers and others while most other African-Americans are sucked down because of them. But, the real rub flies in the face of white Americans.

At the time of its creation, white Americans were virtually unaffected by the negative economic, social and political downward spiral of the life zapping quasi-slave system vortex. However, as is the case at 124 West Ninth Street, time has shown that the vortex's original design of only negatively affecting African-Americans is failing. Events are showing that the powerful leviathan effects of the vortex transcend racial containment and have become transracial.

As it has broken free of its exclusive racial restraints and into the U. S. Treasury with reckless abandon, the unbridled quasi-slave system vortex, like a Frankenstein monster, has become unwieldy and has taken off on its own. By virtue of it having its own inertia, it threatens to swallow and consume not only the African-Americans that it was designed for, but it will get increasingly larger numbers of taxpaying white Americans as well into its destructive chew-them-up and spit-them-out inhalation.

I asked myself many questions: "Does America plan to continue its genocidal activities of economic strangulation in the American black communities?"; "Is America doomed to repeat history in a spectre akin to the American Civil War?"; and, "Will America face massive social unrest because it decided to leave the race sore to fester?"

In dealing illegally and unethically with its black population, there was no doubt that the American government was not taking a reasoned approach to solving the vexing problem of race that confronts it. By default, America appeared to me to be closer to making another failed attempt at shipping its blacks back to Africa, as it did when it shipped many thousands of blacks to Monrovia, Liberia, West Africa beginning in 1822, than it did to committing itself to honest, meaningful and aboveboard changes.

Successively, under both the chattel and the quasi-slave systems in the United States, I knew that African-Americans were continuing to be killed, maimed, scandalized, tortured, dragged, ridiculed, disemboweled, raped, punched, spat upon, pilloried, burned, kicked, hung and bamboozled in order to stop us from having the freedoms that were rightfully ours. Like the chattel slave system of the past that collapsed upon itself due to the constitutional falsehoods that supported it, I also knew that the quasi-slave system of today had to be permanently abolished for the sake of America's economic sanctity and survival.

I knew that, at the end of the day, as with other past threats to America, only the collective efforts of individual Americans would be the deciding factor as to whether or not the quasi-slave system would be abolished forever. In the meantime, I knew that the threatening assault on the historic foundation of the American precept of freedom, liberty and justice for all would continue unabated and unchallenged if I, as a truly caring American, did not continue to take it upon myself to resist.

Chapter 11

Patriot Parallels

"There is a life that is worth living now as it was worth living in the former days, and that is the honest life, the useful life, the unselfish life, cleansed by devotion to an ideal. There is a battle worth fighting now as it was worth fighting then, and that is the battle for justice and equality: to make our city and our state free in fact as well as in name; to break the rings that strangle real liberty, and to keep them broken; to cleanse, so far as in our power lies, the fountains of our national life from political, commercial, and social corruption; to teach our sons and daughters, by precept and example, the honor of serving such a country as America. That is work worthy of the finest manhood and womanhood."

—Henry Van Dyke

I could not help but to be reminded that the main reason why the Roman Empire fell was due to mismanagement and corruption in high places. The barbarians could not have ever gotten in if the Romans themselves did not welcome them. Even though we had been severely retaliated against financially and faced the hidden threat of physical retaliation, Sandy and I were not about to surrender to the barbarians that we knew were at the gates of the U. S. Treasury. For us, holding the line for our homeland, regardless of its problems with race, was not as much a necessity as it was a virtue.

Flagrant contradictions that threatened the land that I loved were all around me; public officials deceivingly swore to uphold the laws of America; there was not freedom and justice for all; and the Constitution was being scuttled. But yet, even more than the individual damage that was done to me via the quasi-slave system was the national ruin that was being exemplified by the President and the Queen's successful Bananagate cover-up.

In thinking about fighting a superior foe, for some reason, my mind kept drifting back to a poem that was required reading for me in high school, Henry Wadsworth Longfellow's epic, "Paul Revere's Ride." From its opening words of "Listen my children and you shall hear, Of the Midnight ride of Paul Revere,..." to its end, I became somewhat mesmerized by drawing a plethora of parallels between Longfellow's depiction of one of the most famous historical events in American history and my Bananagate cover-up experiences.

I also found it to be coincidentally fascinating that the same person who was responsible for naming the Queen City in the first place was the same person whose writing provided me with the perfect literary example for drawing factual parallels between the President and the Queen's federal criminal behavior and my total willingness to dutifully fight back. Some thirty-five odd years ago, I never would have anticipated how a classroom assignment that once bored me stiff would become one of my rallying cries.

I recalled how Paul Revere, a trusted American Revolutionary War Patriot, along with others, set up a network to watch the movements of the British Redcoats who threatened the independence of America. On April 15, 1775, as they noticed a buildup of Redcoats that indicated something was about to happen, Revere rode out to Lexington to advise his friends of the soldiers' activity. On his way back to Boston, he met with some gentlemen in Charlestown and agreed to send a signal when the British army deployed.

> ...He said to his friend, "If the British march
> By land or sea from the town to-night,
> Hang a lantern aloft in the belfry arch
> Of the North Church tower as a signal light,—...

The day when signals were given from the North Church steeple, April 18, 1775, however, had a personal poignancy to me. To the day, it was exactly two-hundred and twenty years later that the oppressive President and the Queen saw to it that I was ordered to vacate my house of sixteen years as part of their real threat to America's Treasury.

In this poem, Longfellow reflected how the American patriots had nothing to lose when they were already enslaved and expected to obey the dictates of an intolerant power without complaint. Just as Paul

Revere did everything within his power in this poem to alert his country that he had distinct proof of a danger to the well-being of his homeland, similarly, I tried to alert my fellow countrymen of how concealed U. S. Treasury theft had metastasized from the Queen to the President. In many ways, Paul Revere's Ride was the embodiment of my experiences with the President and the Queen.

In a poetic parallel between Revere, the country farmers, and myself, we all were protagonists who rightfully resisted and fought back. Likewise, this poem highlights parallels that exist between the President, the Queen and the British, who are all villainous antagonists that posed a looming threat to sleeping Americans. Too, like Revere, I was spurred into action because I was worried for my country and, had I not put up a clamorous resistance, America would not have been warned about an unseen menace.

After recalling this poem, I realized that, with this one life that I have on this earth as an American citizen, notifying the public about the Bananagate cover-up was a rare chance for me to have a positive impact on my homeland. Regardless of the many delays that I endured, and the many legal setbacks that were sent my way, I was determined to not let the President and the Queen send me packing in the manner that they were intending. Like Revere, I had readied myself for action to expose the national danger that I knew was there, as I waited to see the right warning signals to continue to sound my alarm.

> "...One if by land, and two if by sea;
> And I on the opposite shore will be,
> Ready to ride and spread the alarm
> Through every Middlesex village and farm,
> For the country folk to be up and to arm."...

I thought of all of the many lives that had been sacrificed by America's defenders since Revere's time, making it possible for the existence of the best country on earth today. As the bones of countless thousands of veterans laid as a mute reminder of the possible sacrifice that I could have been making for speaking up, I cast caution into the wind and mounted my own charge against those who were making a mockery of their deaths, in order that they would have not died in vain. Longfellow's metaphorical description aptly portrayed the sinister nature and enormity of the President and the Queen's impending danger to America.

...The Somerset, British man-of-war;
A phantom ship, with each mast and spar
Across the moon like a prison bar,
And a huge black hulk, that was magnified
By its own reflection in the tide....

Like Revere, as my life was in danger because of the President and the Queen's dragooning, the specter of death did not frighten me: I felt that my country's life was far more important than mine. As a veteran, I knew that I would have rather died in continual service to this land as her defender rather than to have seen her weakened by those who were robbing her blind internally. Like the Patriot's most trusted messenger, I was not willing to be shanghaied while surrendering what was rightfully mine. In the course of time, as I had become a wilderness fighter who was standing on a lonely front, like Revere, I was a messenger in waiting.

...Till in the silence around him he hears
The muster of men at the barrack door,
The sound of arms, and the tramp of feet,
And the measured tread of the grenadiers,
Marching down to their boats on the shore....

In one of Longfellow's passages, I had a personal interpretation that eerily reminded me of the depth and extent of the President and the Queen's Watergate-like cover-up that was haunting America:

...Beneath, in the churchyard, lay the dead,
In their nigh encampment on the hill,
Wrapped in silence so deep and still...

Just as I witnessed an illegal conspiratorial campaign that had marched through the U. S. Treasury, the poem captured my sense of having seen the invasion of the President and the Queen's expansive army for the first time:

...For suddenly all his thoughts are bent
On a shadowy something far away,
Where the river widens to meet the bay,—
A line of black that bends and floats
On the rising tide like a bridge of boats....

In comparing Longfellow's historic depiction to what Paul Revere saw, I was remindful of the external threat that currently exists to America. Therein, I knew that another parallel could be drawn between what I saw in the entire Bananagate incident and the constitutionally-alien internal invasion of the President and the Queen. As an external defeat is totally unacceptable to me as an American, being defeated from within is even more unacceptable. In either case, I knew that my personal makeup would not allow me to sit by idly.

Like Revere, I was eager to begin my alert and waited to get the proof and the right signs that I needed:

...Meanwhile, impatient to mount and ride,
Booted and spurred, with a heavy stride
On the opposite shore walked Paul Revere.
Now he patted his horse's side,
Now he gazed at the landscape far and near,
Then, impetuous, stamped the earth,
And turned and tightened his saddle girth;
But mostly he watched with eager search
The belfry tower of the Old North Church,...

Once I had amassed an overabundance of federally incriminating evidence against the President and the Queen, I had gotten on my mark. Once I uncovered the federal laws contained in 24 CFR Part 511 that expressly prohibited the type of U. S. Treasury theft that occurred at 124 West Ninth Street, I had gotten set. But once the existence of the Bananagate cover-up was confirmed, I had all of the proof that I needed, and was ready to go.

...And lo! as he looks, on the belfry's height
A glimmer, and then a gleam of light!
He springs to the saddle, the bridle he turns,
But lingers and gazes, till full on his sight
A second lamp in the belfry burns....

Just as President Thomas Jefferson once said, "Eternal vigilance is the price of liberty," I felt compelled to do more. True liberty was taking a beating. As plain as day, I could see how the President and the Queen had become the new Benedict Arnolds. I envisioned my lone voice as a trusted steed that was the only thing that stood between Bananagate's successful cover-up and its public exposure.

... A hurry of hoofs in a village street,
A shape in the moonlight, a bulk in the dark,
And beneath, from the pebbles, in passing, a spark
Struck out by a steed flying fearless and fleet;
That was all! And yet, through the gloom and the light,
The fate of a nation was riding that night;...

Just as President Abraham Lincoln once said, "Let the people know the truth and the country is safe," I knew that the country was not safe under the corrupt leadership of a habitual prevaricator like Bill Clinton. The fact that no one in the national press would cover my important story created an impetus for me to cover myself. In response to the President and the Queen's perfectly concealed federal criminal activity, I created a louder voice by founding a grassroots organization that allowed me to get my message out to the American people, The Cincinnati Watchdog Committee.

...It was twelve by the village clock
When he crossed the bridge into Medford town....
And felt the damp of the river fog,
That rises after the sun goes down....

In their attempt to legitimize the federal crimes that I was exposing, like the invading British regulars that Paul Revere saw, phalanxes of resources kept pouring in to silence my rebellion. In my relentless pursuit of exposing the President and the Queen's raid on the national Treasury, they did not blink—and neither did I. To prevent my complete shellacking, it was incumbent upon me to grab the reins of my destiny to muster up the additional efforts required for me to stay in the fray.

To both shield themselves and to quell my uprising against high federal crimes, misinformation about me and the 124 West Ninth Street cover-up was the biggest strength that the President and the Queen had in their Bananagate assault on America's laws. As their Achilles' heel was the irrefutable evidence of their involvement in a U. S. Treasury theft conspiracy, out of necessity, I had to figure out ways to creatively turn their incriminating cover-up negatives into positives for me.

I responded by self-publishing a fax and Internet based newsletter, *The Watchdog News*, that was sent worldwide. With its professional newspaper format, I was able to efficiently disseminate Bananagate cover-up information that warned Americans of the danger that they faced. It proved to be an equalizer that allowed me to stand toe-to-toe with the President and the Queen on the uneven playing field.

> ...It was one by the village clock,
> When he galloped into Lexington.
> He saw the gilded weathercock
> Swim in the moonlight as he passed,
> And the meeting-house windows, black and bare,
> Gaze at him with a spectral glare,
> As if they already stood aghast
> At the bloody work they would look upon....

Realizing that the lives of innumerable Americans were being threatened, like Revere, I continued to ride hard to reach many more people. Even in the uncertainty of riding in the darkness, I made it a point to clap spurs to my steed to remain an ever-moving target. In putting America's need to be warned in front of the bare necessities of our family, Sandy and I took a calculated risk by diverting extremely scarce money into buying a state-of-the-art computer system that gave us Internet and batch faxing capabilities. As a result, the evolution of our revolution became high tech.

As a beacon of suppressed information, *The Watchdog News* became a thorn in the side of the President and the Queen by shedding light on their exposed underbelly. Like Revere, *The Watchdog News'* singular efforts were not only used as a strong weapon to defuse the federal government's misinformation strategy, but its wide circulation tended to further diminish its chances of keeping Bananagate hidden. I knew that I had reached out and touched someone when Independent Counsel Ken Starr's office notified me via mail that they had received my information, and when the Executive Secretariat in HUD's Washington, D. C. headquarters sent me a fax asking for a free subscription to *The Watchdog News*.

But there were things that *The Watchdog News* did not do. Although it bought me much needed time, it did not stop the success of the Bananagate cover-up. As I became astutely aware that my faxing and emailing did not apply enough pressure on the leadership of a tyrant who had a proclivity to dodge the many bullets of presidential scandals that could have indicted him, I had a pressing need to bring my steed to a full gallop.

> ...It was two buy the village clock,
> When he came to the bridge in Concord town....
> And one was safe and asleep in his bed
> Who at the bridge would be first to fall,
> Who that day would be lying dead,
> Pierced by a British musket ball....

Like a guerrilla fighter engaged in irregular warfare, I constantly gave the President and the Queen different looks that they were not expecting, confounding the skeptics who thought that I had long been whipped into submission by the White House, Lindner, Chesley and the Queen. Astride my steed, I resisted further by putting the Cincinnati Watchdog Committee's twenty-four hour a day web page on the Internet.

> ...How the farmers gave them ball for ball,
> From behind each fence and farmyard wall,...
> ...Chasing the redcoats down the lane,
> Then crossing the fields to emerge again
> Under the trees at the turn of the road,
> And only pausing to fire and load....

In the midst of the battle with the President and the Queen, I recalled memorable sections of the U. S. Armed Forces Code of Conduct that had stuck with me ever since my Army days. When I remembered the section that stated, "I am an American fighting man. I serve in the forces which guard my country and our way of life. I am prepared to give my life in their defense…" As Bananagate's cover-up threatened the way of life of all Americans, I knew that I still had a duty to serve.

But the part of the Code that I remembered most was "I will never forget that I am an American fighting man, responsible for my actions, and dedicated to the principles which made my country free. I will trust in my God and in the United States of America."

...So through the night rode Paul Revere;
And so through the night went his cry of alarm
To every Middlesex village and farm,—
A cry of defiance, and not of fear,...

In knowing that having a strong motivation and belief in one's victory are two of the most important things in a guerrilla war, I set up resistance to Bananagate's perfect U. S. Treasury theft crimes anywhere and anytime that I could. While fate had made the exclusive burden of revealing these federal cover-up crimes mine to bear, my energy level did not flag.

...A voice in the darkness, a knock at the door,
And a word that shall echo for evermore!...

As the President and the Queen were criminals of the highest order, I did whatever I had to do to expose them. Capitalizing on the strengths that kept me as a defender for a long period of time, I used the most formidable weapon that I had in my arsenal: my ability to read, write and articulate words. Like Revere's ride, my language skills gave me the edge that I needed to keep the element of surprise.

There were other similar and dissimilar parallels that existed between my Paul Revere-like efforts and the efforts of other Revolutionary War and present American patriots. Like George Washington, I never told a lie about the federally indictable Bananagate criminal activities that I uncovered. Just like George Washington after Braddock's Defeat, I withstood the licking that was initially meted out to me, only to be able to come back to fight for a larger national ideal on another day.

Unlike George Washington, however, I was erroneously branded as a malcontent and was cast as a liar. Too, unlike George Washington, I was forced to fight alone.

Like Francis Marion (the Swamp Fox) who faced a far superior foe, I fought those that threatened America in the best way that I could with what I had. Instead of continuing to fight them in the openness of a corrupt U. S. Justice Department, I increased my success of exposing their criminal activity by using the cover of facsimile machines and the Internet to snipe at them.

Like Francis Marion did to the British, I showed the 124 West Ninth Street HUD fraud conspirators how they were exposed, vulnerable and could be beaten. Like Francis Marion, my sniping with the truth kept the 124 West Ninth Street U. S. Treasury theft participants confused and worried.

Unlike Francis Marion who shot from protected positions behind rocks, trees, logs and hills, I was illegally steered into defending my country without the protection of a lawyer. Unlike the Swamp Fox who would hit, run and hide in the glen, I was illegally denied the appointment of a legitimate attorney time and time again.

Like retired General Colin Powell (Currently U. S. President George W. Bush's U. S. Secretary of State), I chose a career of my liking, played by the rules and excelled in what I did. Unlike Colin Powell, who put in check an evil foreigner (Iraq's ruler, Saddam Hussein) that threatened the vital interests of this nation, the Treasury thieves from my HUD building renovation project remain on the loose and unchecked, as they break America's laws and threaten its fiscal vitality from within.

Unlike Paul Revere, my voice was not listened to, as it fell on deaf ears. Unlike Paul Revere, the warnings that I cried out into the darkness were dismissed and went unheeded.

Just as Paul Revere fully exerted himself in opposition to an aristocratic crown, I mounted up to parallel his example by resisting the Bill Clinton-like aristocracy that lets corrupt money rule America—instead of its laws. I realized that it would only be through such exertions that we, as a nation, could pass the torch that lights the path of true American freedoms.

> ...In the hour of darkness and peril and need,
> The people will waken and listen to hear
> The hurrying hoof-beats of that steed,
> And the midnight message of Paul Revere.

Chapter 12

Stopping The Hemorrhaging

"Anyone who studies the state of things which preceded the French Revolution will see that the tremendous catastrophe came about from so excessive a regulation of men's actions in all their details, and such an enormous drafting away of the products of their actions to maintain the regulating organization, that life was fast becoming impracticable. And if we ask what then made, and now makes, this error possible, we find it to be the political superstition that governmental power is subject to no restraints."

—Herbert Spencer

In the fell clutch of circumstance, I was able to keep everything in its proper perspective. Like a physician diagnosing a malady, I recognized that the United States of America, with all of its positives, needed to undergo treatment for a serious condition that severely threatened its future.

At the same time, recognizing that the American constitution reflected the true genius of individuals that conceptualized a remarkable and noble experiment on paper, I understood that it was not the system that was at fault: it was the people who were running it. Despite the 124 West Ninth Street federal bludgeoning that I took which opened the Queen syndrome's vista to me, still and all, I remained confident and willing to fight to protect America, determinedly convinced that my homeland could operate efficiently as it was constitutionally designed.

But amidst my optimism, public corruption was on the rampage, illegal political activity had gained a foothold and mistrust of government stampeded across the American landscape. Running counter to my sanguineness, I saw that the Queen syndrome tugged dangerously at the delicate equilibrium of American democracy itself.

In an observable environment of constitutional racial hypocrisy that had been eclipsed by a much more dangerous U. S. Treasury theft breeding ground, I agonized over the prospect of America's unrestrained bleeding. As a nation, I observed that we had the wrong emphasis and approach, and that there were far too many inherent contradictions. I could see that America needed to undergo serious treatment to heal its wounds and to right its path.

From my perspective, I knew that there was an answer blowing somewhere in the wind that could stop the national hemorrhaging. Regardless of all that I had said and done in opposition the President and the Queen, I remained confident that there was a way to snatch America from the jaws of racial and fiscal death.

Currently, as the American populace stands by in silence, an atmosphere exists that perpetuates a sense of not belonging in the United States. America has become a place of "do your own thing" where many say "If it does not directly impact my life, who cares?" It is particularly a sad state of affairs when one considers that the Queen syndrome and the quasi-slave system operate within the broad continuum of illegal activity that stretches from the Queen, through the State of Ohio, into the highest federal realm and then back down into the directions of all States.

When quoting the esteemed Scottish essayist and historian, Thomas Carlyle (1795-1881), at one of the most famous trials of this century, O.J. Simpson's defense attorney Johnnie Cochran said, "No lie can live forever." The American government cannot have it both ways; it cannot profess the broad freedoms of its Constitution while, through sleight of hand and duplicity, it selectively takes them away from its black population.

It is not that America does not have the way to eliminate the quasi-slave system; it does not have the will. In order for America to be cured, the vestiges and remnants of America's chattel slave system must be exposed for what they actually are. As the notion that "everything is fine" is false, major operational shifts are needed to properly do what is best for America.

America's closet race lie is an invitation to social collapse. The negative effects of the quasi-slave system, like a spreading and malignant skin cancer, go much deeper than the eye can readily see. Yet, on its own, it stands out like a sore thumb. From the mute testimony of

African-American neighborhood streetscapes to the glaring diatribes of race hate groups and beyond, America's big race relation lie is there for all to see.

Using history as a teacher, I needed only be reminded of the conditions that brought about the French Revolution. An unfair system of taxation (taxation without representation); opportunities for a privileged few (feudal privileges); social inequality (many people were not allowed to improve their standard of living); a greedy aristocracy; political crisis; a poor judicial system; and an inefficient government were all causes of France's tumultuous revolution.

While this writing has defined a current national condition that describes many of the similar cultural, social and economic conditions that were causations of both the French Revolution and America's Civil War, likewise, it draws attention to rumblings that also threaten massive social eruptions in the United States of America. Just as history can be used to provide an accurate prognosis of America's illness, it can also be used to provide a remedy.

In May of 1997, the Marshall Plan celebrated its 50th anniversary. Established in 1947 by Secretary of State George C. Marshall (1880-1959), it was created by the U. S. government to rebuild a devastated Europe following World War II. Between 1947 and 1952, over $13 billion in food, raw materials, and other financial aid was funneled into many foreign European nations, as their requirements far exceeded their ability to pay for them.

The Marshall Plan chartered a bold new course for American foreign policy: it was a plan to rescue Europe. It forced the Europeans to handle their own recovery. Without the morale lift of the Marshall Plan, Western Europe (in particular, France and Italy) may have collapsed. Regarding the four-year war that had recently destroyed Europe, George C. Marshall was quoted to say, "There is no doubt in my mind that if we decide to do this thing, we can make it happen."

All around me, I could see the telltale signs of institutional racial destruction to African-Americans via the Queen syndrome, the quasi-slave system and the Bananagate cover-up. In like fashion, there was no doubt in my mind that, if the American government decided to do the right thing, almost four hundred years of African-American racial devastation in America could be ended at the stroke of a pen.

Instead of making some type of meaningful amends to a significant portion of its taxpaying public, counterproductively, the United States government chooses to maintain the quasi-slave system. What happened at 124 West Ninth Street is glaring proof that America's federal government is still relying upon expensively misdirected investment and economic policies that are race-based.

In a seemingly everlasting constitutional state of denial, the American body politic continues to rely on a racial policy of diminishing returns. The nation's massive quasi-slave system expenditures, social policies and gross underutilization of the economic potential of the American black citizenry are all indicators that should cause alarm.

From a financial standpoint alone, it is much more practical and realistic for America's national government to focus on a feasible economic policy that gives a profitable return on its investment rather than maintaining a perpetual cycle of unconstitutional race relation destruction that gives rise to consistent financial deficits. A Marshall Plan-type of federal investment is needed in America's black community to offset the ravages of the quasi-slave system.

The fact of the matter is that Cuba and African-Americans are both being financially embargoed. Instead of using a failed quasi-slave system economic policy that resorts to the tyranny of "chopping off feet" in order to illegally remain in force, racially imposed constraints against African-Americans by the American government should be lifted because it is not prudent to do otherwise. Until this is done, America's underutilized black population will collectively (and to a disproportionate extent) be a financial drag on the national economy, as we will not be allowed to pay our way due to racial fears, prejudices and ignorance.

Until that time, the financial potential of blacks as a unit of the population in the United States will continue to be flat, economically untapped, not invigorated, financially stagnated and productively static. When the economic shackles are eventually removed, American blacks will rightfully take their place at the financial table of the free enterprise system by increasingly becoming net producers instead of net consumers.

As a reasoned approach must be taken nationally, America must face the inconsistencies of its contradictions. Some argue that the payment of reparations is the only way to go in solving the African-American racial crisis that America continues to avoid. Be that as it may, and within the historic context of the chattel slave system carry-over that still plagues the viability of the Constitution, America must make a meaningful investment of some type into its African-American community in order to achieve the needed results.

With respect to World War II's Europe, a good German/bad German parallel currently exists in America. In comparing the German public's acceptance of Adolph Hitler's lies and deceptions during the 1930's and '40s to the legacy of former President Bill Clinton's lies and deceptions of today, the status quo in the United States is ignoring the truth like the WWII-era status quo of the German population.

The bad Germans during WWII knew the type of mental attitude that existed in their country as their Nazis marched through Europe. They were aware of the psychology of their nation; how it was part of their normal dialog; what it was doing; and how rampant Naziism was allowed to go on. They did not take to the streets in rising up in protest against the Nazis. All along, while leaving the affairs of the nation into the hands of the Nazis, most of them were hoping, at arm's length, that their nationally perceived problems would somehow, anyhow, get solved—as if osmosis would take over. Truth is always a casualty in a totalitarian state.

In contrast, the good Germans during WWII were immediately detached from directly participating in the national politics of the day. However, in the final analysis, there was no distinction made between the two German groups when the world judged German war crimes. Both groups were colored negatively and blamed together because of the actions of one group. The same holds true for the "good" Americans of today.

Like Hitler once did, former President Bill Clinton used his power to destroy his opposition. Like Linda Tripp, I am a whistle-blower who tried to do the right thing in reporting criminal activities of the President and he used his power to financially destroy me. Like Linda Tripp, I was retaliated against for bringing unwanted criminal exposure upon the President.

It was a very dangerous thing to have a person like Bill Clinton at the helm of America. The lesson that Bill Clinton should have learned a long time ago is that cover-ups, in the long run, do not work. Clinton should have learned from Nixon's national lie in that the truth will always surface.

But Nixon had nothing on Clinton. In comparison to the Arkansan Chief Executive's ability to conceal criminality, Nixon's Watergate was a single-layered, run-of-the-mill cover-up that got "Tricky Dick" Nixon caught. As America's moral decline was exacerbated by Bill Clinton's abuse of power, "Slick Wille" set a new standard for criminal cover-up efficiency.

In complete revulsion, I watched helplessly as (using the word that U. S. Congressman Dan Burton, R-Ind., chairman of the House Government Reform and Oversight Committee, called him) a "scum-bag" president successfully covered-up simultaneous and multi-layered presidential scandals. One scandal involving Monica Lewinsky hid illicit sexual activity in his White House office and the other one, Bananagate, hid his illicit White House activity in the Lincoln Bedroom with Carl Lindner, Jr.

In viewing an August 11, 1999 White House ceremony on television, I tittered when President Bill Clinton thanked former President Gerald Ford for "ending the long national nightmare of Watergate." My tittering continued when, during the last week of September, 1999, I watched television news coverage of the permanently damaged President Clinton forgiving himself for the national shame that he brought upon America in the disgraceful Lewinsky White House affair. From the clarity of my Bananagate perspective, I knew that Bill Clinton had criminally evaded being thrown out of office, unlike Nixon, by the skin of his teeth.

In that he has given new meaning to the words presidential cover-up, the annals of time will not be kind to Bill Clinton. The historical record not only shows that a criminal cover-up muzzle was federally placed upon Sandy and I through Bill Clinton's exertions, but that Sandy and I constantly writhed to break free of our restraints to warn of a true presidential danger to America. Like Nixon, Clinton should have been removed from the White House a long time ago, and into a place where he belongs: disgrace.

Through the lying and dishonesty that is increasingly becoming synonymous with his name, a slick former President has criminally absolved himself from Bananagate's incriminations with a fancy footwork dodge, the likes of which most Americans had never seen before. But, even as he attempts to shake off a dark cloud that naggingly follows him around, the ex-President is hard-pressed to meet the standard of conforming to fact, law and doing what is morally upright, as he has mislead a federal grand jury by urging others to prevaricate on his behalf.

Under Clinton's perverted reign, twisted presidential attitudes about extramarital sex and openly lying to the American public have violated a basic sense of decency and decorum. Under the former President's rule, the honor of the Chief Executive's role to lead America's national character has, like the Queen, fallen into disrepute.

As Washington has been out of touch, drastic change is needed there. The type of incident that occurred at 124 West Ninth Street only bolsters the mistrust and disillusionment that the American public has with big government. Just as society rots from the head down and builds from the bottom up, what has happened in Bill Clinton's White House is a classic example of coin-operated politics functioning over the best interests of America.

In the cheapened political environment that has been the irrevocable hallmark of the Clinton administration, Congress is following the out of whack money grab of America's former chief executive and, in so doing, misses tackling many crucial national problems and central issues. "Show me the money" has become the mantra of politicians and bureaucrats nationwide who are involved in the sleaze of America's current political climate.

While it is the national politicians who make the laws and run the country, it is also they who are the main endorsers, beneficiaries and proponents of leaving meaningful campaign finance reforms alone. With rivers of campaign finance cash that is available to flow into their pockets, they are perplexed to pass the type of weighty national legislation that will cause them to financially shoot themselves in the foot.

Greater still, other fundamental questions should be posed to the American taxpaying public. If white-collar crimes of 124 West Ninth Street's nature can be committed and systematically cloaked through the cunning and stealth of campaign finance incentives as easily as I have personally witnessed, how often do these types of unreported crimes occur? Is HUD a bureaucratically protected sacred cow that is nothing more than a political spoil which is used for graft by the White House? Further, as 124 West Ninth Street's cover-up events continue to indicate, are federal tax dollars being funneled through this out of control federal Department to pad the pockets of greedy politicians?

As a concerned American who has been forced to watch in silence from the inside of a presidential Treasury theft/campaign finance cover-up scandal, it is frightening how desensitized and disinterested politicians have become to what is happening in Washington. As U. S. Justice Department officials, Congressmen and Senators refuse to bring light to the types of white-collar crimes that occurred at 124 West Ninth Street, they are derelict in their Constitutional duties to provide oversight of the executive branch. Like Clinton, by federal law, these public officials should be dealt with accordingly.

With corporate America owning ninety percent of the economic resources of the United States, money-hungry politicians seek the Carl Lindner, Jr.'s of the nation. Whereas current campaign finance trends are inconsistent with good government, a condition of nationally anti-constitutional political insanity has developed. For lobbyists and corporations, money is the name of the game as they give, and give, and give. As they exploit their positions in the chase for conditional money that can, and does, hurt America, lobbyists shake down the congressmen and congressmen shake down the lobbyists in a gone-haywire political money game.

What happened at Cincinnati, Ohio's 124 West Ninth Street is something that should not be taken lightly: it signals a fundamental national problem that requires immediate attention. These types of occurrences place hidden U. S. Treasury theft on the front line of a fight between everyday Americans, who demand that their tax dollars not be taken illegally, and elitist Americans, who think that they can illegally take and use federal tax dollars whenever, and however, they please.

America needs to get a handle on what its politicians are doing. As a good, efficient and non-corrupt administration of federal tax dollars is necessary, Americans must demand honest, effective and, especially, non-biased handling of their federal tax dollars. The 124 West Ninth Street incident shows that national, state and local politicians are playing fast and loose with federal tax dollars. Besides, if 124 West Ninth Street's hidden felonious activity can go on inside of HUD, what about government sanctioned theft in other federal departments?

By definition, politicians are the caretakers of the public's money. However, as the 124 West Ninth Street incident highlights, the obligatory currying-for-favor activities of politicians, bureaucrats, and Sixth

Circuit U. S. Court officials who are in the public's trust are continuing to undermine the moral fiber of America. They have no remorse for letting the country down because that is how they do business. As they peddle their influence, it is more than political patronage for them: it's a way of life.

Even though politicians want to keep hiding from the negative ramifications of campaign finance contributions, we should not let them. As well, we should all be vigilant against the infectiously related Queen syndrome, as its existence also confirms an illegal stratagem that is a further foot in the door for cash-starved politicians who will betray America at the drop of a hat. While the President and the Queen have, so far, been able to get away with picking the pockets of America at 124 West Ninth Street, their days for keeping these scurrilous crimes hidden, which contravene the Constitutional laws of the United States of America, have to be—better yet, must be—numbered.

Moreover, the 124 West Ninth Street incident reveals that the federal government is being ruled by an elite and privileged class...a group that considers themselves to be superior and above the law. Since they operate secretly from the national corridors of power, they are covert tyrants who are bleeding America white as part of a closeted inner circle. Yes, Virginia, there is an American aristocracy...look at Carl H. Lindner, Jr.

When aristocratic influences govern over existing American laws, all American life is cheapened and denigrated—all of it. We cannot have one set of rules and laws for a privileged class and another for the rank and file. Just as much as anything else, the Queen syndrome and Bananagate are about the special privileges of self-perceived elitists.

What happened at 124 West Ninth Street has become an important linchpin as to whether or not the financially powerful and the politically well-connected will be allowed to evade the federal laws that all other Americans must abide by—especially when money is stolen from the United States government. Just as surely as we should be ruled by laws and not by men, what has happened in Bananagate is a test to see if we still have what it takes to keep America's Constitution operational and intact.

The brakes will not be put on this scourge simply because the answer to this national problem is something that we are just going to stumble across, nor is it something that is going to happen by chance:

it has to be willed on and worked towards through deliberate action. First, there should be acknowledgment and recognition of the problem.

Second, the problem should be adequately acted upon, as those who are involved should not be allowed to evade the constitutional laws, statutes, rules, regulations and guidelines that already exist which expressly prohibit the type of federally indictable criminal activity that occurred at 124 West Ninth Street. Accordingly, there must be tighter controls on federal tax dollars. Whenever the words *U. S. Treasury theft* are even whispered, red flags should go up all over the place and loud warning bells should sound to the high heavens.

If Americans do not take it upon ourselves to be part of the solution, we are part of the problem. If we are not part of the cure, we are part of the illness. If we are not acting in the best interests of ourselves, we are acting against ourselves. Instead of reacting on the defensive, we must be offensively proactive. Ambitious attempts need to be made.

Americans cannot afford to have different standards, to different laws, for different reasons and for different races in America. As conflicting national ideals must be eliminated, it is much more prudent for this nation to adopt non-racial policies that will save us quantum amounts of money over what we are spending now to enforce and maintain the quasi-slave system.

America does not need the type of conservative politics of yesterday: it needs a vision of tomorrow. As long as the Queen syndrome exists, American freedom itself is in jeopardy. It calls for a radical new way of thinking that enforces the enlightening precepts of the American Constitution.

Like FDR, the thirty-second President of the United States, a new sense of direction and a new sense of purpose has to be administered by a responsible government official in order to breathe new life into American society. The American public needs to move forward on a solid footing by abandoning its laissez-faire attitude towards the quasi-slave system. The ordinary people who comprise America's commonality, just like during Revolutionary War times, must see through the attempts of many public officials to hide the social and financial tyranny that surrounds them and engulfs their government. America's population must answer to their insides and understand the reasons why they are losing faith in the ability of their leaders to effectively govern the affairs of the country.

The current political climate is the antithesis of what is best for America. The necessity that dictates America's national survival states that we cannot let crooked politicians, like former President Bill Clinton, turn the Constitution on its head. Defiance must be part of a snowballing resolve of America's citizens not to let this type of thing happen. 124 West Ninth Street conspirators should not be allowed to straddle the fence and play both sides. Until choices are made, and until the facts and the evidence are acted upon, the problem will not just simply go away. An example must be set.

We must take a turn for the better by saving ourselves from our own allowed damnation. We must, in some shape, form or fashion, establish a national categorical imperative that commands that we consecrate ourselves to a higher purpose. Old racial hatreds; old racial fears; and old racial doubts: these are the mountains that are blocking our way. As we must be of one mind and of one accord, our fates are inextricably adjoined.

In the meantime, Americans remain victimized by power politics run amok. For example, it stinks to the high heavens when, on one hand, Carl Lindner, Jr.'s Provident Bank is directly involved in stealing dollars from the American government at 124 West Ninth Street. But, on the other hand, it makes millions of dollars by buying an "outstanding" status to do business from the Federal Reserve System through generally shady political campaign contributions.

On top of all of this, the American taxpayer gets the double whammy as Provident Bank is allowed to go unpunished because of its direct political payoffs to the office of the President of the United States. Moreover, this bank of Carl Lindner, Jr. continues to receive America's blessings to hold federal funds, issue U. S. savings bonds and make money—lots of it—by gobbling up smaller lending institutions as if there is no tomorrow.

Americans cannot realistically stave off the inevitable by sticking our heads in the sand. As long as an unrestrained Queen syndrome is known about and is allowed to operate with impunity, America's constitution is a sham. As freedom and justice for all is a moot precept within the sphere of the operationally unconstitutional Queen syndrome, like the completely bogus and government sanctioned HUD building renovation project at 124 West Ninth Street, America is functioning fraudulently.

With the inescapable proof of 124 West Ninth Street presidential corruption, the time has come where we, as a nation, should not deal with the folly of the President and the Queen's criminal cover-up behavior that allures America in a counterproductive national direction. As long as America denies that the sickness is there and fails to effectively operate on it, the cancer will continue to eat away at the supporting foundation of the country itself. History teaches us that.

As powerful American moneymen like Carl Lindner, Jr. control the White House, it is bad enough that a domestic evil genie is out of the bottle. However, foreign money-laundered cash is showing up in American banks. As a result, and with all of the political money grabbing that is going on, American politicians who are aggressively seeking all available cash are opening America up to the greater evils of Central and South American drug lord money—not to mention the rising Russian Mafia and etc.

As the corrosive power of the President and the Queen's genie has been released, self-aggrandizement, at any cost, has become paramount to many greedy politicians, as they sell out America to feather their nests. If the Queen syndrome's downward pull on the United States is not reduced and reversed within a reasonable timeframe, its inertia will carry this country into perilous waters. A course needs to be chartered away from these dangerous straits. As it has gained its own momentum, the Queen syndrome must be forced to lay fallow through innocuous desuetude or, in the best case, be completely terminated.

Will we make the necessary, orderly and fair adjustments within our society, or will we remain stagnant, frozen in our outmoded ways and die as a result of our contradictory recalcitrance? Will we learn from our mistakes of the past, or are we doomed to failure for the lack of the use of reason? Only time will tell.

As the potential exists for the hidden looting of countless trillions of dollars from America's Treasury, through complacency, we are sewing the seeds of our own destruction. Just as long as the United States is gripped and paralyzed by the influence of special interests, we will waste away and languish if the national hemorrhaging is not stopped. Maintainers of the breech cannot move us forward by leading us backwards, down and out.

The tremors of an outlawed American chattel slave system, in all of its wicked ways, significantly rocked the very foundation of the

Constitution one time already in the history of the United States. The racial shock waves need to be silenced to prevent the next earthquake so that our creative energies can be focused on the other inevitable challenges that will surely threaten and test the hard-earned gains that have been paid for in American blood.

The pain that this nation underwent during our Civil War years must not be forgotten. In all of its horror, the American conservative racial ideology was once the cause of an awful tragedy that visited these shores. If we are smart, we will not allow that horror to return again.

As the President of the United States of America is the repository of a special trust that must maintain the purity of the Constitution by defending the rule of law, the presidential oath itself is sacred and must be enforced. If lying under oath is tolerated, the integrity of America's judicial process will be fatally compromised. Bananagate conspirators should be forced to pay hefty punitive and compensatory damages and should be forced to go to prison like other Americans.

As there was—and is—credible evidence that former President William Jefferson Clinton was involved in federal campaign finance infractions that stem from 124 West Ninth Street's U. S. Treasury theft cover-up scandal, it was again interesting for me to hear what Ken Starr said on NBC's July 10, 1999 "Today Show." On this date Starr said, "It is the Independent Counsel's responsibility to follow the law." Then, on or about August 9, 1999, Starr said, "If there is criminal wrongdoing, I will prosecute."

But his words, like those of most other politicians, did not ring true, especially with regard to the U. S. Treasury theft that occurred at 124 West Ninth Street. It did not matter that his office spent almost $50 million in five years before he quit this position as a largely ineffective federal prosecutor. It did not matter that he knew of the government's accountability to the people and that he had a lawful requirement to produce admissible evidence. It did not matter that his office was fully aware of—and did absolutely nothing about—incriminating Bananagate U. S. Treasury theft evidence. Although Robert Ray replaced him on October 18, 1999, Ken Starr's role in history as a prominent federal law officer is inextricably adjoined to a documented Bananagate presidential conspiracy.

Regarding the expiration of the Independent Counsel Act, on March 7, 1999, the Pulitzer Prize-winning columnist for *The New York*

Times, William Safire, said the only thing that will rebuild pressure on the powerful to obey the law, stick to the truth and adhere to ethical standards will be "only the renascence of public outrage." As the Independent Counsel Act expired at midnight, June 30, 1999, it was the last vestige of much needed Watergate reform. Sadly, justice was left up to a politically corrupted former U. S. Attorney General, Janet Reno, to investigate ethics and criminal violations of her boss. God help America!

More than three decades after the Kerner Commission found that America was "moving towards two societies, one black one white, separate and unequal," the unconstitutionality of the quasi-slave system's lingering presence still rears its ugly head. Going back in time, the fact remains that America's racial compass was not sufficiently reset at the end of our Civil War.

Going further back in time, in his first inaugural address on March 4, 1801, President Thomas Jefferson said: "Equal and exact justice to all men, of whatever state or persuasion, religious or political…These principles form the bright constellation which has gone before us, and guided our steps through an age of revolution and reformation. The wisdom of our sages and the blood of our heroes have been devoted to their attainment. They should be the creed of our political faith, the text of civil instruction, the touchstone by which we try the services of those we trust; and should we wander from them in moments of error or alarm, let us hasten to retrace our steps and to regain the road which alone leads to peace, liberty and safety."

With these words in mind, the President and the Queen's Bananagate criminal behavior is a high-handed assault on the American people. Presidents, politicians, corrupt judges and bureaucrats will come and go, but what will remain will be the American nation. Since Bananagate politicians have been left unimpeded and to their own devices, the focal point of immediate consideration for concerned Americans should be the extent to which they have caused damage to this nation in their aftermath.

As long as America's race lie is there for all to see, ideological inconsistencies will exist which will erode the public's confidence in the government's ability to effectively govern. At a time when competent, capable and proficient national leadership is most needed, if for nothing else, America's best interests should come before the racial politics of the Queen syndrome. As long as the Queen syndrome exerts its damaging effects upon the American populace, freedom and justice for all will continue to allude America.

If American laws are truly colorblind, the laws that were put on the books should be obeyed. In the final analysis, if America is to survive, its laws must be followed. Americans are patiently watching and waiting. But just like the American founders of this country experienced under the tyrannical rule of the British, even patience has a tendency to sometimes wear thin.

No matter how much America's national race problem is overlooked and artificially viewed through rose-colored glasses, the fact remains that true constitutional equality, justice and fairness has been wrongfully steered away from me, as it has for most African-Americans. Like a substance abuser that avoids seeking cure by continually denying involvement in damaging and repetitive behavior, American society needs to follow a different course for its own self-benefit.

Even though U. S. Judge Susan Weber Wright found Bill Clinton in contempt of court on July 29, 1999 and imposed a paltry federal fine on him that amounted to nothing more than a mild slap on the back of his hand, the President (Clinton) has figuratively gotten away with murder against the American nation. As many burning questions continue to besiege the already damaged credibility of a historically-scarred Bill Clinton regarding many of his last-minute and anti-American presidential pardons, it remains to be seen whether or not he will be able to maintain his aura of political/criminal invincibility in the face of obvious guilt.

Regardless of his propensity to not have varying prosecutions stick to him (to wit, his "Teflon Kid" and/or "Slick Willie" image), Americans need not look far to reverse this oily trend by forcing criminal guilt to stick to Bill Clinton. Within the covers of this book, there exists enough scathing information and evidence that can set an example to other presidents who will follow Bill Clinton that they should not thumb their noses at the American people by violating our trust, laws and the sanctity of this nation.

Due to the hidden criminal activities of former President Bill Clinton, the essence of *The President and the Queen* is this: what happened to my family and me is but one of the many federal prosecutions that an unscrupulous President has been able to evade. In the wake of the overall damage that this man has caused to the American presidency and the nation, there is a way to make him pay for his national sins by relegating him to a quarter from which he cannot escape.

As the same Syndiçated Columnist, Pulitzer Prize-winning Author and Journalist William Safire wrote about Bill Clinton in an editorial captioned "That Wagging Finger" in the October 29, 1998 *New York Times*, "...a pattern of deceit and other abuses not limited to 'lying about sex' should have the most serious consequences." In writing about the President's photograph that is on the cover of this book, Safire went on to say that it is the "...showing of the film clip that will dog Bill Clinton to the end of his days: looking us right in the eye and wagging his finger in our faces to make us listen to him lie in his teeth....Is it right for this country to let any President, of either party, get away with that?"

If for nothing else, this writing offers conclusive proof that, just as he was responsible for blatantly lying to the American people about his sexual affair with Monica Lewinsky, he has been the commanding force behind the illegally concealed HUD U. S. Treasury theft that occurred at the building that I owned for more than ten years at the Queen's 124 West Ninth Street.

In the final analysis, if all Americans' rights are not protected, nobody's rights in America will be protected. It just simply works that way. If crooked politicians and evil moneymen can secretly steal away my American dream, every American is vulnerable to illegal breakdowns of their constitutional rights as well. Americans must take it upon themselves to be repairers of the breach. We must fix the hole in our nation's heart.